International Issues in Social Economy

Studies in the United States and Greece

Severyn T. Bruyn
and
Litsa Nicolaou-Smokoviti

PRAEGER

New York
Westport, Connecticut
London

Library of Congress Cataloging-in-Publication Data

Bruyn, Severyn Ten Haut, 1927-
    International issues in social economy: studies in the United
States and Greece / Severyn T. Bruyn and Litsa Nicolaou-
Smokoviti.
    p.   cm.
    Bibliography: p.
    Includes index.
    ISBN 0-275-92518-8 (alk. paper)
    1. Management--United States--Employee participation.
2. Human rights--United States. 3. Community development--
United States. 4. Management--Greece--Employee participation.
5. Human rights--Greece. 6. Community development--Greece.
I. Nicolaou-Smokoviti, Litsa. II. Title.
HD5660.U5B78   1989
306--dc19   88-3525

Copyright © 1989 by Praeger Publishers

Library of Congress Catalog Number: 88-3525
ISBN: 0-275-92518-8

First published in 1989

Praeger Publishers, One Madison Avenue, New York, NY 10010
A division of Greenwood Press, Inc.

Printed in the United States of America

∞

The paper used in this book complies with the
Permanent Paper Standard issued by the National
Information Standards Organization (Z39.48-1984).

10 9 8 7 6 5 4 3 2 1

Contents

Foreword by Branko Horvat

Political democracy has been with us in the European countries for about a century and a half. Political democracy means a constitution, manhood suffrage, and responsible government. Women were suffered to vote only in this century, but that innovation has lasted long enough to be granted status as an inalienable human right and has ceased to be an issue. Current controversies about political democracy focus instead on the conflict between the bureaucratic centralism of the modern enormously expanded state and local autonomy. Federal states tend to be more decentralized, with Swiss cantons and Yugoslav općine and republics representing extreme cases. Nonfederal states tend to be more centralized, with France presenting a good example of a thoroughly centrally governed country. In spite of such diversity, however, political democracy seems well established.

Modern economy is organized differently. In fact, there is a glaring contradiction between political democracy and economic autocracy. Free as a citizen, the individual becomes a subject as soon as he or she enters the factory gate. It is politically unthinkable to order citizens to vote a certain way and use one's wealth as a justification; however, that is exactly what happens in the economic sphere. Various theories have been developed to explain (and mystify) the difference, but it is obvious that the schizophrenic behavior of individuals in their capacities as citizens and producers points to a serious deficiency in contemporary civilization.

Things are beginning to change, however. The United Nations has found it necessary to complement the traditional list of human rights (consisting of political rights) with economic and social rights. Countries are experimenting with various institutions, with German codetermination and Yugoslav worker management being, perhaps, the best-known and -studied examples. The natural next step is to undertake comparative in-depth studies. That is exactly what Severyn Bruyn and Litsa Nicolaou-Smokoviti have done.

These authors compare two extremely different countries, the United States and Greece. The former is a huge

military superpower and maintains the strongest economy
in the world; the latter is a small, relatively undeveloped
Balkan country.   The United States is a staunch capitalist
country that recently, under President Reagan, has moved
toward the Right.   Greece, after the electoral victory of
Papandreou in 1981, has undertaken to build a kind of
socialism.   The former is a relatively new country with
only two centuries of state history; the latter is one of
the oldest countries in the world.   As far as the development of economic democracy is concerned, however, the two
countries display fascinating similarities: the trend is
the same, although institutional implementation is different.
In the United States development has been more sporadic
and spontaneous, while in Greece it is more intentional
and planned.

Economic democracy is often associated with producer
cooperatives (as different from consumer cooperatives).
Producer co-ops have existed longer than a century, yet
their economic significance has been marginal.   It is still
marginal, but the trend has changed.   By now, five U.S.
states have enacted special laws to provide a legal basis
for chartering worker co-ops.   Worker co-ops imply joint
ownership and participation in decision making.   Each of
the two components may be developed separately, and that
is what has happened.   In the United States the emphasis
is on ownership, in Greece it is on participation.   There
are now about 8,000 U.S. corporations partly owned by the
employees.   This is mainly the result of special Employee
Stock Ownership Plan (ESOP) legislation intended to save
jobs and to produce "worker capitalists."   Indeed, ESOP
firms have been created at the rate of several hundred
per year.   Frequently firms about to become bankrupt or
liquidated are saved by enabling the employed workers to
buy them.   When capitalism fails to work, worker management (or at least worker ownership) takes over.

In Greece the Papandreou government has initiated a
program of socialization.   The management structure of socialized firms is based on various forms of worker participation prescribed by law.   Here as well as in the United
States, attempts have been made to rescue troubled firms
by engaging workers in management.

As retired U.S. labor leader Irving Bluestone aptly
pointed out, worker participation consists of managing the
job and managing the enterprise.   The former is less of a
threat to the traditional owners and managers and is,

consequently, much more developed than the latter. It is probably not an overstatement to say that worker job management is becoming a recognized sign of modern management.

Worker participation in management increases the role of communal institutions, and so local autonomy gains increasing importance. Community development corporations, community land trusts, and community-based banks complement the democratization of firms. The authors find that

> attempts at community self-governance in Greece have developed a more-integrated process and consistent effort than in the United States. Again, the spontaneous, sporadic development of the United States is largely outside of state control, while in Greece there is commitment of the government for action in restructuring the countryside and an institutional setup that harmonizes with its ideology and seeks to fulfill its purpose: to make a socialist transformation of society.

In order to tackle their subject appropriately, the authors use a blend of economics and sociology (and industrial psychology), which they designate as "social economy." They distinguish between social governance (the way people manage their own affairs at all levels of the economy) and social development (the creative application of human resources to economic affairs that leads to an increase in the capacity to manage corporate activities with some measure of autonomy), when social development is a means for reducing the need for the state control of economic life. The term self-governance refers to the capacity of people to manage their own affairs apart from external controls. The more usual terms of (political) local self-government and (economic) worker self-management are replaced by community self-governance and worker self-governance, which the authors feel are free of ideological connotations.

The contradiction between political democracy and economic autocracy is still very much present, along with the stifling of citizen initiative by the big state. But strong trends are discernible that may lead to overcoming these deficiencies. Worker ownership and worker management are on the increase, and so are job management, enterprise management, and communal self-governance. Socialization in Greece and worker capitalism in the United States move in the same direction. The authors of this study have documented these trends very well and have written an interesting and useful book that no social scientist can afford to ignore. After all, nihil novum sub sole does not prove to be a correct description of the world--fortunately.

Branko Horvat

Preface

Our collaboration in the research for this volume covers over a decade. We have offered papers at international meetings in Europe, Israel, Mexico, and India and have jointly published papers on comparative questions of development in the social economies of the United States and Greece. The formulation of the concepts and our approach in this study are the result of this long preoccupation for a new dimension (perspective) of social development and intensive efforts to trace developments that seem to substantiate our thesis in our two nations. Our work is the product of a creative dialogue and most rewarding exchange of ideas and experiences.

We want to thank our international colleagues for suggestions that influenced our thinking and writing. We are especially grateful to Professor Branko Horvat, whose work in both the theory and policy of industrial democracy has been an inspiration to both of us. Our debt is deep also to Professors George Coutsoumaris, David Ellerman, Dimitrius Iatridis, Chris Jecchinis, Nicos Mouzelis, Constantinos Papageorgiou, Menachem Rosner, Irwin T. Sanders, Steve Savas, Theodoros Skountzos, Nickolaos Travlos, and Evan Vlahos, whose critical reading of parts of the manuscript was extraordinarily helpful. We are thankful to the following colleagues from the Greek and international community who contributed to the documentation of the study: Dimitrios Carantinos, Miranta Damala, Anastasia Gana, Georgia Michalakakou, and Pantelis Pantelidis.

This research would not have been possible without the collegial support of faculty members at the Sociology Department and the School of Management of Boston College as well as the Management Department of the Piraeus Graduate School of Business Studies.

We also wish to thank the many individuals, government officials, and executives in the private, public, and social sectors of Greece who provided us with relevant information and official documents and who kindly gave their time in lengthy interviews.

Invaluable assistance was also provided by the secretaries of the Sociology Department at Boston College,

Barbara Smith and Roberta Nerenberg, for which we express our most sincere appreciation.

And to members of our immediate families--Louise, Dimitrios, Vasoula, Teta--who encouraged us in this endeavor and supported our work in countless ways with patience and understanding, our gratitude and affection.

We hope that this book will bring to our international colleagues and students a message that scholarly cooperation in comparative crossnational research can prove fruitful and can do much to extend international scholarship and fellowship.

It will be a great satisfaction to us if the perspective we develop in this book will prove of some value to those who aspire to a more human society and take action to promote new institutions that upgrade social conditions.

Acronyms

UNITED STATES

A & P	Great Atlantic and Pacific Tea Company
ACORN	Association of Community Organizations for Reform Now
AFL-CIO	American Federation of Labor--Congress of Industrial Organizations
CDC	Community Development Corporation
CDCU	Community Development Credit Union
CDFC	Community Development Finance Corporation
CDFI	Community Development Finance Institution
CEDAC	Community Economic Development Assistance Corporation
CEED	Community Enterprise Economic Development Program
CLT	Community Land Trust
CWA	Communication Workers of America
EDA	Economic Development Administration
ERISA	Employee Retirement Income Security Act
ESOP	Employee Stock Ownership Plan
ESOT	Employee Stock Ownership Trust
FHA	Farmers Home Administration
GM	General Motors
GNMA	Government National Mortgage Association
ICA	Industrial Cooperative Association
JALMC	Jamestown Labor-Management Committee
LODC	Local Ownership Development Corporation
MA	Massachusetts
MIT	Massachusetts Institute of Technology
MNC	Multinational Corporation

NAM	National Association of Manufacturers
NY	New York
PA	Pennsylvania
PACE	Philadelphia Association for Cooperative Enterprise
PIRG	Public Interest Research Group
QWL	Quality of Work Life
R & D	Research and Development
RLF	Revolving Loan Fund
SBA	Small Business Administration
SMSIs	Small and Medium Sized Industries
TOTEM	Total Energy Module System
TWA	Trans World Airlines
UAW	United Auto Workers
US	United States

GREECE

ADEDY	Supreme Executive Committee of Public Servants
AEI	Schools of Higher Education
AMIANTIT	AMIANTIT S.A. (trademark)
ANEK	Crete Maritime Company
ASKE	Representative Assembly of Social Control
ASO	Autonomous Currant Organization
ATE	Agricultural Bank of Greece
DA	Democratic Renovation Party
DEFA	Enterprise Municipal Gas of Athens
DEH	Public Power Corporation
DEP	Teaching and Scientific Personnel
DEPOS	Public Corporation for Housing and Urban Planning

DNE	International Maritime Union of Greece
EBEA	Commercial and Industrial Chamber of Athens
EBEP	Commercial and Industrial Chamber of Piraeus
EFEE	National Student Union of Greece
EKKE	National Center of Social Research
EKP	Piraeus Labor Center
ELAIOURGIKI	Central Cooperative Union of Olive Producers of Greece
ELINDA	ELINDA S.A. (trademark)
ELTA	Hellenic Post Office
EOEM	Greek Company for Organizational and Technical Studies
EOKap.	National Tobacco Organization
EOMMEH	Hellenic Organization of Small and Medium Sized Enterprises and Handicrafts
EOT	National Tourist Organization
ESAP	National Council of Higher Education
ESAP	National Council of Development and Planning
ESYE	National Statistical Service of Greece
ETANAM	Amvrakikos Bay Development Company
EYDAP	Water Supply and Sewerage Systems Company of Athens
GENOP/DEH	General Federation of Public Power Corporation Personnel
GSEE	General Confederation of Workers of Greece
IKA	Social Insurance Foundation
IMEO	Institute for Study of the Greek Economy
IOBE	Institute of Economic and Industrial Research
KEDKE	Central Union of Municipalities and Communities of Greece
KEGME	Mediterranean Women's Studies Institute
KEMETE	Center for Study, Documentation, and Training
KEPE	Center of Planning and Economic Research

KESY	Central Council of Health
KKE	Communist Party of Greece
KKEes.	Communist Party of Greece of Interior
KYDEP	Home Products Handling Cooperative Administration
L	Law
LARKO	Hellenic Mining and Metallurginal Company of Larimna (trademark)
MME	Small and Medium Sized Enterprises
MOP	Integrated Mediterranean Program
ND	New Democracy Party
NEE	Hellenic Chamber of Shipping
OA	Olympic Airways
OAE	Industrial Reconstruction Organization
OAED	Manpower Employment Organization
OATh.	Sewage Organization of Thessaloniki
OGA	Farmers Insurance Organization
OLP	Piraeus Port Authority
OLTh.	Port Authority of Thessaloniki
OSE	Hellenic Railways Organization
OTA	Local Government Authorities (administrative units at the local level)
OTE	Hellenic Telecommunications Organization
OTOE	Hellenic Federation of Bank Employees' Unions
OVES	Federation of Industrial Labor Corporations
OYTh.	Water Supply Organization of Thessaloniki
PASEGES	Panhellenic Confederation of Agricultural Cooperatives
PASOK	Panhellenic Socialist Movement
PENP	Panhellenic Association of Shipping Agents
PRO.MET.	Company for Supplies to Small and Medium Sized Enterprises

PYR.KAL.	Greek Powder and Cartridge Company Ltd.
RHODA	Local Transportation Company of Rhodes (trademark)
SDOEE	Association for the Establishment of an Economic Chamber of Greece
SEB	Association of Greek Industries
SEKE	Cooperative Organization of Tobacco Producers
TEDK	Local Union of Municipalities and Communities
TEE	Technical Chamber of Greece
TPD	Office of Loans and Consignments Funds
VELKA	VELKA S.A. (trademark)

INTERNATIONAL

ECU	European Currency Unit
EEC	European Economic Community
GDP	Gross Domestic Product
GFCF	Gross Fixed Capital Formation
GNP	Gross National Product
HAMASHBIR	Purchasing Cooperative (Israel)
ILO	International Labor Office
IQ	Intelligence Quotient
OECD	Organization of Economic Cooperation and Development
S.A.	Société Anonyme
TNOVA	Marketing Cooperative (Israel)
UK	United Kingdom
UN	United Nations
YMCA	Young Men's Christian Association
YWCA	Young Women's Christian Association

Greek Periodicals Used as Sources

ENGLISH TRANSLATION	GREEK TITLES (in Latin Characters)
Agriculture	Georgia
Agricultural Cooperativism	Agrotikos Synergatismos
Avgi	Avgi Daily
Current Issues	Synchrona Themata
Economic Analysis	Oikonomiki Analysi
Economic Herald	Oikonomikos Tahidromos
Express	Express Daily
Government Gazette	Efimerida tis Kyverniseos
Industrial Review	Viomihaniki Epitheorisi
Profit	Kerdos Daily
Public Sector	Dimosios Tomeas
Review of Labor Law	Epitheorisi Ergatikou Dikaiou
Review of Social Research	Epitheorisi Koinonikon Erevnon
Rizospastis	Rizospastis Daily
Studies	Spoudai
The Cooperative Way	Synergatiki Poreia
Vima	Vima Daily

International
Issues in
Social Economy

1. Introduction

The United States and Greece are so different in terms of
size, politics, and culture that it would seem impossible
and even wrong to compare these cases, and yet it is precisely because of their differences that a joint study is so
important. Indeed, these two vastly different nations, a
giant capitalist nation in a position of hemispheric hegemony and a small nation with a socialist-oriented government, characterized by so many differences and conflicts,
represent the range of key issues in the social development of modern economies. The divergence and convergence
of their developments should cast light on a theory of development that transcends their differences.[1]
      Our intent is (1) to provide a conceptual framework
for understanding selected dimensions of the political economies of nations with such differences in size and political
orientation and (2) to encourage comparative international
research (i.e., the study of different political economies
in the continuum of market systems) that may lead toward
new governmental policies. Furthermore, we believe that
such comparative international research may have implications for constructive relationships between nations and
may even be critical to the issues of world order.
      To do this, we propose a theoretical framework for
examining changes taking place in the 1980s in the economies of these two nations that is set apart from previous
frameworks. Different from such theories as "modernization" or "dependency," theories of centrally planned development, or Marxist theories of development, this framework
takes account of the processes of modernization and dependency and the principles underlying social theories of development without seeking limitation by any one of these

singular approaches. It does not include the traditional presumptions of capitalism or state socialism. Furthermore, we use terms that are different from those of the conventional economist, and so it is important to open this chapter with a discussion of our conceptual framework.

The key concepts that guide our discussion are intended to be a foundation for examining developments in social economy within each nation. Our discussion of this framework will be brief, since it has been formulated in other writings, but we want the reader to understand our thinking. The value of our framework is its potential for evaluating the level of social development in the economies of both big and small nations, as well as of nations with divergent political orientations. We believe that the delineation of a framework to make these evaluations is vitally important today because we live in a time when issues of social development remain largely in the arena of ideological debate rather than in social research and theory.

Our study focuses on certain policies expressed in both countries. We are interested in reviewing those policies germane to our theoretical framework as we trace parallel developments in the United States and Greece, including the intent to give workers greater authority within the corporate economy and attempts to cultivate greater political authority among citizens in local communities.

In this introduction we describe our general framework, which is focused on social economy, and discuss critical developments in and the political history of the two nations of our study. In Part I we describe our understanding of worker self-governance as the background for subsequent chapters in which we interpret what is actually happening in the United States and Greece. In Part II we repeat our pattern of analysis, describing our understanding of community self-governance, and in subsequent chapters we interpret what is actually happening in each nation. Finally, in Part III we evaluate our findings for both countries and point out their implications for policy research and international studies. The broader implications of our study for further comparative studies are included in the Appendix, in which we suggest a basis for comparing the social development of self-governing firms at the community level, for example, Israel (the kibbutzim), Spain (Mondragon cooperatives), and Yugoslavia (labor managed firms).

The key theoretical question we raise in this comparative study is: How can new solutions to problems created by the competitive market be solved within the enterprise system itself? The theoretical direction of our work would suggest the development of a social economy that is mature and accountable to the people it embraces. We are looking toward the possibility that self-governance may develop within the private economy in ways that reduce the necessity for state intervention and regulations.

This theoretical orientation is paradoxically both Marxist and capitalist. Marx was deeply concerned about reducing the power of the state over the economy; he also recognized that many social changes would need to occur before it could actually happen. The political administrations in the United States and in Greece in the 1980s seem to have objectives for decentralization and/or self-determination of people in the economic order of society, albeit with radically different agendas for its accomplishment. The experiences of both countries tell us something about the difficulty of achieving this objective. They also provide us with an opportunity for recommending special courses of action to each nation.

The study of these two nations leads us toward an international picture of social development. Our comparative study brings us eventually to recommendations for social policy related to solving common problems of capitalist-oriented and socialist-oriented nations. Our interest is in taking preliminary steps toward designing a framework that will enable us to interpret international issues that affect the development of a social economy.

From a sociological point of view, this study uses fiscal and statistical data, legal documents, the press, and primary data collected through personal interviews as well as other secondary sources in both the United States and Greece. The 1983–87 Five-Year Plan for Economic and Social Development in Greece and new legislation in both the United States and Greece have been judged as important points for this study because they express the orientations of the political parties powerful in the 1980s in actionable policy. More specifically, the 1983–87 Five-Year Plan, although much debated and questioned regarding its realism and implementation, is a concrete and sanctioned formal document that displays the thought and policy of a particular political party. We do not deal with an evaluation of its implementation (which should probably be the task of a future study) but instead, as with all our sources, are concerned with its expression of the thought, orientation, and views of the government and of its embodiment of their intentions for changes in society.

SOCIAL ECONOMY

Social economy is a field of knowledge rooted in the disciplines of economics and sociology but significantly linked to other disciplines. It represents an important convergence in subject matter that has been steadily developing from a wide range of scientific fields and public-policy programs. It focuses on the economy as an institutional order within society and has links to such fields as industrial psychology, occupational sociology, business administration, scientific management, labor studies, public administration, environmental studies, and consumer research.

Many of these specialized disciplines are challenged by the changing structure of society, and this concern gives impetus to social economy as an integrating field of knowledge. Industrial sociology, for example, must explain the fact that a postindustrial economy is developing alongside traditional industrial organization. Scientific studies in the capitalist tradition have had to come to terms with the growing power of labor organizations, especially in Europe. Although we should recognize that traditional management has certainly been concerned with labor (at least in the last forty years), labor has recently gained such managerial significance around the world that a new integral outlook is required. Industrial psychology must take greater account of the effects of business systems on personality in different cultural settings as business expands its operations domestically and internationally. And industrial management in capitalist societies must recognize the developing field of administration in socialist societies as different types of nations increase their trade relations.

All nations must confront the fact that a new managerial culture is emerging independent of ideologies. Management in socialist countries is coming to terms with capitalist economics as leaders perceive it to be effective and applicable in socialist organization. Business administration has to account for socialist governments as they show evidence of viability in the cultural life of modern nations. In this mix of specialized fields of theory and practice, there is need for an integral perspective. Social economy is the link between these separate areas of investigation. It takes account of the strains and provides a general scientific outlook needed for an integrated approach. Its strength lies in its potential to provide insight into the relationships among special areas of study of different market systems. In other words, the larger structural changes and challenges of modern societies transcend earlier ideological artifacts of management. New management differs in part from old because of the new and imposing demands of such factors as, for example, corporate size, corporate complexity, departmental interdependence, and worker participation.

For our purposes, such factors need to connect with concepts of self-governance, social governance, mutual governance, social federations, and other concepts that constitute what we consider part of the framework of social economy as a field of knowledge. Our special task is quite limited within this general field, but we must begin with the broad concepts that are guiding this study.

Two theoretical concepts within this field of social economy are important to note at the outset. Social governance refers to the way people manage their own affairs through participation in all levels of the economy, including the workplace, the firm, the industry, and finally the entire economy as a human institution. Social development refers to the upgrading of human resources at all levels of the economic order. Ultimately, both concepts involve looking at how material and human resources are interacting in the context of society.

A schematic presentation of the generic concepts in this framework is given in Figure 1.1. No single work in economics and sociology has focused systematically on these concepts as they are applied to the institutional economy, although many studies point in this direction. Our task is not to formulate the details of such a theory here but rather to work descriptively within the meaning of these concepts.

Social governance refers to the way people manage their affairs in all institutions and organizations in the economy. The fact that economic governance is "social" means simply that people manage their own affairs in conjunction with others. This common governance of the

Figure 1.1

Perspective of Social Economy

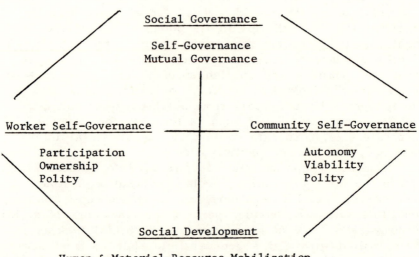

economy includes the state as an institution, but our analytical focus does not find its principal meaning there.
Our primary focus is on the way people manage economic
activities to reduce the need for state controls.

Social governance has two principal concepts, or
dimensions, in all nations. One dimension is the concept
of self-governance, which refers in the broadest sense to
the capacity of an economy to operate relatively independently of the state. The other dimension is mutual governance, which refers, in the broadest sense, to the degree
of joint management of economic affairs through democratic
institutions with minimum state intervention. We use this
concept primarily in reference to social federations (e.g.,
trade associations, cooperative leagues, etc.) developing
within the economies of nations.

Social development implies an increase and/or improvement in the creative application and cultivation of
human resources in economic affairs. It suggests an increase in the capacity to manage corporate activities with
some measure of autonomy and participatory governance.
Put another way, social development is the development of

human authority and responsibility, which reduces the necessity for the formal government to assume the management of economic life. The term development implies a broadening of the organized base of leadership among people working at different levels of a nonstatist economy and signifies an increase in personal and social accountability in the workplace and the marketplace. It also implies an enhancement of the quality of life in the economic order. This enhancement can mean an increase in the level of self-determination and freedom in one's place of work. It often requires some deepening of human sensitivity and some strengthening of needed skills for people engaged in the corporate economy. In general, it points to a potentially higher level of self-knowledge and a greater degree of self-reliance for people working in the economy--a broadening of social consciousness among managers, white-collar workers, laborers, and lawyers, that is, a greater awareness of the interdependence of all institutions operating in the economy. It means, in its broad scope, the creative enhancement of life itself in the social organization of the economy.

Social development is a means of reducing the need for state bureaucracies and federal agencies to control economic life, a decrease in external controls over human conduct and an increase in the level of inner resources to deal with the changing environment. It implies an increase in the power of people to control their own economic activities. Social development means, in the final analysis, an increase in self-determination for people in the economic order of society.

This is the primary issue before us in our study of the economic orders in different nations. We are interested in the development of a social economy, which guides our research independent of size, cultural context, and so forth. The question before us is: How does social development and social governance happen in the economies of big and small nations? A parallel question is: Are any parts of the process the same for different nations in the continuum of market systems?

To move more directly toward the answers to these questions, we must break down our framework into other concepts that will allow us to examine special changes occurring within these two countries leading toward social development and new forms of social governance. The two major areas we have chosen to examine are labor development and community development. Both areas of study have new concepts emerging within them that we wish to introduce here: worker self-governance and community self-governance. These concepts provide us with our special paradigm and our orientation toward social development in the economies of the United States and Greece.

We have mentioned self-governance as a dimension of social governance. Self has both a subjective and an objective side to its meaning. Its subjective side refers to that area of personal identity to which people are most finely attuned in their own consciousnesses. The objective side focuses on whatever area of economic activity we choose to define in relation to our scientific focus of study. When we refer to self-governance in the workplace, we mean the capacity of people within that workplace to manage their own activities apart from outside supervision and regulations. When we refer to self-governance in the corporation, we mean the capacity of this entity to govern itself apart from outside controls. The same meaning applies to the capacities of industry and community to develop themselves as units apart from outside controls.

Self-governance, once again, refers broadly to the relative capacity of people and entities to manage their own affairs apart from external controls. It signifies the skill of people to socially govern their economy at every level. These levels include the individual in the workplace, the workplace itself as a collective entity, the department, the corporation, the industry, and the economy as an institutional part of the society. Each level has its own problems in acquiring greater resources for itself. Each level has challenges to its capacity to operate with autonomy within the larger whole. The problem at the level of the workplace is often in the capacity of the workers to acquire more skills to work effectively without supervision. The problem at the level of a whole industry is often to find a way for firms to collaborate without collusion against others, that is, a way of cooperating that allows them to function effectively together in the interest of the larger society as well as themselves, thus reducing the necessity for outside government controls. Our primary interest in this research, however, is not on industrial self-governance but in the development of worker self-governance and community self-governance.

Worker self-governance involves the relative capacity of employees to manage their own firm democratically and effectively, the key notion here being again that of participatory democracy. The way worker self-governance develops in each nation is different, a very complex process involving many different variables. Two variables that will draw our special attention will be levels of worker participation and ownership of corporations. We assume that an integration of worker participation and ownership in some nations is an essential ingredient to achieve an optimum degree of corporate self-governance. They are not the only factors affecting labor in the economy, but they become important for our purposes of comparing the cultivation of worker authority in the economy. Taking these two factors into consideration, we are then interested in how a <u>democratic</u> <u>polity</u> develops within the life of corporations.

Community self-governance also involves the capacity of people in a locality to manage their own economic affairs apart from outside government controls, but refers to the power of people to create autonomy, viability, and democratic polity in their local economy. These are concepts (as well as goals) to which we will return later in our analysis of local development in these two nations.

Furthermore, we are interested in how social development occurs in the context of both work and the locality. In this respect, we will examine the connection between land, labor, and capital as part of the process of social development. We will also look at the concepts of decentralization and social ownership as a basis for future policy studies of community development. Clearly, labor and communities in most nations are far from realizing the full value of self-governance, but these relative terms serve as a framework within which we can begin to compare aspects of social economy in the context of each nation.

The concept of social federation becomes important as we move our analysis of development from the local firm and the community to other intermediate levels of society. Social federations are developing beyond state controls to assist in governing the economy. They often fail to fulfill their task of representing interfirm relationships in the context of society, but they succeed often enough for us to assume that they have the evolutionary capacity for expressing future modes of social development at higher levels of the economy. If their member firms become increasingly democratized, they offer a basis for developing social governance beyond the firm. Examples in this direction would be trade associations and cooperative federations that develop ethical codes of conduct and tribunals in the market system. These federations represent types of mutual governance that enable people to act judicially and democratically outside direct state controls.

In this period of transition to postindustrial organization for modern societies, our social-economic framework of analysis is a most appropriate perspective from which to characterize the study of economy and society. The term political economy continues to be a vital term to describe certain features of the economy, as we shall see, but today it refers only to specific aspects of the larger field: the study of power and the institutions of the state in their relationships to the economy and the society. Political economy is a special dimension of the general field of social economy.

The disciplines of sociology and economics find common ground in the concept of social economy. This concept suggests an order of study and thought that takes account of the older tradition of political economy and adds a twentieth-century perspective of the social sciences. It assumes that political institutions and the political order constitute only one major characteristic of the economic order in the context of society. The economic order has a political character and a relationship with the state that is fundamental to observe, but the political concept cannot represent all the multifaceted relations of the economy in the context of society. The field of political economy remains a perfect reference for scholars studying power in the relations of the economy and the state.

The scientific concepts that are used in the study of society need to express more completely the total human reality. The social concept, therefore, has an efficacy of its own in this respect. It is basic and inclusive of many other institutional relationships. Karl Marx often interchanged the words social and human. Max Weber defined social as being oriented toward others in action. This orientation could be based on many motives: religious, educational, economic, personal, and political. The usages of Marx and Weber thus include a variety of nonpolitical relationships in the study of economy and society.[2]

The political concept by itself restricts studies to the phenomenon of power and the formal government of the state. The implicit assumption in any theory of political economy is that all human relationships are based on power. However, power is a complicated concept that has yet to be fully distinguished in relation to other great concepts such as community, truth, value, love, and beauty. Some theorists claim truth to be the basis of power, whereas others claim that power can be realized only in community. The community thus becomes the more-critical concept even though linked with the concept of power. Since different basic concepts explain human behavior in the context of society, the social concept is closer to comprehending the relationships of people with their economic order and in this respect has the greater efficacy. Power is examined as one fundamental component of social relations within the economy.

The concept of the community is key to our analysis.[3] The distinction between community and state is important in our conceptual framework as well as the dichotomy between gemeinschaft and gesellschaft.[4] Our analysis takes a special turn here within the study of international issues in social economy. The community has a local and a national, if not international ("spaceship earth"), meaning. People find a sense of togetherness in their neighborhoods and separately in their nation at the same time. Our study is concerned with this relationship between the local and national community. We focus on the process of bottom-up development through labor-managed firms and local communities while also considering the top-down process of policy making that determines much of the direction of local development in each nation.

The process with which we are especially concerned in our research involves building the practical knowledge needed for shaping the economy from below. Nevertheless, we see the decision-making process to be a continuous interplay between those at the bottom and those at the top. The developmental process is never a one-way path of energy transformation and learning. Both the top and the bottom learn from each other in the transition toward a more highly developed society, a process observed in all nations big and small.

Our framework will unfold in the theoretical chapters preceding our discussion of what is happening in each nation. We will be examining the kinds of social ownership and property that appear around the problem of worker self-governance as well as in the context of the community. We are interested in the patterns of worker participation and ownership in corporations and their capacity to lead toward higher levels of self-governance for employees in the context of participation. We are also interested in the degrees to which the economies of local communities can achieve autonomy, viability, and democratic polity in both nations.

Our task now is to describe the differences that exist in the social economy of the two nations of our study. The relevant political context remains essential to our analysis of the social development in the United States and Greece.

THE POLITICAL ECONOMIES OF THE UNITED STATES AND GREECE

The perspective of social economy offers a basis for formulating theories of development applicable to all nations. Many different theories of development can be formulated, but we focus on the social roles of labor and the community in each nation. We believe that they are both critical dimensions of social development in every economy, critical to economic life. In addition, we are concerned with the role of the government in relation to social development, as the government plays a significant role in affecting the lives of the workers and citizens in neighborhoods and towns.

Let us now look at some of the differences between the United States and Greece before we look at their common problems in social development.[5] Table 1.1 describes some key differences that will become relevant in the course of the text. The fact that Greece is a relatively small country with a centralized government, that it has a tradition of state intervention supported by relatively strong unions, and that it lacks depth in managerial expertise in the private economy are important to understand in evaluating the direction of government policies. Readers will see significant disparity, largely because of different institutions, legal traditions and different public attitudes toward government, in the roles of both unions and government in the social development of these two nations.

Table 1.1

Comparisons of the Two Countries
Selective Differences

GREECE	UNITED STATES
GENERAL CONTEXT	
- Small country.	- Superpower.
- Social composition: institutions under development and change.	- Social composition: institutions already developed and relatively stable, but facing new challenge of post-industrial society (flux). Racial and gender tensions.
- An old country influenced in recent history by the European feudal system. Local governance thrived during the Ottoman rule. Strong centralized policies characterize the new Greek state since the 19th century.	- A country developed by immigrants. Institutions have been created under the English influence, from the bottom-up and, therefore, there have been more decentralized policies.
- Current politics: Socialist-oriented government (1987).	- Current politics: Conservative government (1987).
LAW AND ADMINISTRATION	
- Law is of European origin and old Roman-Byzantine, and is related to state intervention from the top.	- Law is Anglosaxon. Interpretive emphasis. Customary law.
- The term "state" is frequently expressed by the civil employees who represent it.	- The term "administration" is used.
- More centralized government.	- More grassroots politics.
- European monistic system.	- Separation of powers (President-Congress). Pluralistic emphasis.
- Relative uniformity of laws and state intervention, developed from historical traditions.	- Different local laws and institutions among States.
MANAGEMENT	
- Less effective management.	- More effective management.
- Relative lack of entrepreneurial support systems.	- Wide range of entrepreneurial support systems.

(continued)

Table 1.1 (continued)

GREECE	UNITED STATES
LABOR	
- The term "worker" characterizes those at the bottom working at the factory level, not those with managerial responsibilities.	- The term "worker" is a more general term, sometimes including management.
- Strong unionization. Political parties are involved and influence unions.	- Most recently anti-unionism and political de-emphasis of labor.
- Most enterprises engage small number of personnel.	- Large numbers of personnel are engaged in many big enterprises.
INSTITUTIONAL CONTEXT	
- Need for new institutions to fit a new urban society, as well as to modernize and adjust old institutions to new conditions. There are institutions dating back to 1800 and a State Budgetary Control System dating back to 1853.*	- Appropriate institutions exist which facilitate economic activity. - Need for emerging post-industrial institutions. - New efforts for cost-sharing.
ECONOMY	
- Western type of a mixed economy with certain chronic and structural problems.	- A capitalist system with some problems of adaptation to the challenges of acute international competition.
. Open economy with large dependency on imports and inflow of capital.	. Open economy with large balance deficit.
. Developing economy.	. Developed (mature) economy.
- Imported technology.	- Development of high technology.
- Economic policy is determined by the central government and affects the entire country.	- Some differences of economic policy among State and city economies (i.e. state environmental regulations, etc.).

* See, George Coutsoumaris, Morphology of Greek Industry (Athens: Center of Economic Research, 1963).

The Vast Differences

We can differentiate briefly between these two countries by referring to statistics on their population, stage
of economic development, and condition of dependency,
while keeping in mind their similarities. Table 1.2 sum-
marizes dimensions of these differences that we discuss in
the following sections.

Table 1.2

Important Economic Indicators, 1984

	Greece	U.S.A.
GDP (Gross domestic product) (in billions of U.S.$) (current prices, current exchange rates)	33.4	3634.6
Total Population (in thousands)	9,900	236,681
Inhabitants per sq. km.	75	25
Foreign Trade		
Imports of goods, cif as % of GDP	27.8%	9.9%
Exports of goods, fob as % of GDP	13.9%	6.7%
GFCF (Gross fixed capital formation) (at consumer prices)		
Average annual volume growth over previous 5 years	-4.5%	2.5%
Structure of the Economy		
Contribution of industrial sector to GDP	26.6%	37.4%
Contribution of service sector to GDP	55.0%	60.0%
Contribution of agricultural sector to GDP	18.5%	2.6%
Employment		
Total civilian employment (in thousands)	3,501	105,005
% of labor occupied in the industrial sector	28.6%	28.5%
% of labor occupied in the service sector	41.4%	68.2%
% of labor occupied in agricultural sector	30.0%	3.3%

Source: Organization for Economic Cooperation and Development OECD: Economic Surveys 1985/86 GREECE. Paris: OECD,
1986; Economic Surveys 1985/86 UNITED STATES. Paris: OECD,
1985; Economic Surveys 1986/87 UNITED STATES. Paris: OECD,
1986.

Population: The two nations are far from comparable in the size and density of their populations. In 1984 the population of the United States was 236,681,000, with 25 inhabitants per square kilometer, while the population of Greece was 9,900,000, with 75 inhabitants per square kilometer,[6] clearly more comparable with the State of Massachusetts than the entire United States. The twentieth century was a period of a large transoceanic and intra-European migration for thousands of Greek people emigrating to North and South America, Canada, Australia, South Africa, and Germany. A poor and inefficient Greek economy could not absorb young Greek farmers and workers, leading more than 2 million people to leave.[7]

Economic Development: The second major difference between these two nations is their degrees of economic development. In 1984 the U.S. GDP was $3,634.6 billion, while the GDP in Greece was $33.4 billion (Table 1.2). Per capita income in the United States in 1984 was $15,356, while in Greece it was $3,378 (Table 1.3). This difference is important because it helps explain such social facts as the emigration of Greeks, the attraction of the United States, the relative political power of the United States on the world scene, and the tendency toward political unrest within Greece.

Table 1.3

Indicators of Economic Growth and Living Standards

	Greece	U.S.A.
Per capita income (at current prices and current exchange rates) (U.S.$)	3,378 (1984)	15,356 (1984)
Private consumption per capita (using PPPs) (U.S.$)	4,118 (1984)	10,214 (1984)
Passenger cars per 1,000 inhabitants	108 (1983)	473 (1984)
Telephones per 1,000 inhabitants	336 (1983)	650 (1984)
Television sets per 1,000 inhabitants	158 (1980)	621 (1980)
Doctors per 1,000 inhabitants	2.8 (1983)	2.3 (1983)
Infant mortality per 1,000 births	14.6 (1983)	11.2 (1983)

Note: PPP = purchasing power parity.
Source: Organization for Economic Cooperation and Development OECD: Economic Surveys 1985/86 GREECE. Paris: OECD, 1986; Economic Surveys 1985/86 UNITED STATES. Paris: OECD, 1985; Economic Surveys 1986/87 UNITED STATES. Paris: OECD, 1986.

The difference in living standards between the two nations is also significant by other measures. The United States is substantially higher than Greece in private consumption per capita, number of cars, number of television sets, and telephones per 1,000 inhabitants and lower in infant mortality rate despite a lower number of doctors.[8] The difference in consumer expenditures is especially clear. In the United States in 1984, private consumption per capita was $10,214, while in Greece it was $4,118 (Table 1.3).

Until the late 1950s, Greece exemplified the classical underdeveloped economy: low productivity in the agricultural sector, a highly inflated and parasitic service sector, and an industrial sector unable to absorb the redundant agricultural labor force.[9] Greek industrialization has been characterized by an important inflow of foreign capital and technology. Furthermore, planning that was formally introduced in the early 1960s never played any important role before 1980. The de facto strategy for economic development has been import substitution and then export promotion of intermediate and final industrial products.[10] Even though Greece has now passed into the category of developed countries, it is still considered as one of the less-industrialized countries of the Organization for Economic Cooperation and Development (OECD).[11]

Another apparent difference between Greece and the United States is Greece's highly dependent economy compared with the relatively self-reliant U.S. economy. In the United States, imports of goods in 1984 represented 9.9 percent of GDP and exports represented 6.7 percent, while Greek imports in the same year represented 27.8 percent of GDP and exports represented 13.9 percent in the same year (Table 1.2). The Greek economy is clearly more dependent on other nations for its development.

Big trade deficits have been a serious problem in Greece for many years, but most recently for the United States. Greece is heavily dependent on capital, intermediate goods, and know-how from abroad for its development. For most of this century the United States has been a surplus nation, but no longer. The trade deficit has grown steadily from a few billion dollars per year in the 1970s to more than $156 billion in 1986 and $171 billion in 1987.[12]

Still another difference between the two nations can be seen in the structure of the economies. In the United States, the contribution of the industrial sector to the GDP

in 1984 was 37.4 percent, in contrast to the service sector's 60 percent and 2.6 percent in the agricultural sector.[13]   In Greece during the same year, the contribution
of the industrial sector was 26.6 percent, with 55 percent
for services and 18.5 percent for agriculture (Table 1.2).
The developmental trend in the United States began with
the emphasis on agriculture, then on industry, and finally
on services, the most recent area of expansion.   (This
tends to be the process for every country.)   Today we see
the United States in a postindustrial stage, moving significantly into the service sector largely at the expense
of industry.   But in Greece, the major drop from the agricultural sector has taken place very recently.   The process
may be the same in the two countries, with a significant
lag, but a key difference between these two countries is
that in the United States the expansion of the service sector is based on intensity of capital, while in Greece it is
mainly based on intensity of labor.   There are also some
important arguments that the service sector in Greece is
excessively developed in relation to the degree of industrial development.[14]   A large agricultural sector, although
with low productivity, is still important to the economy of
Greece and indicates its status as a developing nation.
Trends in modernization, as defined by past experience
and Western models of development, suggest that Greece
should experience a further drop in agricultural activity.

Recognizing that major differences in size and structure exist between these two nations, our task is to point
to the problems they share in the social development of
their economies.   As previously stated, the two areas we
have chosen to examine are in the developmental fields of
labor and the community.   In our theoretical framework,
their respective social development is significantly related
to the role of the government--as we shall see.

The Status of Labor

Ever since Karl Marx pointed to the depressed condition of the working class and its changing role in history,
leaders in every society have had to pay considerable attention to the problems of stratification and power.   A new
social consciousness about social equality and justice arose
in the nineteenth century that cannot be ignored.   The
roots of human alienation, Marx said, were to be found in

the relationship of labor to the ownership of the means of production. He argued that labor has a destiny to be in a position of higher authority in the developing society and that we are currently experiencing a historical stage of development in which labor plays a key role. Put another way, labor's position in society is continually being upgraded, and ignoring that fact can spell disaster for any national leader today. The position of the working class carries a significance to the developmental direction of modern society.

The roles of labor in the United States and Greece are quite different in their respective stages of economic development. In contrast to Greece and most of Western Europe, trade unions in the United States are not linked to political movements and do not carry a socialist ideology. In fact, the mainstream of the union movement has been frequently opposed to "communism" and has attempted at times to eliminate any such ideological tendencies developing among its members. Furthermore, the union movement in the United States has suffered a decline in power and membership in the last decade and has been looking deeply at its purposes while assessing its political role for the future. This situation is partly owing to the fact that American labor faces strong competition from foreign "cheap" labor, especially from Third World nations. On the other hand, it has been argued by management circles that in a postindustrial society with a large service sector worker autonomy and self-realization is increasing in the United States and, therefore, unions have become an anachronism. In Greece the union movement has continued to gain strength, especially in the periods from the early 1960s to 1967 and again after 1974. In particular, since 1984 there has also been in Greece the legal framework for a more significant involvement of unions in corporate decision making in many areas of the economy (Law 1264/84).[15] Unions in Greece have also become significantly involved in the public sector, in contrast to the comparatively weaker role of government unions in the United States.

The political context for union development is vastly different in the two countries. After the fall of the military regime (1974) in Greece, labor was free to develop and was given a bigger role by the socialist-oriented government that came to power in 1981. Labor in Greece has a strong historical and ideological foundation and

participates actively in party politics. Alternately, while
in the United States government does not as a rule openly
resist the labor movement, it has also not based much of
its political ideology on labor principles. Republicans
have tried to not offend labor while actively opposing
labor programs. Democrats have been on much friendlier
terms and the major labor union, the American Federation
of Labor-Congress of Industrial Organizations (AFL-CIO),
has often endorsed the Democratic ticket in national elections. Under the present Republican leadership, however,
unionism has suffered many blows. Indeed, the current
administration has taken the most-overt steps of any
political administration in recent history to undercut the
power of labor as a significant social movement. The fact
that it has been successful in this effort is related partly
to competition from cheap foreign labor and partly to the
position of unions in the changing occupational structure
(service and white collar) of postindustrial U.S. society.
Unions have been tested so severely that they now represent only half the fraction of workers that they did at
their peak.

Labor in the occupational structure of both countries
has been moving steadily in its concentration from agriculture to industry to service sectors. In the United States
during 1984, 3.3 percent of the labor force were employed
in agriculture, 28.5 percent in industry, and 68.2 percent
in the service sector. In Greece for the same year, the
occupational structure was as follows: 30.0 percent in
agriculture, 28.6 percent in industry, and 41.4 percent in
services (Table 1.2). In the United States, labor's organizing efforts have not kept pace with the rapid growth
of the service sector. But in Greece there is every reason
to believe that the labor movement will remain strong as
the nation develops the service sector of its economy.
This is especially valid in the subsectors of banking and
public administration.

Labor should continue to have important union support in both nations in the near future, but the recent
growth in power of the working class (including workers
in public administration and private enterprises) is at-
tributable to many other variables as well.[16] It appears
to be related to trends in worker participation in management and profits, the development of worker ownership,
the participation of employees in decision making in government agencies, and the development of a cooperative

sector that takes into account the employees in the governance of the firm. These are some of the variety of labor-development trends that we will be examining.

In formulating theories about social development for labor and reporting empirical studies associated with new trends, our concern is of course not only with labor itself but also with its relation to capital. The relationship between these two classic categories still remains a major sociological challenge in the twentieth century.

The Status of the Community

If for Karl Marx human alienation is rooted in the problems of labor in relation to capital, it is rooted in problems of community for other sociologists. Emile Durkheim, Max Weber, and other sociologists spent their lives studying the problems of urbanization, industrialization, and bureaucratization as causative factors in the breakdown in community life.

The tremendous growth of cities and urbanization during the last hundred years has been a worldwide phenomenon. Between 1800 and 1982, a period in which the total population of the world expanded about 5.3 times, the number of people living in its cities swelled about 84 times, from about 21.7 million to about 1.8 billion people. In 1980, 26 cities had 5 million or more residents, with a combined population of 252 million.[17] The United States and Greece are no exceptions to this international trend.

Many sociologists are concerned with urban problems and the degree to which the dignity of life is retained. They are concerned that the growing number of densely packed cities are dehumanizing, impersonal, anonymous, and filled with bureaucratic institutions that distance people from one another. Some sociologists follow Wirth's model that increasing size, density, and heterogeneity increase role segmentation and anomie.[18] The question we pursue in our study concerns the degree to which people lose control over the direction of their own lives in the local urban economy.

The reasons for urbanization and the breakdown of community life are complex. In the past 30 years, both the United States and Greece have undergone enormous changes in their social structures and their life-styles. These changes have included a decrease in family size, a loosening of bonds among relatives (not so much for Greece), the exit of women from the traditional environment of the home, change in courtship and marital patterns, and high mobility in both horizontal and vertical directions.[19] These vast changes in social life are factors contributing to the breakdown of the traditional community.

Urbanization and the loss of a sense of intimacy among neighbors originally found in rural areas has been closely connected with industrialization around the world.[20] In the United States, the portion of the population living in urban places (fixed communities with populations of 2,500 or more) grew from about 15 percent in 1950 to 74 percent in 1980. Statistics show that people with lower incomes, less education, and fewer skills are over-represented in the central cities, while people with higher incomes and a higher education have moved to suburbs. Since the 1930s there has been an increase of nonwhite minorities in the central cities. By 1980, 58 percent of the black population lived in central cities compared with 25 percent of whites.[21]

At the same time, in the 1970s the more well-to-do blacks migrated to the suburbs in higher numbers than before, leaving behind the poor. This concentration of poor blacks in the center of the city has added to its financial and social problems. Then, during the 1970s and 1980s, another migratory process called gentrification began to happen. This involves the selective redevelopment of high-quality housing in certain cities and the movement of high-income whites (especially no-children young professionals) into that housing. The gentrification process is alarming to some residents because it drives up the value of land in the central city, making it more difficult for the poor to live there and leaving them with no other place to go.

This urbanization process is also evident in Greece (although differently). During the last 30 years the population of urban areas almost doubled, at the expense of rural areas. Urbanization benefited Athens (total recorded increase of population approximately 120%) and Thessaloníki (134%) the most. The remaining urban areas have experienced an increase of population in the vicinity of 70 percent. In 1951, 38 percent of the total population were living in urban areas. By 1981 the corresponding percentage had increased to approximately 58 percent. During the same year, more than 30 percent of the nation's population were living in the greater Athens area.

The movement from rural areas to the city (and especially to Athens) constitutes an extreme case of over-urbanization and of the dire consequences of an extreme primary city. There have been also significant movements of the population out of the country in a common search for higher-paying jobs. High prices and profits in some parts of industry widened the gap between industrial and agricultural incomes in the decade of the 1970s, and, among other reasons, unemployment or underemployment sent many relatively low-income people in the agricultural sector to nearby industry, concentrated largely around Athens and Thessaloníki, and also to neighboring countries. A parallel trend of high-income people moving into the suburbs is also visible, stimulated in part by the conditions of environmental pollution in the inner city, but there is no suburbanization in the American sense. The "suburbs" of lower socioeconomic level in Greece include illegal settlements (e.g., Perama), and they are not the typical suburbs of the United States. This is owing to a serious time lag in the development of comprehensive planning of housing and zoning in Greece.

The city has often been studied by sociologists from an ecological standpoint, with an assumption that the patterns of the marketplace are natural and inevitable in the modern world. The city is seen to have developed typically according to what are called concentric zones, city sectors, and multiple nuclei. The ecological school of thought assumes that "cities will continue to grow . . . [and] be accessible for these larger populations. . . . The real estate market will continue to be the main mechanism determining land use. . . . Business uses will continue to outbid residential uses in the central neighborhoods of maximum accessibility."[22] The assumptions of this school have been based on the principles of the competitive market and business society. However, while they are still important to take into account, they do not provide the best basis for comparing nations with different social patterns such as the United States and Greece.

Our concern is not so much with ecological evolution as with the problem of community breakdown in the process of urbanization. The loss of community life and the impersonal, bureaucratic structure of the city is a worldwide problem associated with all sorts of other social problems, including drugs, crime, prostitution, delinquency, and class conflict. The lack of community power, like the lack of labor power, is a major sociological problem of the twentieth century.

The roots of the loss of community are located in shifting social structures, new economic policies, corporate bureaucratization, income gaps, new styles of life, and many more factors that need to be investigated. But our focus on the causes for the loss of community life is on the market forces of modern society. In nations that are experiencing a transition in the nature of their market system, we are especially interested in how the competitive forces of that system are related to the problem of community breakdown and how steps can be taken toward the redevelopment of community life in light of this analysis. In our study we recognize the positive role of the market in strengthening the economy and respect the voluntary nature of the relationship between buyer and seller. But our question is rather: How can cooperative relations in market systems be cultivated as the basis for restoring genuine community life?[23]

Another reason for our selection of the competitive market system as a cause (but not the only cause) of community breakdown is because we see a larger problem connected with it. The development of the competitive market has brought enormous progress to modern nations, but it has also created monopolistic and oligopolistic situations that have hindered the development of labor and the local community, and it is necessary to find systemic solutions in order to reorientate this development.

The solution is conceived by orthodox Marxists to be through increased government regulatory role over the economy. The rise of the socialist state is a major example of attempts today to deal with distortions of the market system. But the solution offered--the dominance of the state in the society--has also not worked.

The current governments in Greece and the United States are sensitive to problems of community breakdown and/or state dominance but neither has found a fully satisfactory alternative. Greece in fact has a socialist-oriented government that seems preoccupied with the political answer to these problems; one purpose of the government is to help solve potential market problems of land, labor, capital, and the loss of community life, which are also related to factors of size, density, and heterogeneity, as implied earlier.   The ideological preoccupation with the solution to these most-important questions in modern society explains the focus of our study in Greece.

The most significant fact about the United States and Greece is that despite the divergent political outlooks of their governments in the 1980s, they are both seeking an alternative to the problems of alienation and the increasing complexity of modern life.

The Status of the Government

The United States and Greece have each experienced a continuous growth in government activity in response to the problems of the market system, but the current governments are virtually opposite in their approach.   Both came to power at approximately the same time (in 1981) with a commitment to solve the problems of a free society, as all governments do.   In the Greek case, the main stated goal was the socialist transformation of society and increased regulation of the economy as well as state and social participation in economic activity.   In the United States, the main goal was to reduce government controls and to deregulate the economy.   In other words, the present Greek government proposed to treat the problems of the economy through what it called "socialist transformation," while the present U.S. government sought to reduce government regulations by supporting what it called "supply-side economics."   The paradox is that in both countries the government sector has expanded and government debt has increased significantly over the last few years.

Expansion of government activity in Greece also took place under the administration of the conservative New Democracy party in the 1974-81 period and accelerated under the administration of the socialist PASOK party since 1981.   The annual compound growth rate of the government budget deficit was 35 percent in the 1975-81 period, much higher than the 13 percent growth rate of the deficit in the 1960-73 period.[24]   The public debt reached the highest level ever in 1985, when the government deficit as a percentage of the GDP rose to 18 percent, compared with 15.6 percent in 1984 and 11.5 percent in 1983.[25]   The expansion of government activity came at the expense of diverting economic resources from uses in the private sector.   This has been partly responsible for the Greek inflation rate remaining a two-digit figure in spite of the low rate of 5 percent in the other nations of the EEC.

The annual compound growth rate of the U.S. government budget deficit was 4.3 percent in the 1975–81 period.[26] But if we calculate the growth rate from 1974 to 1981, the growth rate of the deficit was 49.5 percent, a much higher rate than for Greece. (The U.S. deficit was small in 1974.) The deficit of Greece has been increasing more than in the United States in nominal and real terms, but the extent of the difference depends on the years in which it is calculated. The annual compound growth rate in the United States, beginning in 1963 at 0.80 percent, grew in 1973 to 1.09 percent and in 1983 to 6 percent. This represents a major period of expansion.[27]

The growth of government activity during the Reagan years seems not to have slowed down in spite of all the political promises to reduce government. The annual compound rate of federal expenditures during the Reagan years was 8.5 percent during 1981-85, as compared with the Carter administration's 1977–81 13 percent. Adjusted for inflation rates, there is no real difference between these periods.[28]

The United States has recently become a top debtor nation. At the end of 1986, it owed the rest of the world $263.6 billion, more than double the previous year's total. The annual report from the Commerce Department reports U.S. foreign debt rose 135 percent in 1986, outpacing the combined debt of Brazil, Mexico, and Argentina, the three previous debt leaders. Foreigners now own more in U.S. investments than Americans own in foreign investments, something that has not occurred since 1914. Last year (1986), foreign investment in the United States jumped 26 percent to $1,331 trillion, while U.S. investment overseas recorded a smaller 13 percent increase to a new total at the end of the year of $1,068 trillion. Some economists have predicted the U.S. debt total will top $1 trillion by 1990, requiring a transfer of $50 billion annually to foreigners just to meet interest payments on the debt.[29]

Market forces are a factor in explaining the growth of the government activity even though their power is not easily measured. We are proposing that the growth of government agencies in welfare, public aid, consumer protection, labor protection, environmental protection, and conservation of land and natural resources is largely a result of the problems caused by a competitive market that does not operate consistently in the public interest.

The business corporation is becoming more socially motivated in the United States, but it is not structured to be publicly responsible, that is, to help its laid-off employees obtain new jobs, to conserve the nation's natural resources, to protect the consumer in a competitive market, or to enhance community life. It is structured to operate only in its competitive self-interest; hence, the need for government services. Many other types of government growth— police systems, rehabilitation and treatment centers, divorce courts, and prisons—can be attributed in part to the breakdown in community life, in turn spurred by the high mobility of people and the norms of corporate self-interest in a competitive market. This is a complex sociological point of view that informs much of our study. It requires careful scrutiny in further research for its political implications.

The social and economic progress brought about by capitalism has also brought its own set of problems--problems that many believe require governmental solution. The solution to social problems created in the competitive market are sought today through the help and under the auspices of a democratic state. Thus, we see a major institutional cause for the continued growth of government.

However, our references suggest that the solution to the problems caused by the competitive market do not rest in more government controls over the economy. Indeed, the growth of government often serves as another form of bureaucracy and helps destroy not only the free-enterprise system but also genuine community life. It can lead toward a state bureaucracy with more-serious forms of dependency and dominance for the population as a whole. The real question is: How can we overcome the problems of a competitive market without increasing government growth?

The goals of the two political administrations in the United States and Greece are surprisingly similar in one narrow respect: they both want to limit central government growth and maintain a mixed economy. This interest in limiting the power of central government is part of the political platforms in each nation. Indeed it is the rationale of our time for designing new government policies. But the attempt to find solutions to government growth in these two nations, so different in social patterns and beliefs, results in new problems arising to block progress

toward their goals. Thus, the solution to this complex
problem is a central issue in our research.

RECENT POLITICAL HISTORY IN THE
UNITED STATES AND GREECE

The cultural heritages of Greece and the United
States are each notable for their own contributions to our
conceptual framework. Ancient Greece is noted for having
first experimented with the concept of democracy. In ancient Greece, the Achaean League and the Amphictyonic
Council reportedly represent the first invention of a federation.[30] Polybius described the Achaean League, with
its unitary laws, weights and measures, coinage, councils,
and judges, as a voluntary federation of city-states in
which deputies were appointed by citizens. The concept
of the federation stems from these ancient origins and becomes a critical part of our understanding of how modern
economies develop. The United States is noted for being
the latest nation to experiment with democracy on a large
scale, but it is best characterized as a republic, following more the Roman than the Greek paradigm. Its most
notable contribution, however, may exist in the vast number of nonprofit and voluntary associations that have developed there as democratic federations. They constitute
nonstatist examples of how the economy (rather than simply
the polity) is becoming democratized. These many nonprofit
democratic federations (the Young Men's Christian Association [YMCA], the Presbyterian Church, Kiwanis Clubs,
etc.) provide interesting examples of how member corporations can become a part of the larger systems of social
governance.[31]
We now turn to a discussion of the more-recent
political histories of the two nations.

The United States

After World War II, the United States seemed singu-
larly qualified to assume the mantle of leadership in international affairs. Pent-up domestic demand coupled with
the rebuilding of Western Europe and Asia and the Pacific
fueled the American ascent. Greece was among the countries that under the Marshall Plan received American aid
and rebuilt itself.

There are really two economies in the United States, according to John Kenneth Galbraith. There is a market economy, where 14 million corporations and partnerships struggle over 30 percent of market sales roughly in accordance with classic laws of supply and demand. Then there is the "planned economy," where some 800 multinational conglomerates dominate fully 70 percent of all economic activity. Two-thirds of the manufacturing sector is run by oligopolies, that is, a few of these corporations. Fifty of 3,000 banks control one-half of all bank assets. The policies of the present administration have led to a continuing growth in corporate concentration.[32]

Studies show the corporate economy continuing to centralize. A Senate Governmental Affairs Committee staff report found that the largest percentages of stock ownership in almost all major U.S. corporations are held or controlled by as few as 15 financial institutions, notably major banks and insurance companies. Also, a study for the congressional Joint Economic Committee showed that the rise of conglomerates had spread the practice of administered pricing (where one or two big firms establish high prices, regardless of market conditions, for the rest of the industry to follow) to industries that previously were not concentrated.[33] Although this is not true in all industries, there is much evidence to support such a general contention. These developments have led to an awareness of the need for public control over the economy.

Since 1981 and the advent of the Reagan administration, however, a radical shift has taken place. Soon after inauguration, a number of steps were taken to remove government controls over the economy. For example, a cabinet-level committee was appointed to identify and eliminate government regulations deemed unnecessary. Price controls were removed on domestic crude oil, and several industries were deregulated (e.g., airlines, trucking, and communications). In addition, the Occupational Health and Safety Administration dropped over 1,000 pages of regulations and design standards from their books. Opportunities developed to create a more-favorable climate for multinational corporations (MNCs), ranging from "clarifying" the Foreign Corrupt Practices Act to revamping the Export-Import Bank. Legislative proposals were offered to strengthen domestic international sales corporations (by permitting the tax deferral of 100 percent of qualified export income); to retain the foreign-tax credit system and the procedure of not taxing accumulated overseas earnings prior to their remittance as dividends; to permit the organization of trading companies to act as agents for smaller firms; and to beef up federal agencies responsible for developing long-term foreign-trade policies.[34]

The consequences of the policies of the Reagan administration are too recent and complex to evaluate here, but some of them are described in succeeding chapters of this volume.

Greece

The roots of the problems and conditions in Greece can be traced to the historical development of the country. The modern Greek state goes as far back as 1821, the year of the revolution against Ottoman rule. The Greek social system continues to the present as a combination of Western and Levantine elements, traditionality and modernity. Greece has faced long periods of war, requiring painful efforts at economic reconstruction, and has traditionally been an ally of Western powers. Within the last 30 years or so, Greece has made the great jump from being classified as a peasant, underdeveloped country to joining the ranks of developing ones.[35] During this period, the nation enjoyed an unprecedented economic prosperity.

The post-1974 period is most critical to our study. It began with the end of a seven-year period of military dictatorship in Greece and the restoration of a democratic regime in July 1974. It continued with the election of a socialist-oriented government in 1981. Since then Greece has witnessed new developmental efforts, new policies, and political changes that attempt to bring about new structural arrangements in various areas of the social and economic life of the country.

Before we embark on more-detailed discussions, however, it is important to advance a number of caveats that underline our analysis. One has to do with our implicit recognition of rhetoric versus reality. When we use such terms as socialist-oriented in the case of the Greek government, we conform to the descriptive terms adopted by the government or the intentions exemplified in formal documents (such as manifestos, party platforms, or the 1983-87 Five-Year Plan). As indicated previously, we view Greece as in an earlier stage of capitalism (protocapitalist) and as part of the general drift toward consumer-oriented

societies. This view distinguishes it from the strict meaning of the term socialism as the precursor stage of centralized, directed economies.

Since the period between 1974 and 1981, when the
country was governed by the conservative New Democracy
party, there has been policy set for improving wages and
salaries of workers, an expansion of social policy and the
welfare state, and official recognition of the Communist
party (KKE). New trends in the economy were witnessed,
reflecting a growth in the public deficit and the trade
deficit connected with the oil crisis and enlargement of
government activity. Although the movement for Greece's
European participation has been discussed heatedly since
the early 1960s, relative arrangements have been made
ever since Greece became a member of the EEC in 1980.
Membership in the EEC carried the promise of substantial
democratic progress according to the liberal political view,
but it also required considerable adjustment, including
modernizing production and the economic and social structure of the country. This required considerable government
attention and involvement in economic affairs.

The enlargement of government activity continues
under the administration of the Socialist party (PASOK)
until today. The current government has completed the
1983-87 Five-Year Plan prepared by the Ministry of National Economy and the Center of Planning and Economic
Research.[36] This Plan initiated a different planning process from the ones observed in the past, introduced new
concepts, policies, and measures involving popular participation, democratic planning, social control, and a social
sector of the economy. While not implemented in the strict
sense of a plan, this document, with its heavily influenced
ideological interpretations of on-going development and
needed transformations, reflected the underlying premises
and hopes of the ruling party in the early 1980s. The
ideas contained in this Plan are a basic part of our study
insofar as they express the orientation of the government
policy at that stage. The focus of our analysis is not
foreign trade or international competition, but such factors
are part of the political background of foreign and economic relations of the United States and Greece.

Foreign and Economic Relations

Developments in Greece have been influenced by the
external policies of the United States. Opinions and views

as to the degree of that influence and its consequences
are diversified. Some are highly critical and consider
that Greece has been a crucial testing ground for the
postwar role of the United States in world affairs, an
opinion expressed mostly by politicians and scholars of
the left in Greece. According to this view, the power of
the United States was felt in Greece as in many other
small nations around the world. Greece has been considered representative of a small nation existing among other
small nations in the world that must deal with a superpower. On the other hand, scholars dealing with social
change have stressed the continuity of transformation in
the Greek economy. They search out the living core of
Greek tradition, culture, and skills of the marketplace
that influence development in such a way that economic
and other unilinear theories of development need correc-
tion.[37]

Institutional arrangements for trade between the
United States and Greece go back to 1948, when provisions
of the Agreement for Economic Cooperation were signed.
This involved a commitment to free trade between the countries and the avoidance of protectionist policies. The
agreement stipulated that no Greek firm should obtain a
monopolistic position and thereby obstruct international
competition. At the time of the Agreement, no firm had
the ability to obtain monopoly, but the intent of the
Agreement was to guarantee freedom of markets for U.S.
firms in Greece.

This contract foreshadowed the basic Greek law for
the protection of foreign investment in Greece, Law Decree
2687, which has been the major vehicle for the inflow of
foreign investment into Greece. The law provided a basic
property guarantee against expropriation and allowed for
repatriation of imported capital and remittance of earnings,
that is, a "freedom of exit" for foreign investment capital.
It also provided preferential tax treatment involving a
reduction or waiver of import duties, fees, and dues of
various kinds and several exemptions of income taxes on
profits.[38] Greece has benefited from such open economic
cooperation with the United States and other Western countries, but it has also felt the consequences of its heavy
dependence on other economies.[39] Preoccupation with the
dependence of the country has led PASOK to declare a
third path of development in the early 1980s, apart from
the pattern of development of either Western capitalist or

state socialist traditions, to avoid conditions that have en-
trapped nations in the past.

IN SUMMARY

The United States and Greece are clearly dissimilar
in size, ethnic composition, population, economic standards
of living, and many other factors, but they are also similar in ways that make our study relevant to international
issues in social economy.   They are both nations that
have sought to avoid state socialism and to limit the
amount of central government growth in the early 1980s.
The effort to curtail state intervention in economic affairs
has been a main concern in the United States.   But the
irony is that in both nations government growth has taken
place.   Furthermore, both nations increased their level of
indebtedness as an unintended consequence of policies introduced in each administration.   The problem of alienation in the field of labor relations as well as the measures
taken in both countries to treat it are greatly dissimilar;
nevertheless the problems do not seem to have attenuated
and some critics claim the problems have not been significantly addressed by either government.   Nor has the problem of a steady decline in community life been addressed
effectively by either government, even though both governments have a strong interest in treating the problems that
result in part from a breakdown in community life.

Our study is designed to address the issues of reducing alienation in the field of labor relations and
strengthening community life.   Relatedly, we are interested
in methods for reducing the necessity for central government growth insofar as it may be caused by competitive
forces in the market system and may be treated by accenting cooperative processes.   Our contention is that by augmenting the self-governing capacity of labor as an effective part of a productive corporate economy and by
strengthening community life through cooperative processes,
steps are taken to reduce the necessity for central government growth and state intervention in the economy.

Our task now is to formulate a theoretical orientation
for the self-governing capacity of labor and communities
in the economic order of modern nations.   We can then examine the degree to which the United States and Greece in
each case have taken steps toward development of these
two sectors.

NOTES

1. By the term <u>socialist-oriented government</u>, we mean that an emphasis is given to social policy regarding redistribution of income and control by the state of certain economic and public activities. This brief description is made on the basis of consultation with government officials in Greece.

2. Severyn T. Bruyn, <u>The Social Economy: People Transforming Business</u> (New York: John Wiley & Sons, 1977), p. 3.

3. The concept of the community is derived from ancient Greek thought. The <u>polis</u> referred to the political community of the city-state. The early appearance of this concept, however, never fully differentiated between the government and the community. Through the evolution of society, scholars began to make this important distinction. Karl Marx was most clear in distinguishing between the concept of the community and the state in his work.

4. The distinction between the concept of community and society is most clearly made by Robert M. MacIver, <u>Society</u> (Philadelphia: Century Bookbindery, 1937) and Robert Nisbet, <u>The Quest for Community</u> (New York: Oxford University Press, 1953).

5. Organization for Economic Cooperation and Development OECD: <u>Economic Surveys 1985/86 GREECE</u> (Paris: OECD, 1986); <u>Economic Surveys 1985/86 UNITED STATES</u> (Paris: OECD, 1985); <u>Economic Surveys 1986/87 UNITED STATES</u> (Paris: OECD, 1986). For selected references to the Greek economy, see Maria Delivani-Negreponti, <u>Analysis of the Greek Economy</u> (Athens: Papazissis, 1979), in Greek; George Coutsoumaris, <u>The Morphology of Greek Industry</u> (Athens: Center of Economic Research, 1963); J. Papantoniou, "Foreign Trade and Industrial Development: Greece and the EEC," <u>Cambridge Journal of Economics</u> (1979):33-48; S. Papaspeliopoulos, ed., <u>Studies on the Contemporary Greek Economy</u> (Athens: Papazissis, 1978), in Greek; and Theodoros Skountzos, <u>Structural Changes in Greek Economy: A Diachronic Analysis</u> (Athens: Center for Planning and Economic Research, 1980), in Greek. For an analysis of social and economic conditions of contemporary Greece, see the publications of (a) National Statistical Service of Greece, ESYE; (b) National Center of Social Research, EKKE; (c) Center of Planning and Economic Research, KEPE; (d) Bank of Greece; and (e) Institute of Economic and Industrial Research, IOBE.

6. OECD, Economic Surveys 1985/86 GREECE; Economic Surveys 1985/86 UNITED STATES; Economic Surveys 1986/87 UNITED STATES; Dimitrios Tsaoussis, Morphology of Modern Greek Society (Athens: Gutenberg, 1971), in Greek.

7. See Maria Evangelinides, "Core-Periphery Relations in the Greek Case," in Underdeveloped Europe: Studies in Core-Periphery Relations, ed. D. Seers, B. Schaffer, and M. R. Kiljunen (Atlantic Highlands, N.J.: Humanities Press, 1979), pp. 190-91; National Center of Social Research, Developments and Prospects of the Population of Greece, 1920-1985 (Athens: EKKE, 1973); Social Sciences Centre, Essays on Greek Migration. Migration Series No. 1 (Athens: Social Sciences Centre, 1967); Vasilis Filias, Problems of Social Transformation, Ch. 1, "Migration and the Socioeconomic Problem of Greece," pp. 183-248 (Athens: Papazissis, 1974), in Greek; Koula Kasimati, Emigration-Repatriation. The Problematic of the Second Generation (Athens: National Center of Social Research, 1984), in Greek.

8. Results concerning the number of doctors are owing to the so-called peculiarities of development.

9. Evangelinides, "Core-Periphery Relations," p. 185; Constantinos Tsoukalas, State, Society, and Work in Post-War Greece (Athens: Themelio, 1986), in Greek.

10. Marios Nicolinakos, "Transnationalization of Production, Location of Industry, and the Deformation of Regional Development," in Peripheral Countries: The Case of Greece in the Uneven Development of Southern Europe, ed. R. Hudson and S. Lewis (London and New York: Methuen, 1985).

11. See Maria Petmezidou-Tsoulouvi, Social Classes and Mechanisms of Social Reproduction (Athens: Exantas, 1987), pp. 168-81, in Greek; and idem., "Approaches to the Issue of Underdevelopment of Greek Social Transformation: A Critical Perspective," Current Issues 22 (1984):13-29, in Greek; Nicos P. Mouzelis, Modern Greece: Facets of Underdevelopment (London: Macmillan, 1978).

12. Evangelinides, "Core-Periphery Relations," pp. 192-93; U.S. Department of Commerce, Bureau of Economic Analysis, Survey of Current Business, June 1987.

13. Economic Report of the President, 1984 (Washington, D.C.: Government Printing Office, 1984), p. 233.

14. See Takis Photopoulos, Dependent Development: The Greek Case (Athens: Exantas, 1985), in Greek; Constantinos Tsoukalas, "Social Extensions of State Employment

in Post-War Greece," Review of Social Research, No. 50, 1983, pp. 20 ff., in Greek; and idem., State, Society, and Work, pp. 250-59.

15.   Iota Kravaritou-Manitaki, "Labor Relations in Greece," in Manesis et al., Greece in the Process of Development (Athens: Exantas, 1986), pp. 287-306, in Greek; Litsa Nicolaou-Smokoviti, Participation and Self-Management. New Institutions of Labor Relations, Ch. 7, "Self-Management in Greece in the 1980s" (Athens: Papazissis; forthcoming), in Greek.

16.   Ibid.

17.   United Nations, Population Reference Bureau.

18.   L. Wirth, "Urbanism as a Way of Life," American Journal of Sociology 44 (1938):3-24.

19.   For a clarification of the concept of mobility as used here, see Tsoukalas, State, Society, and Work in Post-War Greece; also, see Ioanna Lambiri, "The Impact of Industrial Employment on the Position of Women in a Greek Country Town," British Journal of Sociology 14, No. 3 (September 1963):240-47; and idem., Social Change in a Greek Country Town (Athens: Center of Planning and Economic Research KEPE, 1965); Koula Kasimati, Mobility Trends in Greek Industry (Athens: National Center of Social Research EKKE, 1980), in Greek.

20.   Wirth, "Urbanism."

21.   Neil Smelser, Sociology (Englewood Cliffs, N.J.: Prentice-Hall, 1984), pp. 137, 139.

22.   Jackson Toby, Contemporary Society (New York: John Wiley & Sons, 1971), p. 249.

23.   The eclipse of community life has also developed in state socialist countries where overarching state bureaucracy continues to reign. We focus on the market system because revolutionary socialism emerged in part to promote the development of labor and restore genuine community life that had become eclipsed by corporate monopoly. The alternative of state socialism did not solve the problems. Socialist states must now find their own path toward the development of worker control and genuine community life. One of the problems they must solve is how to maintain freedom in economic enterprise without returning to the distortions of the capitalist market.

24.   See Bank of Greece, The Greek Economy, Vol. 2, p. 94 (Athens: Bank of Greece, 1982), in Greek; and ibid., Annual Report of the Governor of the Bank of Greece for the Year 1981 (Athens: Bank of Greece, 1982), p. 107, in

Greek; also, Center of Planning and Economic Research, The Greek Economy Today (Athens: KEPE, 1984), pp. 31, 35.

25. Bank of Greece, Summary of Annual Report of Governor D. Chalikias for the Year 1985 (Athens: Bank of Greece, 1985), p. 42, in Greek.

26. Economic Report of the President, 1984 (Washington, D.C.: Government Printing Office, 1984), pp. 283, 305-5.

27. Ibid., pp. 223, 305.

28. Economic Report of the President, 1986 (Washington, D.C.: Government Printing Office, 1986), pp. 319, 345.

29. Boston Globe, June 24, 1987, p. 73.

30. Sobei Mogi, The Problems of Federalism (London: George Allen & Unwin, 1931), pp. 21ff.

31. For an analysis of American democracy, see the classic work of Alexis De Toqueville, Democracy in America (New York: Harper & Row, 1966).

32. John Kenneth Galbraith, The Industrial State (Boston: Houghton Mifflin, 1967), Ch. 7, "The Corporation," p. 72ff.

33. These studies are described in Mark Green, Winning Back America (New York: Bantam Books, 1982), p. 53.

34. David A. Heenan, The Re-United States of America (Reading, Mass.: Addison-Wesley, 1983), p. 211.

35. Litsa N. Nicolaou, The Growth and Development of Sociology in Greece (Boston, 1974), pp. 1-2 (mimeographed).

36. Center of Planning and Economic Research, Plan for Economic and Social Development, 1983-1987 (Athens: KEPE, 1985), in Greek.

37. See William H. McNeil, The Metamorphosis of Greece since World War II (Chicago: University of Chicago Press, 1987); and idem., Greece: American Aid in Action 1947-1956 (New York: Twentieth Century Fund Inc., 1957); Evan Vlahos, Modern Greek Society: Continuity and Change (Fort Collins: Colorado State University, Department of Sociology, 1969) (mimeographed).

38. Theodore Couloumbis and John Iatrides, Greek-American Relations (New York: Pella, 1980), p. 76ff.

39. See Theodore Hitiris, Trade Effects of Economic Association with Common Market: The Case of Greece (New York: Praeger, 1972).

PART I

ISSUES
IN
WORKER
SELF-GOVERNANCE

2. The Concept of Worker Self-Governance: A Review of Academic Interpretations

The concept of worker self-governance is becoming significant in university research and at the same time in the
politics of modern nations. The increasing use of the term
makes its definition important. But a problem arises when
the same concept is defined one way in academic settings
and another way in political settings. To define a concept
in the context of an educational institution or for use in
scientific studies is different from defining the same concept in the context of a government or for use in a political movement. Indeed, the use of the same concept in
these different contexts can cause much confusion. A
scientific concept and a political concept can have very
different meanings with conflicting messages. Hence, it is
time to distinguish the basis for developing academic definitions for their special purposes and functions. This task
can begin at elementary levels without any pretense at
being comprehensive. The subject is admittedly complex,
but it is especially critical to have clear definitions for
academic studies that intend to compare the content of
self-governance in different societies.

At the outset, we are using the concept of self-
governance instead of the better-known concept of self-
management so as to change the temper of the inquiry and
outlook on the subject. We want to think of this concept
as part of an intercultural approach to the study of social
development in economic life. We refer to the broad area
to which the term self-management often refers ideologically, and we need a term with some flexibility for scientific
purposes. The concept of self-management has different
political meanings in various nations and carries strong
ideological overtones in each case. It is not our task to

41

evaluate these ideological differences or even compare them. We are more interested in introducing a scientific perspective to studies in this field and in providing a conceptual basis for making international comparisons. Our focus, therefore, is intentionally more academic to stimulate thought for policy research. We want the concept of self-governance to be derived from reason and empirical studies rather than simply from the need to establish an ideological position. Our hope is to do this while keeping in mind the relationship that academic studies have for providing insight into political policy and social action.

In pursuit of the more academic goal for our study, we are interested in reviewing the meaning of self-governance from a theoretical perspective. A theoretical framework will give us a better opportunity to discuss the development of worker self-governance in contrasting cultures as well as to offer suggestions for policy research in an international context.

ACADEMIC INTERPRETATIONS OF WORKER SELF-GOVERNANCE

Modern social inquiry distinguishes types of concepts that help clarify the meaning of self-governance in different national settings. We refer to these concepts as sensitizing, operational, ideal type, philosophical, historical type, and planning model. Once we have distinguished these different types, we can look at the problem of history interpreted by a concept of worker self-governance.

The Sensitizing Concept

A sensitizing concept in the field of sociology is simply a common-sense reference to a publicly recognizable phenomenon. This type of concept allows people to refer to experiences in everyday life without the complications of an operational meaning or a sophisticated meaning in philosophy. This type of concept is helpful in "sensitizing" social scientists to the subjective meanings that people use in everyday life.

The more formal definition of social-scientific concepts frequently comes out of everyday experience in

society. Examples of everyday terms that are used in
sociology would be custom or tradition, without ever defining them formally any further than their common meaning.
Mores and primary group would also fall into this category
of common usage, but their origins are reversed. The
meanings of these terms were derived originally from
sociological studies and then drifted into everyday use.[1]

An everyday definition of self-governance to which
we can refer is "the capacity of people to control their
own direction in life apart from outside controls." This
common idea has both a factual (analytical) and a normative (ideal) dimension.

The factual dimension claims that all people have
this capacity to some degree. No one is totally independent or totally dependent upon outside controls. Inmates
in a prison have a degree of self-governance in the sense
that they choose to do a thousand things each day according to their own direction, even if it means only selecting
a spoon to eat instead of a fork. A bed-ridden patient
who must be fed intravenously still has control over the
direction of his or her own thoughts.

The factual dimension means that we can study the
degree to which self-governance exists for workers in firms
even though the firms are not democratically organized.
The workers may be operating within only relatively autonomous groups that are still under the command of higher
management. By working within this autonomous structure,
they may have a relative degree of choice over the direction of their work, in contrast with another structure requiring constant supervision. It is important to see the
distinction we are making for the term in this sense. It
has analytical value apart from normative and ideological
considerations.

The normative dimension exists in the fact that
people desire to increase this capacity for self-governing
work. The meaning of self-governance in this instance
changes from a factual and analytical perspective to an
ideal. The ideal then becomes formulated in many different ways and can become a part of a political ideology.
This meaning of self-governance can take many shapes,
according to the cultural setting in which it develops.
The concept of self-governance in the political parties of
France (autogestion) has a meaning different from its
meaning in Yugoslavia. These ideological dimensions of
self-governance become a special type of normative concept based on history, as we shall see.

The sensitizing (common) idea of self-governance can be applied analytically to many different institutions and different levels of management. For example, it may apply to the organization of the government, church, and school as well as the business corporation. Each type of organization may be differently developed in its capacity for self-governance. Equally important, each organization has different levels of management to be analyzed. Self-governance exists at the level of the individual, the workplace (as a collective entity), the department, the corporation, the industry, and the economy as a whole. Similarly, the government, church, and school have their own separate degrees of practice in self-governance as institutions. We are likely to find that the Presbyterian Church in the United States is more self-governing in this sense than the business corporation, because it is more democratic in its national organization. The government in Yugoslavia is more decentralized and self-governing in its federal structure than the government in Poland. Municipalities in the United States have been more self-governing in the past than municipalities in Greece, and so forth.

The Operational Concept

The concept of self-governance can be operationalized. An operational concept is defined in measurable and observational terms. This involves identifying a procedure used for measuring the degree to which the phenomenon exists in reality. The operational concept enables social scientists to predict human behavior. For example, the concept of intelligence quotient (IQ) is an operational concept defined by applying the Wechsler-Bellevue test to people under specific conditions. It is different from the concept of intelligence, which is a sensitizing concept. The IQ is simply one measurable dimension of intelligence. We might define worker self-governance in this operational sense as existing in an industrial workshop when no supervisor gives an order to a worker for eight hours a day for three days of observation each week for two months. The operational concept is useful for comparative studies that seek to obtain statistical results but should not be confused with other concepts of worker self-governance; it serves the purposes of empirical research and scientific prediction, in contrast with other concepts that offer higher levels of understanding and social insight.

The Ideal Type Concept

An ideal type defines the nature of a phenomenon by its general attributes formulated from historical data. An example would be Weber's ideal type of bureaucracy. This type of concept yields insight at middle-range levels of understanding. It has special value for comparative research of the same phenomenon in different cultural settings. It improves our understanding of institutional phenomena even though it may have less predictive power than an operational concept. Worker self-governance in this sense can be compared between institutions and cultural settings in ways that yield insights at higher levels than the operational concept.

The attributes of bureaucracy have been studied for the degree to which they exist in different corporations. For example, we should expect a corporation to have a hierarchical organization with different office rankings in a linear line above one another. Each office should contain certain specifications of duty, privileges, and power in reference to other offices above and below it. A set of rules based on reason should provide legitimacy to the power of these offices to discharge their duties. Given such attributes, the researcher may find that not all of them exist in reality. A corporation may not have offices organized in perfect linear relationships, insofar as professional departments (e.g., engineering and law) may have an independent and comparable status in the firm. The decisions may take place more typically on the basis of collegiality rather than hierarchy. Furthermore, the rules for a corporation in one cultural setting may be vastly different from those of another setting. The researcher does not judge the morality of the two cases as much as the effects of the differences on the occupants of the two organizations and the range of discretion people are given in making decisions. The concept of bureaucracy thus allows us to compare institutions and gain insight into the nature of human organization.[2]

Similarly, the concept of self-governance can be conceived of as an ideal type. Let us say that self-governance is a pattern of organization in which people are self-directing in their work according to certain external and internal criteria. The details of these criteria are not so important here as simply indicating the character of this social type for comparative research. We would suggest that the criteria extend much beyond what the current literature suggests is important.

The external criteria would include the premise that people in self-governing firms have relative freedom from state controls and the institutional right to free speech. This stipulation was central to the creation of self-management in Yugoslavia.[3] But the external environment is also complexly related to other organizations that can inhibit or advance the self-governing capacity of a firm. These other external organizations include unions, competitors, trade associations, customers, suppliers, municipalities, and creditors as well as the government. The capacity for self-governance of firms is advanced and inhibited in some measure by the relationships established with each of these external organizations. The formulation of the external criteria involves examining the way in which the firm typically finds reciprocity with these organizations. For example, we know that governments control firms in some measure as well as liberate them for independent operations through their charters. At the same time, governments benefit from the existence of firms through job creation, taxes, the production of needed goods and services, and so forth. Similarly, trade associations can dominate their member firms if they become too centralized, but they also provide support for their firms through such activities as trade fairs, courses in accounting for members, protection from foreign imports through government lobbying, and the like. Unions can also dominate firms through corporate buyouts, appointing members from their own administrative hierarchy to the board of directors instead of electing employees of the firm itself. At the same time they can also advance the self-governing capacity of firms by offering low-interest loans, supplying grievance consultation to employees, and providing a basis for establishing pension funds on a broader geographic basis than one firm by itself could afford. The elaboration of the traits typifying these external relations that support or inhibit the self-governing capacity of firms has yet to be done in self-management research. When it is accomplished, the findings should provide insight into the external conditions supporting self-governance among firms in different countries.[4]

Drawing from the studies of Paul Bernstein, the <u>internal criteria</u> would include

1. participation in decision making in significant areas,
2. frequent economic returns to employees,
3. guaranteed individual rights (e.g., free speech),
4. an independent board of appeals, and
5. a particular set of attitudes and values sustaining the organization.[5]

Bernstein defines these attributes in more detail on the basis of historical cases, but in any case, we would not necessarily find that the details fit the reality of particular firms claiming to be self-governed. The task of the researcher is to compare the differences in separate historical contexts. Thus the purpose of the concept is different from that of a political concept as it is designed heuristically for scientific studies. Knowing the given attributes allows a researcher to make intercultural comparisons.

These attributes are seen not as political expectations but as the conceptual foundation for research where the findings are often surprising. In studying the external criteria, for example, we may find in some instances that the sale of products is government restricted, such as the sale of pornographic literature or the sale of people into slavery. At one time the production and sale of bikini bathing suits in Yugoslavia was in dispute, thus limiting the fulfillment of the expected attribute of free enterprise. In studying the internal criteria, we may find that the need for frequent economic returns to employees has much less meaning for the practice of self-governance in Mondragon, Spain, than in the United States. We may find that a formally democratic firm does have guaranteed individual rights although it does not have an independent board of appeals. This elicits an interest (rather than a moral judgment) on the part of the researcher as to why a board was not created. In addition, the researcher could find that these typical attributes themselves (e.g., an independent board) may not be sufficiently definitive and may need further elaboration. As Weber indicated in his original concept, these attributes leave room for interpretation in concrete instances. For example, Alvin Gouldner discovered the lack of an attribute he called "representative bureaucracy" in Weber's original formulation of bureaucracy. He found a need to extend the meaning of bureaucracy to include this new attribute, offering the idea that a degree of self-management could develop in a bureaucratic setting.[6]

The attributes of an ideal type are not defined in very precise terms. The more precisely they are defined for empirical measurement, the closer the concept comes to being an operational concept. Yet the ideal type has its own inherent value without requiring operationalization. Further definition in measurable terms may allow it to gain in the power of predictability at a low level of abstraction but it loses in other respects: it loses its power of ideational insight based on comparative studies. The quality and level of insight gained from this middle-range concept is of primary importance for building social theory and establishing political policy.

The Philosophical Concept

Scholars can also formulate a broad social theory—or develop philosophical ideas—about self-governance. This provides another conceptual level of understanding of self-governance still different from the others. For example, Mihailo Marcovic develops a philosophical meaning for the concept of self-management to help explain the meaning of other general terms like liberation and praxis in a new way. In this case, a more-abstract level of understanding is achieved. This conceptual work is important because it bears fruit in the formulation of ideal types and political policies at middle levels of abstraction. Its value rests in its power to inspire thought at the higher level of the professions and the society.[7]

An ideal (scientific) type of self-governance does not give us the dynamic meaning, in terms of its organizational attributes, that its philosophical meaning would offer. On the basis of understanding a philosophical interpretation like that of Marcovic's, we would then be interested in looking at how the corporate structure of self-governance liberates people. Let us say that the philosophy of self-governance in connection with the concept of liberation—following Marcovic—requires the development of the inner resources of the participants in the corporation. The aim of self-governance is to maximize human resources—the imagination, sensitivity, and skills of corporate members. We now have some ideas that could

make an important addition to our ideal type. Our task
now is to look for these instances in empirical reality.
The philosophy of self-governance helps us see conceptually
the kinds of attributes important to the "progressive specification" of the ideal type.

The philosophic concept of self-governance should be
evaluated on its own terms. It is thus different from the
ideal type in the sense that it need not be subject to the
tests of empirical research. The ideal type may prove to
be so far removed from social reality that it becomes more
of a utopian concept and is not useful empirically, but a
philosophical concept may gain value by its social logic
and vision. It need not be studied empirically, but it
may be challenged on epistemological, metaphysical, and
ontological standards of philosophy. It must connect logi-
cally with other great concepts (like liberation or justice),
be coherent descriptively within itself, and provide a
fruitful direction to new theory.

The Historical Concept

Defining self-governance in the context of history
involves a different method and leads to a different conclusion. This definition directs the meaning of the term
to a particular time and place. But it too, must be distinguished from ideology. For example, federalism had a
certain configuration of meaning within the time of James
Madison and Thomas Jefferson in the colonial period of the
United States. It has had a different historical meaning
in the time of Ronald Reagan and the literature on this
concept today. In each of these two periods, it has operated for ideological purposes. But it becomes a historical
concept when we gain a proper distance from it and take
it as an object of research. It is understood as a historical type when we utilize it as a basis for comparing
historical periods.

Federalism can be seen, therefore, as a historical
construct that has attributes useful for comparative study.
In this sense, it is close to the ideal type in its purpose
but different in emphasis. The attributes of an ideal type
are designed for comparative study, but they go beyond
the limitations of a brief historical period. Bureaucracy
can be observed in ancient Egypt as well as in the modern
corporation. It is different than a type of historical

configuration identifiable within a particular time and place. The ideal type has more universal traits in contrast with the more-time-bound traits of a historical type. But both types are different from ideology in the sense that they do not lay any passionate claim to truth.

For example, the concept of self-management in Yugoslavia can be conceived as a historical type even while it may retain an important ideological dimension. It was originally defined in the Constitution of Yugoslavia (April 7, 1963) as constituted by "free associated labor with socially owned means of production . . . self-management in the work organization shall include in particular the right and duty of the working people to: 1) manage the worker organization directly. . . ."[8] This historical definition continued to develop through a new constitution in 1974 and the Law of Associated Labor in 1976. It continues to be studied by other nations such as Greece, Hungary, Poland, China, and the Soviet Union. It carries a power and a political message in its time. Greece has sent numerous observers to Yugoslavia to obtain ideas for its own socialist development. Hungary has developed a market mechanism close in type to that of Yugoslavia. China has sent teams of observers to Belgrade. In March of 1983, Soviet Party Secretary Andropov, supporting the early Hungarian innovations, said that "the Soviet Union should learn from economic reforms in other countries."[9] This historical pattern is having a significant influence on political policies in other nations. But other nations have different histories and cultures.

This historical type of self-management in Yugoslavia can thus be interpreted over time for the kinds of changes that take place within it. It functions academically like Weber's "Protestant ethic," a construct studied by researchers to document its influence and its change in different cultures and historical stages of development. Thus, the Yugoslavian type of self-management has undergone its own changes and continues to be studied by historians. It has had it own influence on other countries, which remains an important part of future research.

The Planning Model Concept

A construct of self-governance can be formulated at any system level for development purposes. In this case,

the concept of self-governance serves the purpose of planning for future developments and comes closest to having a
political meaning. A political planner may design a whole
system of institutions around legislation aimed at creating
self-governing values in the society. Here the political
scientist and politician may work closely together, but
planning for self-governance may also take place outside
the state through what may be called generically social
planning. For example, a community planner may design
a model of self-governance for a locality in collaboration
with local leaders seeking greater institutional autonomy,
as is attempted in Greece today, or a corporate planner
may design a model for a department store in collaboration
with employees and owners, as happens in many countries,
including the United States. In such cases the planner
usually begins with a semblance of what exists in the
analytical terms of self-governance and builds attributes
that could develop through the cooperation of the members
of the organization.

Such planning for decentralized worker control has
been occurring within Yugoslavia since its initiation of a
decentralized system of "basic organizations of associated
labor." It is also happening in the United States in
selected instances where self-management consultants work
with firms to develop producer cooperatives. But planning
for the cultivation of authority in lower management and
for worker participation has occurred many times in capitalist firms. When workers cannot take full control but
see the opportunity for advancement into management territory, this kind of planning is seen by some observers as
a reasonable alternative.[10]

Let us take a company like Sears Roebuck in the
United States to illustrate the social-planning concept.
The planner recommends that the following external criteria, representing authority to be developed by store
management within the context of the big corporation, be
developed by retail stores: (1) complete authority to hire
and fire workers, (2) complete authority to buy and sell
goods, (3) ability to establish credit for customers, (4) authority to establish a works council, and (5) the right to
be represented as a store on the board of directors. Sears
stores have developed a degree of self-governance for the
first three criteria but could advance further along these
lines without too much difficulty. The major leap for
training and preparation exists in the last two criteria.

It takes time to develop workers councils and board representation, but the plan proposes that steps could now be
taken to implement these things without disturbing the
productivity of the firm.

Then, the internal criteria established within the
plan are based on the premise that self-governance exists
to the degree that store employees have (1) equal participation in decision making within a works council, (2) a
training program developed to prepare workers for self-
management skills, (3) a local judiciary for employees, and
(4) a profit-sharing plan that offers workers shares in the
company.

A more-advanced step toward self-governance would
be the complete divestment of the local store from the authority of the corporation. The possibility for this happening would depend upon the degree of union power and
leadership and the possibility that legislation would offer
tax advantages for the divestment. The big firm might
find it profitable where it is losing money and a special
contract for sales could be established with local stores.
There would still be a delicate balance between the local
store management and higher management in the corporation. Yugoslavia has taken the lead in this experiment
through its law allowing basic organizations of associated
labor to develop within the context of the big enterprise.

Even though a workers council is established in a
formal sense by top management, it takes careful planning
to involve effective worker participation. The old establishment may continue to assume the leadership without
the new energy and skills and imagination of other employees. The store is then self-governed only in a formal
sense and not in an informal sense.

Recent studies have shown that the informal structure
can be the most-important factor in determining influence
in decision making. For example, David Taylor and Mary
Wright Snell report on direct observations of decision making on the regional boards of the United Kingdom Post Office in which union representatives participated with management. In this case, management felt that the copartici-
pation had been imposed upon them and used subtle means
to circumvent full participation. For example, they avoided
bringing the most critical issues to the attention of the
board and brought other issues forward too late for effective action. Furthermore, researchers found that management spoke most of the time. "Often the way they handled

the meeting and even their 'body language' meant that they, in effect, dominated the meeting." The chair rarely asked for opinions from union members and generally failed to give sufficient consideration to the formulation of an agenda. Researchers concluded that both management and labor needed training to participate effectively together.[11]

A conventional firm may operate informally with greater worker participation than is the case for a formally democratic firm. Executives in a conventional firm may consult frequently with employees on issues and be sensitive to their concerns in establishing corporate policy in contrast with formally democratic managers who may not consult at all and may even be quite dictatorial. Scientific research shows that both the informal and formal structure are important to such modeling. Self-management consultants point out that the formal structure remains more important than the informal structure in any planning, because workers always have the power to act on the informal system once the formal rules are established. But the interdependence of the two structures (formal and informal) are fundamental to understand in planning and refining the concept of self-governance.

Comparative research has demonstrated that it is vitally important to establish the formal structure of participation as the base line for developing worker self-governance. One of the more-important studies verifying this matter involved a group of international scholars who studied comparative systems of worker participation in 12 European nations and found that the formal (de jure) system was much more critical to determining the actual influence of workers than the informal (de facto) norms that existed in these nations. "The institutional norms which regulate the involvement of workers, managers, and representative bodies have the major impact on power equalization." Researchers concluded that the "institutional norms have great positive effects on workers' influence on medium- and long-term decisions and on the influence of representative bodies and they inhibit the influence of top management."[12]

Reviewing these academic studies in self-governance together, we conclude that certain attributes have been frequently omitted from the literature and should be recognized as important for future research. First, references to worker self-governance need to be clear about what level of analysis is being represented. The concept usually refers to the level of the corporation, but the term can include other levels ranging from the individual in the workplace to workshops, to departments, and beyond firms to industries and the economy as a whole.[13] The term worker self-governance is a subconcept of social governance and the latter concept carries increasing significance as interpretations of worker self-governance go beyond the firm to include industries, communities and the economy as a whole. At higher levels of analysis, the worker has only one decision-making role among many others--buyers, customers, creditors, citizens--all of whom must be recognized as playing a significant part in determining the social governance of that unit of the economy.

Second, we should recognize that the definition of worker self-governance has a certain flexibility. It can be interpreted as a sensitizing or operational concept, a historical or ideal type, a philosophical idea, or a planning concept. The task of the scientist defining the concept is to recognize the difference, and the duty of a reader is to interpret the concept according to the appropriate standards for each definition rather than merely criticize it on the basis of a political ideology.

Third, scientific studies have pointed to the significance of certain dimensions surrounding the concept that cannot be ignored. These dimensions include the factual and normative, the individual and social, the external and internal, the formal and informal, as part of the reality of worker self-governance at any level of analysis. In the final analysis, each of these dimensions of worker self-governance becomes important to the development of theory.

If we look at academic interpretations of worker self-governance in history we face a more complex problem. Here we must examine the limitations of interpreting history on the basis of any single theoretical principle.

HISTORICAL INTERPRETATIONS OF WORKER SELF-GOVERNANCE

History is always written from some kind of perspective and is often interpreted on the basis of a single theoretical principle. For example, some historians have interpreted all human events from the standpoint of class structure and miss the autonomous and intrinsically valuable development of culture. Some historians have assumed a deterministic view of events and missed the basis for the development of freedom. Some historians focus on the record of governments and believe that a history of politics and the elite is representative of what happens in the society as a whole while ignoring the role and the contributions of the working class.

We are interested in looking at how the concept of self-governance can be more adequately portrayed in history. A few historians elevate the concept of self-governance as the principle for interpreting epochal development, while others move in the opposite direction and denigrate the meaning of self-governance by interpreting history as the story of dominance. We begin with an interpretation of self-governance as the key principle for interpreting history and then proceed to examine special interpretations based on critical and liberal perspectives of history. Understanding the relationships among these historical perspectives is essential to reach a clear interpretation of worker self-governance in capitalist and socialist countries today.

The Epochal Picture

Professor L. S. Stavrianos is a Princeton historian who describes historical development based on the principle of self-management in a manner that can illustrate our point. As a scholar of medieval European institutions, he is very familiar with the Dark Ages that followed the collapse of the Roman Empire. He asserts that the period was anything but dark relative to the age that preceded it. The Dark Age was in fact a "liberating decentralization" and "an age of epochal creativity" in comparison with the decadent Roman Empire. People came to live in a new world contrasting with the bureaucratic dominance and economic imperialism of Rome. People at all levels of society became more important in the new system: small-scale technology began to flourish, the plow and harness developed, three-field rotation began to restore fertility to the land, and serfs became freer than the slaves had been and were real members of the community with a stake in its welfare. A new form of "autonomy and self-management blossomed." People developed a new level of self-management in society.[14]

Stavrianos goes much further than this exemplary effort to document the transition between the Roman Empire and feudalism. He also develops a vision of the future based on his historical analysis. He believes that we are now entering a new age that parallels the transition to the medieval period from the Roman Empire; we are witnessing the breakup of modern empires like the Soviet Union and the United States. The new age will not be based on centralized technology and imperialism as we know it today. Instead, we are heading for alternatives to the hegemony of big capitalist and socialist states. Stavrianos envisions a decentralized technology for the Third World that will serve basic human needs rather than profit-making corporations and bureaucratic elites in the big nations--a new age that will increase the potential for self-management beyond any period in history. It will not be a return to the primitive tribe or to feudal life but will be based instead on a liberal use of science and a new technology that will make very small demands on capital and the physical environment.

This interpretation of self-management developing throughout the whole of society provides an important contribution to our understanding of social change, but the use of this single idea for the interpretation of history can lead to distortions. It leads to a very partial view of the medieval period and a partial view of the future. In terms of the past, for example, it fails to show us the degradation of serfdom and Church dominance as well as other problems of exploitation. In terms of the future, it offers a very optimistic view without careful consideration of the regressive possibilities of nation-states or the real possibility of a nuclear catastrophe ending life on earth.

Karl Marx maintained a progressive picture of social evolution as he interpreted epochal changes in the status of labor. He saw the status of labor improving in each succeeding epoch. Each epoch from ancient times to empires, to feudal kingdoms, and finally to capitalist institutions revealed an advance in the self-governing power of the working class. Each step revealed a higher level of self-direction and authority for labor. But unlike other progressive historians, Marx claimed that each epoch had its own forms of exploitation and dominance that had to be overcome.

Marx's interpretation thus shows signs of balance in this sense, because he does not rest his case on this

singular principle of self-governance. In effect, the historical proposition is that people in the working class
have become more self-governing in society over the centuries in the face of continued exploitation and dominance.
Each stage of societal development reveals a greater degree of freedom in the new system, but each stage is filled
with class dominance. Marx recognizes the opposing principles of freedom and dominance operating simultaneously
in society. The position of the serf was more free and
self-directing as a rule than that of the slave; the serf
could not be bought and sold on the market or tortured so
easily as a slave. The laws changed and the attitudes
of people changed progressively in successive epochs while
the basic motif of class dominance never changed.[15]

Our argument is that self-governance is best interpreted historically from the standpoint of a theory expressing contradictory principles. Without proposing a
dialectical theory of history--far beyond our purposes--we
want to demonstrate how opposing interpretations of history
can lead toward a more-objective picture of self-development. By seeing opposing interpretations together, we can
construct a more-comprehensive picture of the development
of worker self-governance.

Let us call our opposing perspectives critical versus
liberal history. The role of labor in history can be interpreted from a critical perspective that assumes that the
world is explained by institutions based primarily on dominance over labor, or it can be interpreted from a liberal
perspective that generally assumes that the world is progressively getting better. Not all historical interpretations can be divided into these two simple views, but
their depiction is nevertheless useful for our purposes.
We want to see the extremes in order to obtain a more
comprehensive picture of worker self-governance as a historical concept.

Both the critical and liberal standpoints carry important elements of truth, as we shall see. This is partly
because scholars in each tradition are not quite so rigid
in their interpretation of history as to fall simply into
either category. But critical and liberal scholars are so
heavily conditioned by their singular standpoints that they
often misinterpret the meaning of worker self-governance
in history.

The role of labor in corporate hierarchy, for example,
is especially important to consider in relation to worker

self-governance. Some social historians ask: Has corporate
hierarchy existed in history for repression and domination
of workers? Other historians ask: Does hierarchy exist to
provide order, effective work, and ultimately liberation?
The answers to these questions contain presumptions underlying a theory of history. And the answers are essential
for understanding the historical development of self-
governance.

The Critical Perspective of History

The critical perspective of history accents the reality
of dominance and exploitation in human events and everyday life. The outlook of critical historians like Harry
Braverman, Richard Edwards, Stephen Marglin, Paul Baran,
Paul Sweezy, Nicos Poulantzas, Perry Anderson, and many
others depict this reality in their writings. Corporate
hierarchy is interpreted as a pattern of dominance and is
linked to a wider set of contradictions in the system of
capitalist exchange. Their arguments for change are per-
suasive and have influenced many union and government
leaders to seek political revolution and reform following
the Marxist tradition.
Scholars in this critical tradition have pointed out
how management policies that promote worker participation
in decision making are really a sham. Their premise is
that any corporate system based on class-oriented hierarchy, without electoral processes or democratic recall of
top corporate officers, must be designed only to preserve
and extend itself as a system of dominance. Any executive interest in offering greater management authority to
workers through labor-management committees, quality-of-
work-life programs (QWL), or autonomous groups is done
only for devious reasons. Such projects only strengthen
the hand of management and these new policies serve simply as a subtle expression of domination. They argue that
any idea for increasing the level of worker authority and
self-direction proposed by management would be done only
to protect the system and maintain control over workers.
This position grows from a historical view couched largely
in the Marxist tradition.
Harry Braverman argues that scientific management,
initiated by Frederick Winslow Taylor in the first quarter
of the twentieth century, is at the root of all modern sys-

tems of management. The essential principle underlying scientific management is its goal of controlling the labor process to maximize output. Even though managers in this century may have changed their methods to include workers in a more-humane and self-directing position in the workplace, the goal of management to control the labor process has never changed basically in the corporate system.

Braverman describes how workers had more skills and were in effect more self-managing in precapitalist times. They were spinners, weavers, glaziers, potters, blacksmiths, tinsmiths, locksmiths, joiners, and bakers whose productive crafts gave them a relative degree of power and self-authority. Early capitalism did not immediately destroy those skills. Braverman points out that the early workshops were simply agglomerations of smaller units of production, reflecting little change in traditional methods, and the work thus remained under the immediate control of the producers [workers] in whom was embodied the traditional knowledge and skills of their crafts. Even as late as the 1870s, many workers retained skills in ways that signified a degree of self-direction, because their immediate employers were frequently subcontractors intervening between themselves and the capitalist.

Braverman sees three principles in Taylorism as a philosophy of management. The first principle is to dissociate the labor process from the skills of the workers. In other words, the gathering of knowledge about the labor process must be separated into the hands of management. The second principle is to divorce the conception of the work to be done from its execution. That is, the conception of how tasks are to be carried out is the total prerogative of management and not of the workers. The third principle is to use this monopoly of knowledge to control each step of the labor process and its mode of execution. Braverman argues that this principle became part of the accepted routine and custom of management in the historical development of capitalism.[16]

With the rise of capitalism, management policies supported the separation of workers from their control over the labor process and made possible new technical controls over their work life. These technical controls emerged significantly in the first half of the twentieth century and continue in large measure today. The development of assembly lines and other technologically based ways of supervising workers contributed, Braverman argues, to a process of deskilling and to new forms of managerial control. The conditions of workers were worsened as management took over the whole system of decision making.

At the same time, management created a problem for itself as workers were organized in technical factories and became conscious of their collective predicament. In automobile production, radio assembly, electrical machinery production, and other technically controlled work processes, the plants became subject to union resistance and work was paralyzed periodically by labor strikes.

Richard Edwards describes this relatively unstable period of technical control over labor as ending soon after 1945. At that time another form of control became necessary. Technical control was replaced gradually by a more-effective bureaucratic control. This form of control over labor emerged with the development of large corporations and introduced an even more insidious and invisible method of controlling work life in middle and lower levels of the corporate hierarchy. Bureaucratic control differed from the previous forms of control by personal management. It was not based on personal relationships between workers and bosses. It also differed from technical control, which was rooted in the design of machines as promoted by management. Bureaucratic control became rooted in the organizational structure of the firm itself and was a much more reliable and permanent mode of control over labor.[17]

Bureaucratic control was built into the corporate definitions of job categories, work rules, promotion procedures, wage scales, and responsibilities. It carried the impersonal force of "company rules" and "company policy." The logic of bureaucratic control was embedded in fixed penalties for specified categories of offenses. Punishment flowed from organizational rules and procedures. Sanctions were still applied by supervisors, but their application was subject to review by higher levels of supervision and grievance machinery. It was a much more legitimate form of hierarchical control through a rationalized set of rules everyone could understand together.

Edwards argues that bureaucratic control rationalized and institutionalized the exercise of capitalist power. It was embedded legitimately in the nature of organization itself. Hierarchical relations were changed from relations between people with unequal power to unequal relations between job positions. The ability to establish rules therefore provided capitalists with the power to determine the terrain, the conditions around which struggles were to be fought. The rule of law in the firm replaced rule by supervisory command.

Critical scholars in this tradition do not believe that corporate hierarchy developed because it was more efficient, as some liberal historians believe. It emerged instead as a method of bourgeois control over labor. The new corporations survived not so much on their ability to be more efficient or to elicit peak performance as by their ability to organize the routine, normal efforts of workers. The capitalist firm was created to control labor and did not emerge as a natural process of people searching for greater mode efficiency. On the basis of this critique of history, efficiency cannot be an argument for maintaining capitalist systems of management.

Stephen Marglin, a Harvard economist, stresses this point. Marglin argues that the separation of workers from control over the labor process in the bureaucratic corporation was based on an interest of the capitalist class to "gain a larger share of the pie at the expense of the worker, and it is only the subsequent growth in the size of the pie that has obscured the class interest which was at the root of these innovations." Corporate hierarchy did not arise because of its superior power in technical efficiency but because it served a class interest. Put another way, according to Marglin, the rise of the modern division of labor and corporate hierarchy did not happen because of any principle of greater efficiency in production but because the capitalist had no essential role to play in the postfeudal production process. "Separating the tasks assigned to each workman was the sole means by which the capitalist could, in the days preceding costly machinery, ensure that he would remain essential to the production process as integrator of these operations. . . . It was simply a problem of 'divide and conquer.'"[18]

Marglin declares that it is wrong to ascribe the growth in fixed capital gained from the putting-out system (subcontracting by domestic labor) as the basis for the rise of industrial capitalism. It is true that machinery was prohibitively expensive for the individual workman, but then earlier craft machinery had been less expensive and the guilds did not develop a putting-out system. The guilds gave way to the putting-out system because it was more profitable to the class that was able to interpose itself between the producer and the market. The early profits from the putting-out system then provided the nascent capitalist class with the political power to break down the institutional arrangements of guild organization. The rise of capitalism (and corporate hierarchy) has been a result of class struggle and is not explained on a principle of efficiency.

Marglin continues that since we know historically that the need for greater efficiency was not the cause of corporate hierarchy, it should be more logical to make fundamental changes in corporate governance today. The resistance to change is now with management and with labor itself. Marglin argues that "present-day unions lack the will for change, not the strength." Unions have accommodated themselves to "bread and butter issues" and the price has been steep. Unions have "become another cog in the hierarchy . . . [and] the institution of property has itself sufficed to maintain workers in a subordinate position."

Marglin confesses that even though it is true that corporate hierarchy rose as a case of class domination, it is impossible to evaluate the alternatives to corporate hierarchy today without actual experiments in nonhierarchical enterprise. Such experiments should allow us to measure the differences in efficiency.

> One would design technologies appropriate to an egalitarian work organization, and test the designs in actual operation. . . . But social science is not experimental. None of us has the requisite knowledge of steelmaking or cloth-making to design a new technology, much less to design one so radically different from the present norm as a serious attempt to change work organization would dictate. Besides in a society whose basic institutions-- from schools to factories--are geared to hierarchy, the attempt to change one small component is probably doomed to failure.[19]

Other scholars in the critical tradition argue that many historical experiments have been made to demonstrate efficiency within nonhierarchical systems of management without the need for new experiments to test the case. For example, Menachem Rosner argues the efficiency and the effectiveness of such organizations simply on the basis of the 70-year existence of the kibbutz communities and extensive research on these enterprises. The 260 kibbutzim, with their nonhierarchical cooperative production, consumption, and education, although constituting only 3.5 percent of Israel's population, produce almost 40 percent of its agricultural output and 6 percent of its industrial goods, as well as generating 11 percent of its GNP.[20]

Following close on the heels of Marglin's argument, Edwards claims that the most significant historical change was in the fact that bureaucratic control came to blur the distinctions between "them" and "us." Workers came to be no longer distinguished from bosses. The "workplace culture" came to express less of the workers and more of the firm. The notion of a family (the IBM family) included both management and workers. With this change in the culture of the workplace, workers began to lose the original meaning of the term we. It was no longer used to refer to the workers as a class but, rather, to the firm itself. Their ability to make their own class culture was slipping away. Bureaucratic control then became more like totalitarian control, in the sense of involving the total behavior of the worker. Under bureaucratic control, the employees owe not only a hard day's work but also their loyalty and affection to the corporation.

The consequences of these critical interpretations of the role of labor in corporate history are various, but together they stand in contrast to liberal interpretations based on presumptions about progressive development in the institutional economy. While critical historians conclude that changes in the position of labor in the economy have simply strengthened the position of management and worsened the position of labor, liberal historians see management becoming more humane and workers more knowledgeable. Critical scholars see the pattern of dominance becoming more subtle and insidious while liberals see increased worker participation and authority in the corporate system as a promise for the future.

When the workers organized unions and established collective bargaining, critical historians saw the action as a lost battle. The labor movement "caved in" and colluded with the capitalist system. Unions lost their vision and began to take over the values of management. They became interested largely in the dollar and in fighting for higher wages instead of fighting for a new society based on equity and social justice. Edwards describes how unions today continue to support the bureaucratic system that dominates them by agreeing to the specification of pay rates, work loads, and job descriptions in bargaining for union contracts. Union leaders help legitimate the system and the conditions of the struggle are set by the power of management in the corporate hierarchy.

This critical position is not unique to these historians; it is true of some union leaders as well. Some union leaders oppose projects in the quality of work life and the creation of autonomous groups because they tighten managerial control over the labor force. Like many critical historians, union leaders see these programs as schemes of management to gain greater control over workers in the bureaucratic system. Like Braverman, an increasing number of union leaders claim these programs hide the real motives of higher management in controlling the labor process in the interest of maximizing output.

In this picture of history, the outcome can be only resignation, revolution, or revolutionary reform. For those who look into the far-reaching future, the contradictions of bureaucracy and capitalism can only lead toward an institutional collapse. The final outcome of managerial efforts to maintain the status quo are doomed. In the words of Richard Edwards, "Bureaucratic control thus establishes an explicit structure around which broader struggles in the political arena coalesce."[21]

We have been describing a critical perspective that informs the thinking of a group of scholars who see basic contradictions in the system. This perspective tells us something about the distance that we have yet to travel to achieve the dimensions of social justice and equity that undergird these views of reality. But we must look at the liberal perspective before tackling a more-comprehensive picture of corporate history.

The Liberal Perspective of History

A different interpretation of history is made by scholars who assume that small changes in the course of historical events have value and may even add up to major breaks in history in the long run. These scholars assume that there is some virtue to be found in the present system and examine historical events in the light of the relative values they find rather than from a long-range vision of social equity and justice. It is impossible to make any sharp distinction between critical and liberal scholars in all cases, and in many ways their separate views of history overlap. But the distinctions are significant enough to allow us some insight into the complexities of social change. Together they help us to draw our own conclusions on policy and research on worker self-governance in the coming decades.

Liberal scholars like Alfred Chandler, Adolf Berle, Richard Eells and social scientists like Elton Mayo and Douglas McGregor tend to see history as a process in which people overcome problems pragmatically in the economy. Social change is more gradual and there is an overall assumption of incremental progress in social and technological systems. This progressive picture does not contradict the position of the critical historians in the long-range picture of evolution. The difference rather comes in the assumption by many liberal scholars that history is a series of small-scale improvements that have incremental value without interpreting them from the perspective of deeper contradictions underlying the system as a whole.

Alfred Chandler interprets corporate history quite differently from the critical historians. Chandler's eight propositions about the way business developed tell a story about development based on an increasing efficiency in the division of labor. His first proposition is that the modern multiunit bureaucratic enterprise replaced small enterprise when coordination between units permitted greater productivity, lower costs, and higher profits than coordination by market mechanisms.[22]

This position contrasts markedly with that of Marglin, who argues that the original steps toward capitalism in the putting-out system were based on class rather than a principle of efficiency. In the simple practice of wage advances, Marglin asserts, the capitalist was able to force the worker into a position of dependency. The use of wage advances was a legal means for the capitalist to maintain worker dependence and hierarchical control over production. This first stage of capitalist development provided a basis for political power over workers that continued to develop in subsequent stages of corporate history. He argues that the key to the success of the factory was the substitution of capitalists' for workers' control and that discipline and supervision reduced costs without being technologically superior.[23] The factory then afforded a system of discipline and supervision that was impossible under the putting-out system.

Chandler, on the other hand, argues that the advantages of internalizing the activities of many business units within a single enterprise became realized with the advent of a managerial hierarchy. Top managers helped to coordinate the work of middle managers and began to take the place of the market in allocating resources for future production and distribution. This made it possible for modern business enterprise to reach a level that made administrative coordination more efficient and more profitable. In fact, it became more efficient than the market as a system of coordination. Then, he argues that "once a managerial hierarchy had successfully carried out its function of administrative coordination, the hierarchy itself became a source of permanence, power, and continued growth."[24]

From a critical perspective, Chandler's history ignores the development of exploitation through corporate monopoly and oligopolies. Chandler never really investigates the destructive character of this administrative coordination. The critics would argue that the rise of megacorporations entrenched workers even further in the mire of dependency and distanced them still further in the stratification from top management.

Chandler comes close to the history of the critical scholars as he notes how the careers of the salaried managers who directed these hierarchies grew more technical and professional. Following close to the historical picture of Edwards, Chandler describes how the new business bureaucracies were increasingly based on specialized skills, training, and performance rather than on family relationships or money. The multiunit business, Chandler continues, grew in size and diversity as its managers became more professional and finally, management separated from ownership. This introduced a new type of capitalism fundamentally different from all past types but not more exploitive.

Adolph Berle and Gardiner Means are best known for their analysis of this new type of corporate capitalism. They found the corporate system changing from "family capitalism" to "financial capitalism" (symbolized by banks that provide capital to firms placing representatives on the board) and "managerial capitalism" (where managers simply took over all policy making). Their famous study

(The Modern Corporation and Private Property) conducted in
the 1930s, demonstrated how the creation and growth of
enterprises required large sums of outside capital. The
selling of shares to the public changed the corporate structure. As corporations went public, ownership became widespread. The new stockholders did not have the influence,
knowledge, or commitment to take part in the high command. Salaried managers began to determine long-term
policy as well as manage short-term operations.[25]

Berle later studied the structure of ownership developing after the mid-century and found it located primarily
in fiduciary institutions such as pension funds, insurance
companies, and mutual funds.[26] These institutions have
acquired enormous sums to buy and sell stock on the market and thus have the potential for great voting power to
influence corporate boards. Berle's class analysis approaches a critical perspective at this point, but his study
does not comprehend the role of labor in relation to corporate
power. In contrast to a critical perspective, Berle's liberal perspective led him to be concerned about the centralized power that these financial bodies might gain over
corporate management. Out of his concern, he suggested
that certain forms of legislation should be considered to
constrain the newly gained power of fiduciary institutions.
His conclusions about power in the corporate system in this
case were that the concentration of power was shifting away
from management and back to capital.

The liberal historians totally missed the significant
role of labor in history and thus could not be fully accu-
rate in anticipating the future, but they did analyze the
structure of ownership in a manner that was missed by the
critical historians. It is this structure of ownership that
today is critical in assessing the role of labor in the
governance of the corporate system of the United States.

Peter Drucker's 1976 study of these fiduciary institutions found that workers owned one-third of the stock in
all the industrial and financial firms of the United States
through their pension funds. By 1985 they would own over
half of the stock and we would be living with "pension
fund socialism." Indeed, he was correct about the rapid
accumulation of ownership in the pension funds. Today,
these funds amount to well over $1 trillion and represent
the largest storehouse of capital in the world.[27]

Workers have participatory control over a small percentage of the pension funds. At present about $100 billion

are jointly managed by worker and management representatives.[28] The AFL-CIO is seeking to obtain a greater degree of control recognizing that the courts have judged these funds legally as delayed wage payments. They do not belong to management. Thus, their dispensation can be argued technically to be under the proper jurisdiction of the workers as owners. The outcome of this battle, of course, is not likely to result in full labor control over capital allocation, but it could mean that representatives of labor will play a significant role in decision making. The AFL-CIO has recommended control by a tripartite commission composed of labor, management, and government.

A liberal scholar tells us how the structure of power is changing outside the corporation, and liberal social scientists have demonstrated how managerial power has been changing inside the corporation. The social-scientific studies of Douglas McGregor, Frederick Herzberg, and Rensis Likert differ fundamentally from studies in the Marxist tradition. McGregor, for example, showed how managerial attitudes were becoming altered in a positive direction. Managers had maintained certain assumptions about worker motivations, which he described as Theory X. He said that managers had frequently assumed that workers have an inherent dislike of work and hence need to be closely supervised. Many managers had thought that workers must be coerced, controlled, directed, and threatened with punishment to give a fair day's work. McGregor disputed the reality of such assumptions and found managerial attitudes developing based on the idea that workers wanted to exercise self-direction and seek responsibility in work. Theory Y managers assumed that workers had a high degree of imagination and creativity.[29] While neo-Marxists called the new attitudes patronizing, if not insidious, liberals believed that it was a progressive advance in the development of labor-management relations.

McGregor, working in the 1950s, represented a change in thinking that came to be called the human-relations movement. It led eventually to the creation of the new modes of autonomous work and the quality circles that critical historians describe today as a trick of management to achieve its own Tayloristic ends of maximum output for the worker.

Liberal studies tend to support experimental change on a small scale and also lead toward legislation that would provide incentives for social reform. The outcome is not revolutionary, nor even what Andre Gorz once called revolutionary reform. Social scientists do not generally design their research with a long-range social vision. Their small-scale experiments include projects that alter the structure of the workplace or stimulate new sociotechnical systems but they do not entail experiments in full worker control.

The critical and the liberal perspectives are important to examine for the comprehensive insight they provide together. A theory of history is implicit in what we are about to conclude, although we have space only to point to its implications for interpreting worker self-governance.

The singular focus of some critical historians on the subordination of labor to a pattern of corporate dominance in history advances our understanding of the human realities, but it also prohibits us from seeing the positive developments taking place. Those positive developments included basic changes in the structure of worker ownership and a recognition of the power of unionized labor to bring workers toward a new position of struggle for labor self-management.

The singular focus of the liberal historians on the history of bourgeois management is instructive about the nature of the new division of labor but inhibits us from seeing that there are other less-exploitive routes to effective systems of work. Liberal historians do not see the significance of labor in the development of a humane economy, and indeed studies deny such scholars insight into how labor's own self-management plays the key role in creating order, efficiency, and productivity in the firm.

The critical fact is that the so-called progressive step in creating autonomous work groups can be a manipulative strategy of management. It is especially true if workers make no further advances toward self-management. The progressive "advance" then fossilizes at the point of an autonomous group and could thereby weaken union leadership unless it is made a part of a long-range union strategy toward democratic management and ownership.

Given this larger perspective on history, how would scholars in these two traditions view hierarchy and power? The answers become important not only to writing corporate history correctly but also in planning and designing research for new models of worker self-governance.

The Meaning of Corporate Hierarchy

Hierarchy is generally viewed corporately as a linear system of unequal positions in which the people at the top determine policies guiding the activities of the people in positions below them. It is more complex in reality but this picture shapes much of the historical and conceptual thinking on the subject. The critical historians see hierarchy to be dominating and exploitive and argue that any corporate policy of management has a class-based motive to maintain the system of power. The liberal historians, on the other hand, see hierarchy as the basis for maintaining efficiency, discipline, and continued productivity in the corporation.

If we keep both perspectives in mind, we would say that hierarchy is typified by a linear set of unequal positions that can serve many different functions. These functions can involve domination and exploitation to the advantage of those at the top. Hierarchy can also involve some measure of efficiency, order, and discipline, but these things need not only occur only in the capitalist order as though that explains why it evolved. It can also occur in labor-managed systems—to the economic advantage of everyone. Furthermore, hierarchy can also serve deeply positive functions. One is to provide greater self-direction and power to workers. It begins to happen most significantly in planning the long-range development of self-governing firms.

The way power is exercised within the hierarchy makes the difference.[30] Hierarchies can be efficient and inefficient as well as repressive and liberating; they can suppress or promote human development. It depends upon the values and purposes of the people in office.

In other words, power need not be conceived of only as expressed typically through capitalist or statist hierarchy but also as a dynamic expression of development, that is, defined as the capacity to effect change toward self-governance. In this developmental view, power assumes a social direction and a progressive value. Power can be a means to develop human resources and the collective skills necessary for workers to be more independent within the larger community—whether it be at the level of the workplace, the department, the firm, the industry, or the economy as an institution.

Hierarchy exists in all egalitarian organizations even though it may not be so visible in the formal organization where workers are equal in their voting power. We have noted that hierarchy is always evident to observers of the informal organization because people differ in the capacities to effect change in self-governing firms, then, the normative function of all hierarchy (formal and informal) is to create greater autonomy and self-direction for workers at all levels of the corporation. The task of each worker is to help create a basis for increasing levels of effective self-direction on the job. Most significant for our purposes, hierarchy can be applied to planning development in the context of capitalist or self-managed firms.

The practical value of this perspective on hierarchy is seen among a few labor leaders in the United States facing dominance in the capitalist system.[31] These labor leaders hold that it is acceptable to participate in quality-of-work-life programs as long as workers gain some new measure of control over work, they learn some skills of self-management, and the union is strengthened as a principal party in the developmental process. The union thus remains involved and keeps workers from being "sucked into" an identity with business management in ways that would destroy their own collective identity as workers. At the same time workers retain a respect for the function of management. They see the need for labor-management training at all levels. Indeed, union leaders are planning the long-range strategy for the management of pension funds as well as direct ownership of corporations. As we indicated earlier, the AFL-CIO has publicly committed itself to the objective of establishing a tripartite commission for the allocation of pension fund capital. The power to allocate this capital--amounting to $4 trillion in the 1990s--would be shared by labor, management, and the public. Thus, some leaders see steps toward autonomous groups as precedents to worker councils and union management of regional pension funds as precedents to forming a national basis for allocating capital in the interest of the larger society.[32]

In Greece, various government departments, academic institutions, and representative labor and management organizations have introduced proposals for the development of new educational programs that are conducive to tripartite cooperation for the solution of problems of mutual concern and the establishment of appropriate new institutional arrangements for participative management.[33] As we shall see, various efforts have already been made to include labor in the management of corporations as well as representation on boards of directors.

In sum, small steps toward worker self-management at lower levels of the hierarchy make sense when they are a long-range strategy for labor to participate in the governance in the larger economy. This vision is very limited, and yet it is visible in certain sectors of labor, management, and government in capitalist nations like the United States and small nations with a socialist agenda like Greece. The future social economy is developing in partial form in many nations around the world. The future clearly includes not only the development of new forms of labor management but also the formation of intercorporate relations through social federations of labor-managed firms or socially constituted trade associations. At the regional level, it may include what Piore and Sabel call "yeoman democracy," that is, a flexible system of specialization in which "property is held in trust for the community."[34] Thus, the vision includes taking steps toward what we call community self-governance.

This vision need not exclude owner-executives as a factor in the implementation of a long-range plan. There are executives and capitalists in every country that come to see the significance of worker self-governance. This includes company owners like Jim Gibbons, who helped transform his insurance company to a worker-owned-and-managed company in the United States; Ernst Bader, who turned over his stock to the workers in a chemical firm in England so that they could together organize a producer cooperative; John Lewis, who turned over his firm to 24,000 employees in London; Victor Bewley, who gave the ownership and management of his business to the employees in Dublin, Ireland; and many other cases around the world. Today retiring owners in the United States are offering their firm to workers for ready cash through Employee Stock Ownership Plans (ESOPs).[35] The synthesis of elements in the critical-liberal outlook keeps us open to many possibilities for the development of worker self-governance in everyday affairs.

We have said that critical historians view hierarchy as a system of dominance and liberal historians view it as a device to maintain efficiency, but self-management

theorists often take a still different position. They argue
that dominance exists in all command systems and does not
formally disappear until the development of democratic
firms. They would say that formal dominance disappears
but that hierarchy itself does not disappear. It changes
qualitatively into a "coordinating hierarchy." Hierarchy
is no longer based on any formal dominance. This is because the basic policies guiding a self-managed firm are
made by all the employees in a general assembly and it
becomes the responsibility of management to carry out
these policies. As Branko Horvat has said, "Once a policy
decision is reached, it becomes a directive for management.
The management acts as an executive committee of the
working collective and implements policy decisions by
translating them into the day-to-day operations of the
firm.[36] Managers are in the service of the workers and
are mandated to coordinate the work of the firm to fulfill
the objectives of the workers. They simply act on behalf
of the workers.

We would argue that a fourth view needs to be added
to make a theory of hierarchy still more fitting to a concept of worker self-governance. This fourth view assumes
that the will of the workers is an essential but not sufficient attribute by itself in evaluating self-management
policy. It assumes that a theory of values must also develop as a part of self-management philosophy. Managers
of worker-owned firms need a theory to evaluate their own
performance independent of the idea that they must follow
the will of the workers. We do not suggest that management theory should be separate from the workers but that
it be coincident with the concept of self-governance. A
concept of worker management must be evaluated in the
context of the larger community and the society and not
simply in the value context of the firm itself.

A theory of hierarchy in self-managed firms would at
best assume that the basic task of managers at all levels
is not only to fulfill the objectives of workers but to consider still other values of social development as a part of
management responsibility. One of these values is to review daily the possibilities for increasing the level of
self-governance among all workers, even though some workers may resist. Put another way, each manager has a
responsibility to examine how to increase the level of self-
direction on the job with workers under his or her supervision. We assume that the firm can always change toward

higher degrees of self-governance at each lower level of hierarchy. This view assumes that the firm is always moving toward higher levels of self-governance through processes of joint review and reorganization in ways that do not interfere with the overall effectiveness of the firm. This view does not assume that workers alone set policies without a philosophy of self-management operating to stimulate the leadership and their own thinking.

This principle of decentralization was part of the reasoning behind Yugoslavian policies enacted in the Amendment of 1971, the Constitution of 1974, and the Associated Labour Act of 1976. These political decisions were made in part to decentralize authority through the creation of "basic organizations of associated labor." This was an attempt to legitimate the independent enterprise activity of divisions, departments, and large workshops of enterprises so that workers would have greater decision-making authority. The political decision has yet to be fully evaluated, but some Yugoslav observers have claimed that in some regions it has led toward chaotic conditions that require greater controls by the political party to stabilize the new economic order. Hence, the need for management philosophy within the firm that leads internally toward greater decentralization on a rational and voluntary basis from within the firm itself without requiring political initiatives and party controls.[37]

This view of management hierarchy assumes that representatives of workers and appointed directors have a responsibility to act with a philosophy of self-governance apart from the sole directives of workers. It assumes that good management must take account of the impact of the firm's work on the environment, the safety of products for the consumers, the conservation of natural resources, and many other values that are important to the development of the larger society.

The same principle is found in classic theories of democratic government in which it is assumed that representatives, once elected, are not mandated to follow only the opinions of their constituencies but to follow values inherent in the public interest and the concept of democracy itself. Managers have their own integrity in making judgments apart from being simply obedient to the workers who put them into office. There is a set of values associated with management philosophy that permeates self-governing work in the context of the community that is still to be developed and studied.

In conclusion, studies in the tradition of worker self-governance suggest that a more-comprehensive theory of hierarchy is in the making. This new theory must take account of not only dominance and oppression in the critical tradition but the interpretations of self-development in the liberal tradition. Furthermore, a more-comprehensive theory of hierarchy in self-managed firms should be forthcoming in light of how the firms operate best in the marketplace and the context of the larger community.

IN SUMMARY

Our concern has been to review academic studies of worker self-governance as they orient us to the need for new research and cast light on social policy and practice. The advantage of a varied conceptual technology to the study of self-governance rests with its capacity to comprehend selective differences among countries and to compare the grounds for social development in both capitalist and socialist nations. It is important to allow the experiences of people in each nation to be understood in their home settings while establishing a broader framework for comparative analysis of development.[38]

The comparative study of self-designated capitalist and socialist nations guided by a concept of self-governance needs to be understood on its own academic grounds without confusing the interpretation with rigid ideology-- as important as passionate beliefs may be in building a political movement. The task of writing history is difficult enough without the additional problem of science being determined by the politics of nations. While the methodology of social science always expresses values and special interests itself, it can be judged on its own terms rather than in the terms of national ideology. Given the opportunity for future studies in capitalist and socialist nations, there is reason to believe that many new learning opportunities will develop in the years ahead.

In light of these opposing perspectives on the history of worker self-governance, we want to examine the political economies in the United States and Greece. The integration of these perspectives provides the basis for our conceptual framework, permitting us to compare the process of social development in each nation.

NOTES

1. Herbert Blumer, "What Is Wrong with Social Theory," American Sociological Review 19 (1954).
2. Max Weber, Economy and Society (New York: Bedminister Press, 1968), pp. 20-21.
3. Branko Horvat, The Political Economy of Socialism (New York: M. E. Sharpe, 1982).
4. Studies have shown a variety of ways in which outside organizations have advanced or inhibited the development of self-governance in firms, but the findings have not been reviewed for the kind of external criteria useful for a typology of corporate self-governance. For example, trade associations and trade unions collaborated in Norway to study the quality of employee representation and personal participation on the boards of companies. This represents a model relationship for the advancement of worker self-governance through research. See Elinar Thorsrud and Fred Emery, "Industrial Democracy in Norway," in Self Management: New Dimensions to Democracy, ed. Ichak Adizes and Elisabeth Borgese (Oxford, England: Clio Press, 1975). In the United States, the United Food and Commercial Workers was a precedent setter in helping to establish a self-managed firm called the Rath Meatpacking Company in 1980 and contributed leadership and funding support for the worker takeover of the A&P stores in Philadelphia. See William F. Whyte, "Philadelphia Story," Society, March-April, 1986, p. 36ff. The trade-union movement in Poland (Solidarity) initiated the dispute with government authorities over the development of self-management. See Lena Kolarska, "The Struggle about Workers' Control: Poland, 1981," in International Perspectives on Organizational Democracy, vol. 2, ed. Bernhard Wilpert and Arndt Sorge (New York: John Wiley & Sons, 1984). On the other hand, unions have also blocked the development of self-governance among firms in many ways. Some unions in West Germany have purchased firms and leaders have sought to control corporate boards in opposition to elections from employees. In Israel, the Histadrut has also purchased and controlled firms from the outside without planning internal development toward self-governance among employees of the firms themselves. This problem is reportedly being treated in the Histadrut today. For a discussion of the issue of external union control over firms covered by codetermination laws in West Germany, see

Wolfgang Streeck, "Co-determination: The Fourth Decade," in International Perspectives on Organizational Democracy, vol. 2, ed. Bernhard Wilpert and Arndt Sorge (New York: John Wiley & Sons, 1984), p. 408ff. The study of the types of external relationships that inhibit or advance the capacity of firms to be self-governing is badly needed today in order to formulate a more-comprehensive picture of what constitutes a self-governing firm.

5. Paul Bernstein, Workplace Democratization (Kent, Ohio: Kent State University Press, 1976).

6. Alvin Gouldner, Patterns of Industrial Bureaucracy (New York: Free Press, 1954).

7. Mihailo Marcovic, "Philosophical Foundations of the Idea of Self-Management," in Self-Governing Socialism, ed. Branko Horvat, Mihailo Marcovic, and Rudi Supek (White Plains, N.Y.: International Arts and Sciences Press, 1975).

8. The legal and institutional framework of the system of workers' self-management in Yugoslavia is described by D. Gorupic and I. Paj, Workers' Management in Yugoslavia (Geneva: International Labor Organization, 1962). For social studies, see I. Adizes, Industrial Democracy: Yugoslav Style (New York: Free Press, 1971); and Adolf Sturmthal, Workers' Councils (Cambridge, Mass.: Harvard University Press, 1964).

9. Stephen Sacks, Self-Management and Efficiency: Large Corporations in Yugoslavia (London: George Allen & Unwin, 1983), p. vii.

10. Alfred Chandler documents the efforts by higher management in the history of corporations in the United States to decentralize authority with great resistance from middle and lower management in Strategy and Structure (New York: Doubleday, 1966). Sears Roebuck and General Motors are major examples of this "divisionalization of authority." The current model of decentralizing self-management for consultants working with the Industrial Cooperative Association can be seen in Jan Saglio and Richard Hackman, "The Design of Self-Governance in Worker Cooperatives" (Industrial Cooperative Association, 58 Day St., Suite 200, Somerville, Mass., n.d.).

11. David Taylor and Mary Wright Snell, "The Post Office Experiment: An Analysis of Industrial Democracy Meetings," in The Organizational Practice of Democracy, ed. Robert Stern and Sharon McCarthy (New York: John Wiley & Sons, 1986), p. 100.

12. International Research Group, Industrial Democracy in Europe (Oxford, England: Clarendon Press, 1981), p. 179.

13. The term self-management is generally used to refer to the Yugoslavian model and to refer to the level of the enterprise operating independently of the state. For example, Elisabeth Mann Borgese says: "What is self-management? . . . Self-management is the kernel of Yugoslav political theory. . . . [it] politicizes the economic enterprise by transforming it into a community which is not bent on profit-making exclusively but on articulating the social and political as well as the economic decision-making process of its members, workers, and managers alike." Ichak Adizes and Elisabeth Mann Borgese, eds., Self-Management: New Dimensions to Democracy (Oxford, England: Clio Press, 1975), p. xix. This view pervades much of the thinking on this concept. But we are distinguishing the term for its broader use, recognizing Yugoslavia as a historical type and recognizing the operational use of the concept at other levels of analysis.

14. Leften S. Stavrianos, The Promise of the Coming Dark Age (San Francisco: W. H. Freeman, 1976).

15. It is true that a full statement of history is missing in Marx's perspective. For example, the contributions of the upper classes to the advance of science, music, and culture--the contributory role of emperors, kings, and presidents to development--are missing. But Marx is not writing history so much as making a point about how conventional scholars misinterpret history.

16. Harry Braverman, Labor and Monopoly Capital: The Degradation of Work in the Twentieth Century (New York: Monthly Review Press, 1974).

17. Richard Edwards, Contested Terrain: The Transformation of the Workplace in the Twentieth Century (New York: Basic Books, 1979).

18. Stephen Marglin, "What Do Bosses Do? The Origins and Functions of Hierarchy in Capitalist Production," Review of Radical Political Economics 6 (Summer 1974):33-60.

19. Ibid.

20. Menachem Rosner, "Theories of Cooperative Degeneration and the Experience of the Kibbutz" in Annals of Public and Cooperative Economy 56 (Oct.-Dec. 1985):527-38.

21. Edwards, Contested Terrain.

22. Alfred Chandler, The Visible Hand: The Managerial Revolution in American Business (Cambridge, Mass.: Harvard University Press, 1977).

23. Marglin, "What Do Bosses Do?"

24. Chandler, The Visible Hand.

25. Adolph Berle and Gardiner Means.

26. Adolph Berle, Power without Property (New York: Harcourt, Brace, Jovanovich, 1959).

27. Peter Drucker, The Unseen Revolution: How Pension Fund Socialism Came to America (New York: Harper & Row, 1976).

28. Carol O'Cleireacain, "Toward Democratic Control of Capital Formation in the United States: The Role of Pension Funds," in Eurosocialism and America, ed. Nancy Lieber (Philadelphia, Pa.: Temple University Press, 1982).

29. Douglas MacGregor, The Human Side of Enterprise (New York: McGraw-Hill, 1960).

30. Power is generally viewed as the capacity to exercise one's will so that others follow. Both perspectives are in accord with this idea but give conflicting variations on this meaning. The critical perspective emphasizes power as a form of dominance. The liberal perspective also sees power as coercive but presumes that it can also be based on persuasion and enlightenment. People may follow leaders persuasively and voluntarily (not only coercively) even though they do not benefit from their own action but also in some cases when they do benefit.

31. Some examples of the creative steps being taken by labor today can be found in William F. Whyte, "Philadelphia Story," and Neal Q. Herrick, "Learning from Mistakes," Society (1986):36–44.

32. The effort of union leaders to gain national control over pension funds can be seen in "Making Our Money Work for Us" (editorial), Labor and Investments (AFL-CIO Industrial Union Department, n.d.), p. 4.

33. Chris Jecchinis, Preconditions for the Success of Workers' Participation in Management (Athens: Manpower Employment Organization, 1986). For an analysis of the trade-union movement, see Chris Jecchinis and Theodoros Catsanevas, The Trade Union Movement in Greece (Athens: Manpower Employment Organization, 1985).

34. These authors do not stress a concept of worker self-governance as an essential part of their study, which weakens their argument. But their concept of a self-

governing regional system of enterprises rooted in community life shows promise as part of a vision. It simply needs future study as the idea connects with self-managed firms. Michael Piore and Charles Sabel, The Second Industrial Divide (New York: Basic Books, 1984), p. 305.

35. For examples, see Fred Blum, Work and Community: The Scott-Bader Commonwealth and the Quest for a New Social Order (London: Routledge & Kegan Paul, 1968); Will Conrad et al., The Milwaukee Journal (Madison: University of Wisconsin Press, 1964), p. 175ff; John Spedan Lewis, Fairer Shares: A Possible Advance in Civilization and Perhaps the Only Alternative to Communism (London: Staples Press Limited, 1954); and Corey Rosen et al., Employee Ownership in America (Lexington, Mass.: D. C. Heath, Lexington Books, 1986).

36. Horvat, The Political Economy, p. 190.

37. A fuller description of the overall purpose of these political actions taken in a historical context is found in Janez Prasnikar and Vesna Prasnikar, "The Yugoslav Firm in Historical Perspective," in Economic and Industrial Democracy (London: Sage, 1986) 7:178ff.

38. Our argument in part is that historical and scientific findings can be instructive beyond the traditional ideologies of self-management today. For example, certain democratic corporations in a capitalist nation can be more self-managed in their internal life than in a socialist nation when judged in an ideal-typical sense; the internal life may also show social innovations, such as in social audits and committees on affirmative action, that are in the interest of the society but not evident in self-managed firms in socialist nations. On the other hand, certain market areas in socialist nations can show a greater degree of freedom and effective coordination of pricing in the interest of the region than so-called free-market areas in capitalist nations. Academic studies, released from the traps of traditional ideology, help to show these comparative advantages.

3. Development toward Worker Self-Governance in the United States

INTRODUCTION

Workers in both capitalist and socialist nations are beginning to assume higher levels of responsibility in management and are also becoming owners of the firms that employ them. These trends toward worker participation in management on the one hand and worker ownership on the other are taking place in the private and public sector of many nations today and they show signs of gaining momentum in certain cases. Governments are also providing new legislative incentives for private enterprise to develop patterns of self-management. Our task now is to discuss how these trends are taking place in the United States and to interpret the meaning of these changes for the development of social policy.

We use the term worker participation as a dimension of worker self-governance in which employees increase their level of decision making and degree of managerial control over policies in their firms. This trend can involve various levels of decision making, starting in the workplace and continuing through middle management to top management and the board of directors. We view these changes as developmental processes that can be the foundation for constructing self-managed firms, or, on the other hand, they can simply be devices that strengthen managerial control over workers in conventional companies without any real plans to advance the participatory process to higher levels. Those modes of worker participation that increase the level of self-determination of employees are most significant to us, as they have the potential to be a step toward self-governance.

At times we will refer to the term <u>self-management</u>, using the normative meaning, which refers to an optimum degree of integration between worker participation and ownership or complete democratic worker control of the firm. The optimum process of integrating worker participation in management with some pattern of worker ownership to achieve worker control at all levels of corporate life is complex. We propose that in the United States this includes a process of integrating subtrends toward worker ownership and worker participation in management with certain government supports and union participation (in those labor-organized industries). It also involves sharing some measure of influence over corporate conduct with the union, the trade association, the local community, and the government. On a broad scale, U.S. consultants often use worker self-management to mean optimally developing employee control over economic enterprises as a whole, which in turn become socially regulated to operate in the public interest. Consultants in the United States argue that this process may take place slowly or rapidly in conjunction with many different cultural factors and types of government policy that advance or repress this process.

Our task is first to examine patterns of worker participation in the United States with an eye to comparing steps taken in this nation with steps taken in Greece. Our focus will be on the organizations that are in a position to help, hinder, or alter the process of gaining worker control in the context of the community. These organizations include unions, industrialists, political parties, and local communities. In the United States, we are interested especially in the kinds of problems faced by people dealing with new structures of worker participation. We conclude with an evaluation of what has happened in firms so far and make suggestions for establishing new patterns of education and social research to help resolve the problems that have arisen in the U.S. experience.

THE ORIGINS

The first worker-owned-and-managed enterprise in the United States can be traced to 1791, when a group of Philadelphia carpenters gathered together in Independence Hall to form a cooperative enterprise. But we can say that there was no broad interest in the idea of worker control until the 1870s and 1880s, when a labor union called the Knights of Labor began to organize producer cooperatives. The Knights organized around 200 co-ops and incorporated the cooperative philosophy into their labor movement. The union had revolutionary designs on changing the character of the capitalist economy. However, the Knights lost their battle for survival in a competitive union struggle and a hostile political environment. As a result, the loss in union support and membership led also to a decline in the numbers of producer co-ops. Other producer co-ops, of course, continued to be formed in small numbers in each succeeding decade of the next century but without ever becoming a significant social movement.

A significant social movement did develop for consumer-oriented and market-based cooperatives. In consumer co-ops, the customers control the board and in producer co-ops, the workers control the board. There are over 50,000 cooperatives in the United States today involving over 40 million members. These include telephone, credit, housing, retail, and banking co-ops that are customer owned. One of the larger consumer co-ops in the United States is Recreational Equipment Incorporated, with 300,000 members and branches organized in many cities. In addition, there are many marketing and supply co-ops that have become quite large and profitable. The large marketing co-ops include Sunkist, Ocean Spray, and Land O'Lakes. The workers in these companies are not normally given the privilege of voting for the board of directors even though the consumer and marketing corporations are democratically based in regard to their respective members.[1]

The trend toward producer (or worker) co-ops has progressed at a much slower pace with smaller companies. There are no precise statistics on the number of worker co-ops, but studies suggest that there are about 1,000 in the United States.[2] Their numbers appear to be relatively small compared with the other millions of enterprises, but there are signs that current changes in corporate structure are leading in the direction of this co-op prototype. Employee-owned-and-managed firms appear to be critical for social development in the United States in the coming decades. They may contain the germinal structures within which new policies encouraging worker self-management may be formulated in the corporate economy.[3]

Put another way, many U.S. corporations are developing new forms of worker ownership, while others are developing new forms of worker participation. These subtrends toward ownership and management participation
suggest that a meeting ground for integrating worker ownership and management is likely in the coming decades.
The prototype for the conclusion of these two trends is the
worker cooperative.

The Subtrends

There are over 9,000 corporations in the United States
that have become employee owned in some degree. This
has happened through the incentives provided by legislation called the Employee Stock Ownership Plan, and this
pattern of ownership covers over 9 percent of the U.S.
workforce. Worker ownership, however, does not necessarily mean majority ownership in these companies. Employees
own an actual majority of shares in only about 800 of
these ESOPs. Furthermore, employees have full democratic
control in only a handful of ESOP companies.

The advent of worker ownership is significant for
public awareness and the legitimacy it supplies in the
United States for establishing policies leading toward the
cooperative prototype. Public acceptance of worker ownership as legitimate and as an effective policy for enterprises is thus a significant step in the transition to self-
management. The airlines and trucking industries are
trending toward employee ownership. For example, key
transportation corporations are developing worker ownership, including Transcon Trucking (49%) and Chicago and
Northwestern Railroad (22%). Many other industries have
also made significant steps in this direction.[4]

When a firm is organized as an ESOP, it does not
lead automatically to democratic cooperation but the action
increases the possibility for taking these steps. An ESOP
firm can become a democratic cooperative enterprise easily
with proper legal counsel. The recognition of workers that
they are owners has in some cases led them to pressure
management in this direction. The significance of ESOPs
for a movement toward self-management therefore rests to a
large extent with the favorable publicity given to worker
ownership and growing acceptance of its legitimacy in the
United States. Examples of ESOPs that have become organized

Table 3.1

Major Employee Ownership Companies (Examples)

Company	Location	Line of Business	# of Employees	% Owned
Publix Supermarkets	Lakeland, FL	Supermarkets	37,000	100
Ashland Oil	Ashland, KY	Oil Refinery	32,000	27
FMC Corporation	Chicago, IL	Industrial Manufacturing	31,000	32
Colt Industries	New York, NY	Manufacturing	22,400	30
P-I-E Trucking	Jacksonville, FL	Trucking	20,000	38
Kaiser Aluminum	Oakland, CA	Aluminum Products	15,000	20
Lowe's Companies	N. Wilkesboro, N.C.	Lumber/ Hardware	14,000	30
E-Systems	Dallas, TX	Electronics	9,500	25
Ruddick Corporation	Charlotte, NC	Holding Company	9,360	38
Dennison Manufacturing	Framingham, MA	Office Supplies	9,000	21
Weirton Steel Company	Weirton, WV	Steel Mfg.	8,500	100
Marsh Supermarkets	Yorktown, IN	Supermarkets	7,000	20
Michigan Nat'l Bank	Bloomfield Hill,MI	Banking	7,000	30
Parsons Corporation	Pasadena, CA	Eng. & Const.	7,000	100
Science Applications	La Jolla, CA	Research & Dev.	7,000	85
Amsted Industries	Chicago, IL	Manufacturing	6,900	98
Austin Engineering	Dallas, TX	Construction	6,500	60
Dan River Company	Greenville, SC	Textile Mfg.	6,500	70
Avondale Industries	New Orleans, LA	Shipbuilding	6,000	70
Smith's Transfer	Staunton, VA	Trucking	6,000	49
Kerr Glass	Los Angeles, CA	Glass Mfg.	5,000	20
National Health Corp.	Mufreesboro, TN	Nursing Homes	5,000	20
The Journal Company	Milwaukee, WI	Newspapers & Radio	4,900	90
Thomson-McKinnon	New York, NY	Securities Broker	4,130	76

(continued)

Table 3.1 (continued)

Company	Location	Line of Business	# of Employees	% Owned
American West Airlines	Tempe, AZ	Airline	4,000	20
Lifetouch	Minneapolis, MN	School Photography	4,000	100
Transcon	El Segundo, CA	Pipeline Operators	3,700	57
Dentsply	York, PA	Dental Supplies	3,610	33
Transco	Houston, TX	Trucking	3,350	20
American Sterilizer	Erie, PA	Hospital Supplies	3,500	20
Dunlop Tire	Buffalo, NY	Rubber Mfg.	3,500	20
Davey Tree Expert	Kent, OH	Tree Service	3,200	100
American Cast Iron Pipe	Birmingham, AL	Pipe & Fittings Mfg.	3,100	100
CF&I Steel	Pueblo, CO	Steel Mfg.	3,100	38
W.L. Gore Associates	Newark, DE	High-Tech Mfg.	3,000	95
Granite Construction Co.	Watsonville, CA	Highway & Heavy Const.	3,000	51
Quad/Graphics	Pewaukee, WI	Printing	2,700	37
Int'l Data Group	Framingham, MA	Computer Magazines	2,600	20
OTASCO	Tulsa, OK	Retail, Home/Out	2,600	100
Federal Hoffman	Anoka, MN	Ammunition Mfg.	2,500	100
CH2M Hill, Inc.	Corvallis, OR	Eng. & Architects	2,300	100
ABC Liquors	Orlando, FL	Liquor Stores	2,100	100
U.S. Sugar	Clewiston, FL	Sugar Processor	2,100	47
Jerell, Inc.	Dallas, TX	Textile Mfg.	2,000	Maj
Okonite Company	Ramsey, NJ	Wire/Cable Mfg.	1,800	100
Continental Steel	Kokomo, IN	Steel Mfg.	1,700	37

Company	Location	Industry	Employees	Ownership %
Ormet, Inc.	Hannibal, OH	Aluminum Mfg.	1,700	49
Adam Metal Supply	Elizabeth, NJ	Metal Dist.	1,500	100
Bureau of Nat'l Affairs	Washington, DC	Newsletters & Reports	1,500	100
Cinabro Corp.	Pittsfield, ME	Heavy Construction	1,500	43
Katz Communications	New York, NY	Communications	1,500	100
Crucible Specialty Steel	Syracuse, NY	Specialty Steel Mfg.	1,400	Maj
Matthews International	Pittsburgh, PA	Marking Devices Mfg.	1,300	Maj
National Refactories	Oakland, CA	Heat Resis. Mat. Mfg.	1,300	20
North American Rayon	Elizabethton, TN	Textile Mfg.	1,300	100
Tony Lama Company	El Paso, TX	Boot Maker	1,250	20
Alco-Gravure	Rochelle Park, NJ	Printing	1,200	70
Denver Yellow Cab	Denver, CO	Taxicab Co.	1,200	100
Halmode Apparel	Roanoke, VA	Textile Mfg.	1,200	89
TDI Industries	Dallas, TX	Heating & AC Supplies	1,200	100
Texas Foundries	Lufkin, TX	Pipe, Castings Mfg.	1,200	45
Holly Sugar Corp.	Col. Springs, CO	Sugar Processor	1,800	20
Columbus Foundries	Columbus, GA	Foundry	1,100	20
Duff Truck Line	Lima, OH	Trucking	1,100	45
Kolbe & Kolbe	Wausau, WI	Glass & Window Mfg.	1,000	67
Robertson Factories	Taunton, MA	Textile Mfg.	1,000	61

Data primarily from public sources. Some figures are estimates. Not all employees are necessarily owners. *1,000 employees or more and at least 20% employee owned.

SOURCE: This table is adapted from the Employee Ownership Report. [a publication of the National Center for Employee Ownership] 7 (1987): 6&7.

in the fashion of producer co-ops include Republic Container, Chase Brass, Seymour Specialty Wire, and Solar Center.

We have said that the trend toward self-management also includes the subtrend of worker participation in higher levels of management. This subtrend is important because worker ownership is of limited value if employees are not adequately trained in management. Therefore, many self-management theorists recognize that the increasing instance of worker participation in management is an important part of the process toward gaining effective worker control over production.

In the United States, we can see widespread efforts toward establishing worker participation. First, at low levels of the corporate hierarchy, this trend is expressed largely as projects in quality of work life and experiments in autonomous groups. These projects and experiments include thousands of firms. While many of these programs are recognized by unions as simply devious attempts on the part of higher management to gain greater control over worker sympathies and get rid of unions, in other cases union leaders and executives claim them to be genuine attempts to strengthen unions and to teach workers new skills in self-management. Second, the use of labor-management committees in middle management has continued since the mid-twentieth century as a method for improving productivity. This has given workers a taste of middle-management skills in maintaining productivity that are necessary when a company takes steps toward worker ownership. Third, workers have become represented in high management on boards of directors. Well-publicized examples have been Weirton Steel and South Bend Lathe. The various degrees of worker ownership and worker management that have been developing in the United States are a part of a change in American attitudes toward the meaning of work and the role of employees in determining management policies in U.S. enterprise.[5]

We want to examine in more detail how different organizations affect these two trends in the United States. These cases become instructive to us in evaluating education for self-management in the United States and in Greece.

Government

The subtrend of worker ownership has been stimulated especially by two types of federal legislation: 1) the ESOP and 2) a series of laws stimulated by plant closures that involve special types of government actions favoring worker control.

The ESOP was introduced into Congress by Senator Russell Long as a method of redistributing income by sharing the material benefits of ownership. The idea originated with Louis Kelso, an attorney, as a method for distributing asset wealth in substitution for welfare payments. His hope was to give incentives for newly created capital to be more widely owned by people and at the same time to provide a larger source of equity financing for corporations. This plan made the provision of shares to workers in the firm a profitable venture: companies that needed new capital could get it more cheaply by providing stock to their employees.

Following this plan, a company organizes an Employee Stock Ownership Trust (ESOT), whose members then arrange a loan from a bank to fund the capital needs of the company. The trust uses the loan to buy stock newly issued by the company and then the company guarantees repayment of the trust's debt, agreeing to contribute annually to amortize the loan. As the loan is paid, the stock held by the trust is allocated on the trust's books to the accounts of individual employees, usually in proportion to their compensation in the company. The stocks become "vested" according to a formula often based on the length of employment in the company. The acquired stock is then distributed directly to the employees (or the estate) upon their retirement, disability, or death. Dividends paid on stock in the trust are added to the individuals' trust accounts. In conventional loans, only interest payments are tax deductible; under an ESOP, both interest and principal payments to the ESOT are deductible, up to certain limits.[6]

A second type of legislation is associated with plant closings. Representative Peter Kostmayer and his associates aligned themselves with Senator Long and the small-business lobby to introduce the Small Business Ownership Act in 1980. This provided for loans up to $500,000 to be administered through the Small Business Administration (SBA). These loans were to finance employee buyouts of closing companies and give employees the opportunity to own them. The bill passed the Senate unanimously and was signed into law in July 1980.

A closely associated piece of legislation is the Chrysler Corporation Loan Guarantee Act of 1979. Federal loan guarantees not exceeding $1.5 billion were provided to Chrysler because it was on the verge of bankruptcy. The federal loan was made conditional upon matching contributions totaling $2 billion from a broad class of individuals and institutions characterized as "persons with an existing economic stake in the health of the Corporation." Unionized employees were asked to contribute $460 million, nonunionized workers $125 million (in the form of concessions on pay increases), and creditors $500 million. Employees would then acquire equity in Chrysler through the legislation of an ESOP. To secure its investments, the federal government assumed priority liens on Chrysler's assets. Also part of the deal was the acceptance on the board of directors of the president of the United Auto Workers, Douglas Fraser. Though Fraser chose not to continue on the board after his retirement, the precedent was set in this case for a major company to become partially owned by its workers and for a union president to serve on the board of directors.[7]

Various government agencies have become involved in loans for employees seeking to purchase their companies. The Small Business Administration, the Farmers Home Administration (FHA), and the Economic Development Administration (EDA) have all made loans for employee buyouts. For example, the South Bend Lathe Company obtained a $5 million loan from the EDA to the city of South Bend, which in turn loaned the money to the newly created ESOT in the company. The company itself then raised over $4.5 million for the worker buyout. The Vermont Asbestos Group obtained a loan from the SBA. The Library Bureau Corporation in New York borrowed $2 million from the EDA, while $2 million more came from employees, the local community, and local banks. The Saratoga Knitting Mill became worker owned on an SBA loan guarantee covering 48 percent of the purchase price of the plant. The remainder involved 20 percent of shareholder equity and first and second mortgage loans for 26 percent. The federal government in these ways has been an active participant in enabling firms in the United States to become more democratically owned and managed by the workers.

In sum, state and city governments have provided special support for worker buyouts and worker control in at least five different ways:

Feasibility studies: Employees at various plants, such as Weirton Steel in West Virginia and the O & O Markets in Pennsylvania, have received financial support from their states for feasibility studies of worker buyouts.

Reduced interest rates: The Connecticut legislature created an $8 million fund to reduce interest rates for worker-owned firms.

Technical assistance: California authorized the state's Business Development Department and local development offices to provide technical assistance for employee-owned firms under its Employee Ownership Act of 1983.

Educational assistance: Michigan, New York, and Massachusetts not only offer technical assistance to help in securing financing for worker buyouts but also help to advance workers' understanding of employee ownership.

State charters: Cooperatives can be chartered in some form in all states, but seven states have enacted special laws to provide a sound legal basis for chartering worker cooperatives. These states are Connecticut, Maine, Massachusetts, New York, Oregon, Vermont, and Washington.

Unions

Union leaders have had mixed opinions on the subtrends in worker participation and worker ownership in the United States. We will illustrate some of these opinions and then describe cases in which particular unions have become directly involved in these subtrends.

Some union leaders are very much opposed to ESOPs. They point out how they can be misleading to workers insofar as they do not usually offer employees real voting powers. In addition, ESOP votes are generally offered on the basis of the number of shares owned, and this gives wealthy managers an edge over the workers. Also, ESOPs appear at first to workers as though they could be a substitute for pension plans, but in reality they do not serve that purpose. In general, these leaders argue, ESOPs are deceptive to labor unless they can be transformed into democratic structures.[8]

Some union members do not want to become involved in ESOPs even when they are democratically organized because it introduces a new role for unions that is not fully understood and tested. Democratic worker ownership can be threatening to unions unless a whole new strategy is undertaken to address the fears that unions are no longer needed under these new circumstances. The answers are forthcoming on this question as workers begin to see that unions can still play an important role in collective bargaining in their own democratic firm and also remain an important part of the larger labor movement protecting their rights at the national level. But this process of learning what constitutes the role of labor unions affiliated with democratic firms is still evolving in practice. Leaders are learning through their participation in current cases where they are helping to convert firms to democratic worker ownership.

Still other union leaders have questioned the very idea of organizing democratic firms. They have claimed that producer co-ops have a tendency to fail, as did those organized by the Knights of Labor in the last century. Other leaders have argued in opposition to this position, saying that all firms show risks and democratic firms are in the same position as other firms. It is noted, for example, that some 50 percent of conventional businesses fail within the first two years of startup and that 80 percent of the firms close within five years. Therefore, co-ops are simply a risk like any other enterprise. Their success depends as much on the nature of the market as it does on the organization of management.

Let us look at some examples of democratic changes in ownership and management that are beginning to occur through ESOP legislation, with union support, in the United States. A General Motors plant in Clark, New Jersey, had been losing money because G.M. management was shifting the bulk of its production from rear-wheel drive to front-wheel vehicles. The Clark plant was manufacturing ball bearings for rear-wheel drive automobiles and was no longer needed. Management was planning to shut it down when union leaders took the initiative to secure their rights in both ownership and management of the firm. Executives in G.M. could see some advantage in helping to keep the plant open, since it was not abandoning all rear-wheel drive production. Local leaders of the United Auto Workers (UAW) took the lead in pushing the idea of a worker buyout. They tried to raise money from workers for a feasibility study but were narrowly defeated by the failure of their members to support them.

Then, key members of local management decided to join with labor to propose a joint union-management employee-ownership committee. Union leaders accepted their plan and subsequently worked with local management to raise money for a feasibility study. Everyone who wished to work for the employee-owned company was asked to pledge $100. More than half of the workers on the payroll signed up, pledging $120,000. The feasibility study then showed that the company could be viable if it employed half of those currently employed and if workers would agree to a 25 percent pay reduction. The study committee said further that its success depended upon a contract agreement with G.M. to buy a major portion of the plant's output for a three-year transitional period.

A long period of negotiation followed this study in which a New Jersey attorney, Alan Lowenstein, played a major role. Lowenstein believed that to secure the financing for the new company it would be necessary to grant management full control of the firm in the early years of its existence. The union leaders agreed, especially since the stock generated by the ESOP would not be vested for ten years. The union also accepted Lowenstein's proposal on the structure of the company board. The board of directors, he said, should seat three people selected by the union, three by management, and seven prominent outsiders selected initially by Lowenstein.

Local management of the plant debated a number of issues with union leaders. Management leaders wanted the vested stock to be distributed in relation to salary levels so that the employees with higher salaries would obtain more stock. This is often done in an ESOP, but the union insisted that the stock be distributed equally regardless of salary. The union demand prevailed on this issue but lost on another issue in which union leaders wanted to establish a trust designed to consolidate worker voting power. The union agreed to a 25 percent wage cut, which was still above prevailing rates in that area. They did not win their argument for a profit-sharing plan, but they won their jobs and a significant new role in the power structure of management.

The joint committee was strong in the issue of maintaining pension benefits, while G.M. was reluctant to continue pension arrangements because of its potential liability for the plan (which could be as high as $60 million). The issue was finally resolved when the parties agreed that one-quarter of this sum, $15 million, would be added to the purchase price. General Motors agreed to take $10 million in nonvoting stock, thus reducing the price by that amount, and provided $15 million in interim financing until the loan from Prudential Insurance was approved. Finally, G.M. signed a contract based on its estimate of car sales requiring the type of wheel bearing made at the Clark plant. This would take up to 80 percent of the plant's output for the first three years. The local labor-management committee had succeeded. Local managers were largely in control, but they agreed with unions to develop an active program of worker participation through the help of outside consultants. This program would take account of the fact that labor had three representatives on the board of directors.[9]

This case is instructive because the Clark plant did not finally succeed in continuing its operations. A major reason was that G.M. decided not to continue its contracts with its former plant-subsidiary because it needed to switch its production entirely to front-wheel drive cars. The fact that G.M. no longer needed to maintain its contracts with the Clark plant was a devastating blow and a major factor leading to the bankruptcy of the plant.

But it was also true that the new Clark management had not prepared itself for this event. It was not able to reinvest and diversify its products in time for it to become self-sufficient. It was still learning to manage itself under the new autonomous arrangements, that is, it was slow in seeking measures that would make itself fully self-reliant. It was difficult for management and employees to understand together the critical importance for a quick reinvestment in the face of a pending G.M. pullout. Unable to move decisively and quickly on its own behalf, the firm was forced to close.

The case is interesting partly because of its analogue with the family in which a parent must work with an adolescent becoming an adult. In this New Jersey case, it meant that the parent company needed to help the adolescent subsidiary without itself losing money in the process. Indeed, the best situation would have involved the leadership in both parent (G.M.) and subsidiary (Clark) companies thinking together about how to make money during their disengagement. The Clark subsidiary simply needed time to diversify its own product lines in order to survive and to obtain its own identity. This process of disinvestment clearly has its value to the parent company as well as to subsidiary employees and the local community but it requires new patterns of learning in a new frontier of corporate management.

A similar kind of employee takeover occurred with the union associated with Great Atlantic & Pacific Tea (A&P) with success. This company had been closing down its supermarket food stores throughout the country and union leaders were concerned about their jobs. The store closing struck the Philadelphia area particularly hard, and local union employees became very concerned. Leaders of Local 1357 of the United Food and Commercial Workers (UFCW) talked with managers about the possibility of a buyout. After negotiations, they reached an agreement to reopen many of the A&P stores around Philadelphia under the name Super Fresh Food Centers. Today, 23 stores have been reopened successfully. Workers agreed in this case to cut their wages from $10 an hour to $8 an hour and to cut overtime pay from double time to time-and-a-half. The union also bargained for the right of first refusal on the purchase of all future closed stores before they are sold to outsiders. If feasible, the union will continue buyouts of future stores.[10]

The steel industry has been in trouble for many years. One reason is that top management has let machinery become obsolete while foreign competitors have updated their equipment and imported their steel at competitive prices. Another reason is that wages of workers are relatively high in relation to other countries, thus boosting the costs of production. Still another reason is that foreign governments have subsidized their steel industries, putting U.S. steel manufactures at a disadvantage.

National Steel was one company hit by the industrial decline. In March 1982, it announced its intention to close its subsidiary in Weirton, West Virginia. Before closing out, however, management offered employees the opportunity to buy the company. Reportedly, most of the equipment was modern and the company was not in serious financial trouble. A study was conducted by a firm called McKinsey and Company that indicated that an employee-owned firm would be feasible under certain conditions. The conditions were that the workers agree to a 20-percent wage and benefit reduction with an additional 12-percent wage-benefit deferral for a maximum of four years. McKinsey also recommended that the current level of employment of 8,200 be reduced to 7,000 over a ten-year period. This meant that about 3,300 workers currently laid off had little chance of being reemployed, but the pay reduction was not too difficult to accept. Since Weirton's pay and benefits for workers was about $2 above the average for workers covered by the United Steel Workers, the new contract would still leave Weirton workers in a reasonable income position.

The Independent Steel Workers Union of Weirton is a company union and not affiliated with the United Steel Workers of America. It will have the difficult task of introducing self-management processes in the structure of the plant. The negotiations between the union and the company have been completed but the whole story has yet to be told. The primary issue remaining to be resolved is how to maintain a pension fund plan for which National Steel still has unfunded liabilities.[11]

Employees have also become involved in the purchase of companies without union participation. At the Saratoga Knitting Mill, for example, members of a management team invested $4,500 each to save their firm, while rank-and-file workers averaged about $600 each. Some 60 percent of employees invested in the new firm. Saratoga employees now hold a majority interest (70%) in their plant, but the primary control rests with management. The rest of the stock (30%) is shared among 26 local outside investors. In this case of employee buyout, the management hierarchy remained the same. There were no internal changes leading to greater responsibilities for workers in plant management.[12]

Many other similar cases exist. For example, a specialty steel plant in Dunkirk, New York, experienced heavy losses for about 15 years and was ready to close out 2,000 workers when the employees saw the opportunity to buy the plant. Since the company had such a poor commercial record, bankers refused to help them. Eventually, however, 35 employees were able to meet finance requirements with the help of a $10 million loan from the EDA. The new company, called Al Tech Specialty Steel Corporation, represented again a management purchase. Following the purchase, the plant increased in size and productivity rose by 9 percent. It has since continued to be profitable.[13]

The plywood cooperatives of the Pacific Northwest are perhaps the oldest firms without union organization. They originated in the early 1920s. About 32 plywood co-ops have been known to have started since 1930. Most of them were able to survive the Depression by lowering wages while other conventional firms failed. By 1978, 16 plywood co-ops were still operating, with about 200 employees in each plant. Their productivity levels are about 30 percent above average for the industry.[14]

The Community

The local community can become actively involved in assisting firms toward worker control. For example, local leaders in Jamestown, New York, a manufacturing community of 40,000 people, became concerned about their main industries when the local economy began losing ground. The decline had been gradual. At the beginning of the century, there were 34 plants manufacturing wood furniture, but by 1972 the number had dropped gradually to 14. The employment figure for Jamestown's manufacturing industries as a whole showed a steady decline for 18 years prior to 1972. People claimed that the reason for this decline was that local labor was aggressively unionized. The town had not been able to attract industry because of a reputation for having a bad labor climate. Strikes were frequent. The fact is that there had been a gradual shift in company ownership to outsiders, and this was helping to cause the unrest. The situation was going from bad to worse in 1971 when a local labor attorney, Ray Anderson, began talking with the Federal Mediation Conciliation Service about the problem. The talk turned on the fact that a Toledo, Ohio, labor-management committee had been successful in reversing their image as a bad labor town to one that was attractive to outside interests. They continued to talk about how the town problems had become acute in 1971 with the announcement of the closing of the Art Metal Plant. This plant had been in the community for 70 years and was the largest employer, with as many as 1,700 on the payroll at times.

At this point the idea of a labor-management committee for the community was brought to the attention of the

mayor. Stanley Lundine had been elected mayor in 1970
and was ready to take some initiative with leaders from
labor and management. He began consultations on the
problem. After a series of stormy sessions together, the
group began to see their way to a solution. They formed
the Jamestown Area Labor-Management Committee (JALMC).
The committee decided that they had to work fast to stop
the local crisis and reverse the steady decline. In the
next 18 months, JALMC was instrumental in staving off five
other threatened plant shutdowns, preserving over 1,300
jobs. Three of the five were transformed from conglomerate corporations to local ownership and one plant, called
Jamestown Metal Products, was purchased by the employees.

Jamestown Metal Products was ready to close when
workers who were stirred by recent community action mobilized resources to buy the company. Within a month of
the decision to close, a purchase plan was drawn up involving financially about three-quarters of the 120 workers.
Initially, the new employee-owned company experienced
problems associated with a steel shortage and problems in
pricing inherited from previous owners, but it soon over-
came these problems and picked up speed toward recovery.
Today its sales have increased some 55 percent and the
book value of the company has tripled.[15]

Other communities have also played an important role
in facilitating worker buyouts. In Herkimer, New York,
Sperry-Rand announced the shutdown of a furniture factory
under the name of Library Bureau. Management planned
to close even though Sperry-Rand had been making a profit
with it during 19 of the first 20 years of ownership. The
company was making profits, but they were below the level
considered satisfactory by top executives.

When Sperry-Rand announced the shutdown, two
groups became interested in its purchase. One group was
headed by people who had management and marketing experience with the company, and the other group had expertise in financial operations. Each group lacked the
expertise of the other. Fortunately, the two competing
groups were brought together by an outside mediator; they
agreed to work together and hired a consulting firm to
make a feasibility study. They obtained the assistance of
professional staff from the EDA-supported Economic Development Center of the State University of New York.

When the organizers saw that it was financially
feasible to buy the plant, they went into a broad-scale

community campaign to raise funds. Sperry-Rand had required a nonrefundable deposit of $200,000 to test the seriousness of their interest. With leadership from John Ladd, the Mohawk Valley Economic Development district director, the group conferred with local management people and with leaders of the white-collar and blue-collar locals of the International Union of Electrical, Radio, and Machine Workers. The group then presented the opportunity for a buyout to all employees at a local high school. Local union leaders cooperated and the organizers raised $193,000 within several days. Sperry-Rand agreed that this was sufficient for their purposes. The organizers then sought to borrow $2 million from banks in the region, giving them first mortgage on plant and equipment. (The banks could hardly lose because even with bankruptcy, the company assets would be well over $2 million.)

They asked the EDA to provide an additional $2 million in loans by means of a second mortgage. The leaders then sought to broaden the equity base by selling stock to local citizens. They realized that it would be impossible to raise the additional $1.75 million they needed from employees alone because they represented a work force of only 200 people. They decided to take the sales to the community.

Ladd and his organizers led the community campaign for stock sales. It was conducted like a United Fund drive. They divided the territory among themselves for sales strategies and set targets for money to be raised through meetings in each area. The organizers launched a media blitz with news stories, radio and television interviews, and paid announcements. Brokers in the area agreed to sell the stock without commission. Before the end of 45 days—a deadline set by Sperry-Rand—the sales campaign had brought in 3,350 investors in an area with over 13 percent unemployment at the time. Most of these investors had never bought stock before. They did not fully understand the meaning of voting for corporate board members and receiving dividends, but they did see themselves contributing to the welfare of the workers and the community.

Conclusions from the U.S. Experience

We have seen from these cases that there are benefits in taking steps toward higher levels of worker participation

and ownership and that various organizations have helped
to advance this process in the United States.   The findings
of empirical studies also demonstrate that these benefits
give reason for Congress to provide enabling legislation
and tax incentives to encourage more efforts in this direction.   It is also clear that many workers remain ill informed about the whole process and more education and
training is essential to make this process more effective.

There has been limited interest on the part of the
Republican administration to take steps to implement legislation to advance worker participation and worker ownership, but there have been significant signs among Democrats seeking office.   The evidence gained from these
selective cases in worker participation and ownership can
provide the basis for new social policies in the future.

Let us propose some conclusions from these studies
in the United States suggesting that benefits accrue from
worker participation and worker ownership.   First, studies
suggest that employee takeovers can be highly successful
when adequate feasibility studies are conducted.   Key
questions that must be answered are whether the firm can
be viable in the existing market with its financial resources and whether employees want the new democratic
venture.   According to a U.S. Congressional Select Committee on Small Business (1979), no U.S. buyout stemming
from corporate divestiture failed during the 1970s.   Observers of this process know of some unrecorded failures,
but the significant point is that success has been frequent.
Furthermore, when buyouts fail to develop successfully, it
has been primarily owing to market problems and not to
problems in the new democratic structure of the business.

Second, this same select committee tells us that
worker buyouts that avoid plant shutdowns can be considered an important method for preserving jobs at the national level.   The total job-preserving effect of U.S. worker
buyouts in the decade of the 1970s was estimated by the
committee to be between 50,000 and 100,000.

Third, employee-owned companies tend to maintain
their profitability and productivity in the United States.
Conte and Tannenbaum compared the ratio of profit to
sales for 30 firms reporting such information in a panel of
98 firms with substantial employee ownership.[16]   The
profitability of these employee-owned firms was slightly
higher than a sample of paired conventional firms.   The
difference was not at a statistically significant level, but

the important point is that they did not lose money. Furthermore, studies show that firms that experiment with increasing the level of worker participation also experience a rise in productivity. Part of the reason may be the experimental nature of these events, which gives employees a new feeling of dignity in their work. We do not know the extent to which this improvement in productivity is lasting, but it is clear that increasing worker authority in management at this point does not show decreases in productivity.[17]

Fourth, these worker-owned firms also show good relationships established among employees. Conte and Tannenbaum report a positive attitude to employee ownership on the part of management. Good industrial relations were generally felt to prevail within ESOP firms. Grievances were few and employee cooperation was frequently observed to contribute toward reduced levels of wastage.[18]

Fifth, the practice of converting troubled plants into viable worker-owned-and-managed firms reduces government costs. The buyout eliminates the need to lay off workers and this saves major welfare payments and unemployment compensation. The welfare costs in some cases can amount to more than the loan capital of a bank (or state agency) that may seek to save a company. It is worth the risk where market studies suggest the firm will retain its viability in a buyout. Furthermore, the conversion of a shut-down plant to worker ownership also saves the income base of employees who now are able to continue to provide taxes to the state. The elimination of welfare costs in addition to the gaining of taxable income for the government makes a big difference in determining government policy.

Sixth, studies show that shut-down plants impact negatively on the personal lives of employees and their families. Research is beginning to reveal the importance of a job in supplying the human dignity and self-respect important to people living in communities. Research shows that unemployment has a strong negative effect on the personal lives of the jobless. Job loss can result in the debilitation of family life and even serious depression or suicide as well as be a contributory factor in the etiology of physical diseases.[19]

Seventh, business closings also have a negative impact on the community. Studies show that in the long run the cumulative effects can be measured in terms of a rise in the crime rate and an increase in delinquency, drugs, and prostitution. The result is calculable in the financial loss of schools, hospitals, and small businesses, which suffer because of their close interdependence with large corporations making big layoffs. The problem of unemployment is frequently associated with big corporations that have no concern about the well-being of the local community when they move their plants to another country or to another U.S. city because labor costs are lower. The public is increasingly becoming aware of the fact that worker-owned-and-managed firms provide local communities with a greater degree of security for maintaining local institutions and continuity in community life.

Summary

All told, experience with worker participation and with self-managed firms in the United States has been limited but productive. It has been leading to considerable public interest in the idea of employee ownership, with these cases being given attention in the mass media. Attitudes have been favorable in those cases where the action is taken pragmatically to save firms or where there has been harmonious collaboration between management and workers toward these ends. At the same time, the selective manner in which these changes are occurring is also indicative of the long way that has yet to be traversed.

The idea of worker ownership may become popular, but the idea of worker management in association with it has not yet become significant in the public mind. Indeed, the type of stock issued to workers has to be fully understood and studied by management consultants. The problem with conventional stock is coming to be understood by union leaders through experience with ESOPs. Union leaders are learning that corporate stock does not automatically give them any more power or security. Furthermore, worker ownership under conventional stock plans can simply disappear when shares are open for purchase on the public market. The company can simply be sold away to outside purchasers by approaching individual workers who need the money.

This sellout of stock by the workers happened in the celebrated case of worker ownership in the Vermont Asbestos Group and the Kansas City Star (a newspaper), both of

which had become so profitable that wealthy outside interests came along and purchased the firms from the workers
at "top dollar." The Vermont Group is now owned by a
wealthy local businessman who purchased controlling interest from employees, and the Kansas City Star is now owned
by a New York conglomerate whose top executives assumed
final authority in determining the editorial policy of their
newspaper. These reverse buyouts are gradually coming
to be known more widely by the public. We discuss how
they can be avoided in Chapter 8.

Some national resources have developed to support
the trends toward worker participation and worker ownership. For example, educational resources have developed
to train people in self-management and also to aid the
producer cooperative as a prototype for integrating these
two trends in the United States. Academic degree programs have developed to train students in the field of
democratic self-management: Guilford College offers a
bachelor's degree in Democratic Management and Employee
Ownership; Boston College offers a graduate program that
combines a joint MBA-Ph.D degree in the field of social
economy, specializing in the field of worker self-management; New Hampshire College's School of Human Services
offers a joint Bachelor-Master's degree in Community Economic Development with faculty who conduct research on
self-management; faculty at Cornell University—including
Jaroslav Vanek and William F. Whyte—have initiated research programs in worker self-management and worker
ownership. The key organization for information on worker
ownership is currently the National Center for Employee
Ownership. Private consulting agencies have been organized
to advance the development of producer cooperatives, including the Industrial Cooperative Association in Somerville, Massachusetts and the Philadelphia Association of
Cooperative Enterprises (PACE) in Philadelphia, Pennsylvania. These agencies provide technical and educational
assistance as well as loan funds to aid the development
of producer cooperatives.[20]

A slow learning process is taking place in which
labor and management are integrating worker participation
and ownership in corporations. While there are no real
signs at the moment that the process is going to make any
big leap forward, there are also no real signs of turning
back or that the trends will stop. Indeed, President
Reagan has endorsed the idea of worker ownership and

the Democratic party has placed the concepts of worker participation and worker ownership in their political platform. It appears to be simply a matter of time before the political context changes favoring legislation that will quicken these subtrends of worker participation and worker ownership toward an integrated national trend.

NOTES

1. Peter Jan Honigsberg, Bernard Kamoroff, and Jim Beatty, We Own It (Laytonville, Calif.: Bell Springs, 1982).

2. Robert Jackall and Henry Levin, Worker Cooperatives in America (Berkeley: University of California Press, 1984), p. 88.

3. Daniel Zwerdling, Democracy at Work (Washington, D.C.: Association for Workplace Democracy, 1978); Ronald Mason, Participatory and Workplace Democracy (Carbondale: Southern Illinois University Press, 1982).

4. Corey Rosen et al., Employee Ownership in America (Lexington, Mass.: D.C. Heath, Lexington Books, 1986).

5. William Foote Whyte, Tove Helland Hammer, Christopher Meek, Reed Nelson, Robert Sterne, Worker Participation and Ownership (Ithaca, N.Y.: ILR Press, Cornell University, 1983).

6. Severyn T. Bruyn, The Social Economy: People Transforming Business (New York: John Wiley & Sons, 1977), pp. 193–94.

7. Keith Bradley and Alan Gelb, Worker Capitalism Cambridge, Mass.: MIT Press, 1983), p. 71.

8. James Smith [United Steel Workers], "The Labor Movement and Worker Ownership," Social Report 2 (1981):2–3; Glen E. Watts [Communications Workers of America], "New Challenges in Collective Bargaining and Worker Participation," Social Report 2 (1981):4–5; and Christopher Meek, "Employee Ownership and Union Activism: The Rath Packing Company Case," Social Report 3 (1983):4–5, Boston College Program in Social Economy.

9. Whyte et al., Employee Ownership, pp. 110–13.

10. Ibid., pp. 113–14.

11. Jonathon Rowe, "Buying Out the Bosses," Washington Monthly 15 (1984).

12. Bruyn, The Social Economy, pp. 220–21.

13. Bradley and Gelb, Worker Capitalism, pp. 101–2.

14.   Paul Bernstein, Workplace Democratization (Kent, Ohio: Kent State University Press, 1976).

15.   Whyte et al., Worker Participation, chap. 2.

16.   Michael Conte and Arnold S. Tannenbaum, "Employee-Owned Companies: Is the Difference Measureable?" Monthly Labor Review (1978).   See also Arnold Tannenbaum, Employee Ownership (Ann Arbor: University of Michigan Survey Research Center, 1980), p. 3.

17.   Paul Blumberg, Industrial Democracy (London: Constable, 1968); Karl Frieden, Workplace Democracy and Productivity (Washington, D.C.: National Center for Economic Alternatives, 1980).

18.   Conte and Tannenbaum, "Employee-Owned Companies."

19.   M. H. Brenner, Mental Health and the Economy (Cambridge, Mass.: Harvard University Press, 1973); Estimating Costs of National Economic Policy, report prepared for the Joint Economic Committee of Congress (Washington, D.C.: U.S. Government Printing Office).   See also "Influence of the Social Environment on Psychopathology," in Stress and Mental Disorder, ed. J. Barrett (New York: Raven Press, 1979); E. Kelly and L. Webb, eds., "Plant Closings" (Washington, D.C.: Conference on Alternative State and Local Policy, 1980); S. Cobb, "Some Mental Health Consequences of Plant Closing and Job Loss," in Mental Health and the Economy, ed. L. Ferman and J. Gordus (Kalamazoo, Mich.: Upjohn Institute, 1979); Ramsay Liem and Paula Rayman, "Health and Social Costs of Unemployment," American Psychologist 37 (1982); and S. Kasl and J. R. P. French, "The Effects of Occupational Status on Physical and Mental Health," Journal of Social Issues 17 (1962):67–89.

20.   Some magazines carry articles periodically on worker self-management, including In These Times, Social Policy, and Dollars and Sense.   Organizations designed to consult with firms on worker participation in management include the American Center for the Quality of Working Life (University of California, L.A.).   More-detailed case studies of fully self-managed firms in the United States can be found in Severyn T. Bruyn and James Meehan, eds., Beyond the Market and the State (Philadelphia, Pa.: Temple University Press, 1987).

4. Development toward Worker Self-Governance in Greece

INTRODUCTION

The following analysis presents the most-recent developments in critical sectors of the Greek economy where there has been enlargement of the leadership role of the workers in decision-making and expansion of self-determination and autonomy of workers and social groups. Lack of sufficient sociological studies in the field limit us mainly to the examination of legal documents that establish new institutions designed to enhance labor's role in the economy and in society in general.

THE EVOLUTION OF WORKER
SELF-GOVERNANCE IN GREECE

Claims on behalf of the right of workers to participate in decision-making at the level of the enterprise date back to the early 1900s.[1] Such claims were first made in 1918 by the Greek Socialist Party of Workers (SEKE) and the General Confederation of Workers of Greece (GSEE). Nevertheless, no enabling legislative provisions were ever voted to implement worker representation in administrative bodies, and participation at the level of the enterprise

---

This chapter is strictly descriptive of the situation in Greece. We consider its inclusion here as necessary in order to document our thinking and also to inform the reader who is not familiar with developments in the area of labor of a small country in the process of social change.

was never realized. Some forms of participation did occur, however, such as the organization of workers into autonomous work groups at the Emery Mines at Naxos[2] and some worker participation in the administration of legal entities and corporate bodies of the public sector.[3]

The 1978 report of the International Labor Office on labor relations in Greece (known as the Blanchard Report) stated that in Greece there has been no change concerning labor relations at the level of the enterprise and no development of participatory representation. The limited role of labor in the production process observed in Greece up to the 1980s may be attributed mostly to political developments (civil war in 1945-49, military regime in 1967-74) that polarized relations of capital and labor, a polarization that not only inhibited but also prevented the evolutionary process that took part in other European countries.

Nevertheless, in the 1970s claims for labor participation at the enterprise level were strongly propounded by the Hellenic Federation of Bank Employees' Unions (OTOE), and in the early 1980s new forms of organization of labor, i.e., socialization and participation, were widely considered by the labor unions. Labor unions (the General Federation of Public Power Corporation Personnel, GENOP/DEH; the General Confederation of Workers of Greece, GSEE; the Hellenic Federation of Bank Employees' Unions, OTOE; the Federation of Industrial Labor Corporations, OVES; and others) organized national and international conferences whose main topics centered on participation and worker self-governance.

On the other hand, participation at the macro level--committees for labor and social policy--were functioning in Greece as early as 1911. Labor representatives participated in the Supreme Labor Council (Law 3932/1911) and later in the Labor Council (Presidential Decree, November 9, 1931). After World War II, participation by labor representatives with issues related to social and economic policy has been found, for example, in the Council of Social Policy (Law 3229/1955), the Council of Technical Education, the Council of Social Insurance (Royal Decree 479/65, arts. 4 and 5), the Consultative Council of Labor and Social Policy (in 1976 by decision of the minister of coordination), and the Council of Social and Economic Policy (in 1978 by decision of the prime minister).

In Greece up to the 1980s, therefore, we can speak of some cases with various degrees of worker participation only at the experimental level. After 1980, however, some isolated cases of worker participation in management can be found in both the private sector and the public or socialized sector of the economy.

In the post-1981 period, when a socialist-oriented government came to power, the issues of worker participation and self-management came more into public discussion, first as a political slogan and second as a commitment of the government in its Five-Year Plan for Economic and Social Development, 1983-87. This document states that

> the state is to play an active role in the productive process in mobilizing resources for the purposes of development through a full-scale socialization of the state. It is expected that in this way the state apparatus will become capable of functioning rationally and effectively for the benefit of the entire society.[4]

Furthermore, among the objectives of industrial policy is the realization of a new balance in the relations of the productive forces, a balance based on a socially equitable distribution of the benefits of economic progress, the rights and responsibilities of the workers in the production process, new forms of enterprises (especially cooperatives and communal enterprises that are self-managed by the workers), and the like. It should be noted also that the establishment of humane work conditions is recognized as essential to a high quality of life. Participation of the trade unions and the workers in decision making was expected to decisively add to the improvements in working conditions.

Although before coming to power the present government was referring to self-management, the term slowly disappeared in governmental and political circles, and discussion mostly shifted to worker participation. Relevant provisions for the former were not made in the 1983-87 Five-Year Plan. But the trend toward worker and citizen participation in the 1980s in Greece has been stimulated by the government's provision for a new legal framework regarding socialization of public enterprises and public utilities, establishment of supervisory councils in some industrial branches, restoration of problematic enterprises, syndicalist freedoms, and democratic operations of cooperatives and other organizations.[5]

DEVELOPMENT OF WORKER PARTICIPATION AND
SELF-MANAGEMENT AT THE MICRO LEVEL

The new developments are socialization of the public
sector, supervisory councils, and syndicalist freedoms,
phrases that refer basically to the legal arrangements that
enact the new structural arrangements (institutions). Subsequently we discuss the practice and application of various forms of participation and self-governance in Greece,
as well as the positions taken by the syndicates, the employers, and the political parties on the matter.

Socialization of Enterprises of Public
Character, Public Utilities, Banks,
and Insurance Companies

Because socialization as a form of economic organization constitutes the subject of theoretical investigation
among scholars, there are several definitions of the concept of socialization. The Greek government has made
clear its position on the meaning of socialization with Law
1365/1983, according to which socialization of public organizations and enterprises has been legislated.[6]
The term "socialization" seems to define a process by
which social control of public enterprises is to be achieved.
Such social control is to be exercised by a wide scheme of
participation, i.e., workers at various levels (enterprise,
industrial branch of the area, or at the national level)
and representatives of the state, local government, and
social organizations that are served by or have vested interests in the public enterprise.
Socialization, as indicated by the above definition,
does not relate to the shared capital and the property of
the enterprise. The shares of those enterprises belong
entirely or by absolute majority to the state. From a
share-holding point of view, public enterprises and organizations are already socialized.
Socialization of public enterprises has the following
goals: to serve the interest of the entire society; to harmonize the operation of the enterprise with national, regional, and local plans for economic and social development
and the physical, social, and cultural environment; to
save resources and effectively manage them; to increase
productivity and effectiveness for the benefit of those

working in the enterprise; to improve the services offered
to the social whole; and to increase participation of workers in decision making.

Presidential decrees define the structure, the role,
the kind of management, the operation as well as the synthesis of the participative administrative organs, the programs, and the control that will be exercised in the
socialized enterprises according to the special character
of each enterprise. They also define the new labor relations that derive from socialization and new privileges
and obligations for the workers.

The above law took effect from the very moment that
the presidential decrees were announced for the socialization of the Public Power Corporation (DEH), the Hellenic
Telecommunications Organization (OTE), and the Hellenic
Railways Organization (OSE). The procedure for the socialization of public enterprises and public utilities was
completed for the above three enterprises in the middle
1980s and, according to government declarations, seven
more enterprises are in the process of being socialized.[7]

The organizational structure of the socialized public
enterprises include the following collective organs of social
control and administration (see Figure 4.1):

1. a Representative Assembly of Social Control (ASKE) with
   corresponding regional assemblies in every prefecture;
2. a board of directors with the participation of the
   workers, and
3. an administrative council of technocratic nature.

The Representative Assembly of Social Control (ASKE)
is appointed for a three-year period and is composed of
27 members as follows: nine representatives of the state;
nine representatives of the workers of the enterprise; and
nine representatives of such different social institutions as
the General Confederation of Workers of Greece (GSEE), the
Association of Greek Industries (SEB), the Central Union
of Municipalities and Communities of Greece (KEDKE), the
Commercial and Industrial Chamber, the Panhellenic Confederation of Agricultural Cooperatives (PASEGES), the
Handicraft Chamber, the Technical Chamber of Greece, the
Economic Chamber, and the General Farmers Cooperative.

The main tasks of ASKE according to the law are
middle-range planning (particularly in investments),
finance, price fixing, and industrial relations. It also

Figure 4.1

Socialization of Public Enterprises

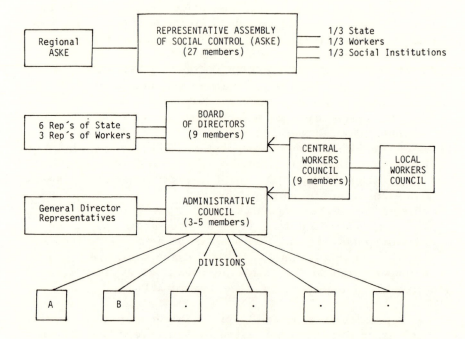

exercises control over the course of the implementation of
these goals and the evaluation of their attainment.   Its
operations are public to ensure full visibility and open-
ness.

Social control is effected not only at the central
level, but also through the Regional Assemblies of Social
Control, which have been established to give consultation
to ASKE on matters of planning at the local level, in order
to harmonize the operation of the enterprise with local
plans for economic and social development.

As the most-important innovation of the law relative
to other participative schemes that are limited to the presence of the workers as representatives in the administration only, ASKE has created some controversy.   According
to certain syndicalists of the DEH, that enterprise has
shown that the social agencies and institutions participating in ASKE are characterized by inertia;[8] other syndicalists complain that socialization is undermined since the

workers are not well informed about the reasons for their representation in the organs of socialization. Because of the lack of information and the inexperience of managers, of the worker representatives, and of other social institutions, mistakes are expected when such participative schemes are tried for the first time. According to other economists, ASKE is a decorative rather than a substantial organ, which, in their opinion, will not be able to carry out its controlling function.[9] Others believe that ASKE's problems relate mainly to its area of jurisdiction and derive from obscurities and inefficiencies of the law that needs further clarification.[10]

With the new institutions of socialization, more social groups participate in the management and control of public enterprises and public utilities. In this sense, socialization can be considered an extension of worker participation, since participation of other social categories (like state representatives, representatives of regional and local self-government, representatives of the industrial branch, and others) is also involved. Also among these participating categories are groups that are served by the enterprise (consumers, for example) or have vested interests in the enterprise (legal and physical entities owning shares, supplies, etc.).

The board of directors consists of nine members: six representatives of the state and three representatives of the workers in the enterprise. It has jurisdiction over the course of operations and over the implementation of enterprise plans by the general management.

According to the law, the central workers' councils consist exclusively of elected worker representatives. They are organs through which workers exercise social control and management that operate within the framework of the enterprise at the local and regional level. These councils have decisive and consultative functions. They handle decisions on issues related to conditions of work, work environment, hirings, transfers, promotions, training, and discipline, and they make recommendations on issues related to production, productivity, organization of work, representativeness, and the like.

The concept of socialization faced very severe criticism. Certain scholars observed much confusion around it.[11] Some political parties and other political and syndicalist organizations voiced their criticisms of socialization as a concept and as an institution, but they were

not very specific. The GSEE has not taken any position
on the concept of socialization.

The definition of <u>socialization</u> as provided by Law
1365/ 83 also faces intense criticism. Some believe that
distinction from the term <u>nationalization</u> is not justified,
since property is not taken from the state and given to
the workers or to a social institution. The public enterprises continue under state control while what has changed
is the synthesis of the board, with broader representation
of the social sector in the administration of the socialized
enterprises. This view was confronted by the assertion
that the difference between socialization and nationalization is the fact that socialized enterprises must be profitable and competitive; in other words, they must operate
within private-sector criteria. Whereas a nationalized
company that belongs to the state may try to equalize
total revenues and total cost by maintaining low product
prices and covering losses with the resources of the national budget, in no case must a socialized enterprise
operate at a loss.[12]

A former syndicalist of GENOP/DEH who is at present
an elected representative of the workers to the board maintains that no one has dared to say what is "real" socialization and that the reason is simple: the form and the
extent of socialization as a sequence of given sociopolitical
conditions and a long-term developmental process in each
country are realized only when approved by the majority
not only of the workers but of the whole society.[13] A
substantial dialogue with the workers can create the appropriate climate for the application of modern management,
decentralization, new incentives, and increased productivity.[14]

Socialization as a new institution should be evaluated on its implementation of positive or negative effects
upon labor relations, the work climate, and productivity.
It could be argued that socialization as implemented up to
the present in the public sector has no real extended participation by outside constituencies, whereas participation
by employees in the enterprise is more substantial. Such
unbalanced real participation in the administrative organs
of socialized organizations could be criticized as corporatism.

Supervisory Councils

The spirit of socialization is also demonstrated in the institution of supervisory councils (Epoptika Symvoulia). Because mineral wealth is a nonrenewable natural resource that must be utilized in the social and national interest, they were first established for the mines and quarries. Recently, supervisory councils have been extended to other branches of industry as well, for example, shipyards.

Supervisory councils were established by Law 1385/83 and constitute collective organs with worker participation in the social control of groups of enterprises in selected branches.[15] They consist of representatives of the state appointed by the Ministry of National Economy, worker representatives, and representatives of employers and the local government or other social institutions that are influenced by the activity of the supervised enterprises. According to Article 6 of Law 1385/82, worker participation in the supervisory councils constitutes a variety of syndicalist activity and is protected by Law 1264/82, which provides for syndicalist freedom. Supervisory councils refer to groups of enterprises or to single enterprises of the branch and, consequently, have a branch and local character.

The supervisory councils constitute a practical application of the law vis-à-vis socialization but at the level of an industrial branch in the private sector of the economy. The representatives of the workers participate in the control and the management of the mineral wealth and the other physical resources of the country and have as main goals the harmony of the economic activity of those enterprises with the economic and social plans of the government, the supervision and investigation of the shaping of prices of imported and exported goods, the protection of the environment, the examination of productivity, the improvement of labor relations, and the submission of proposals for the improvement of industrial relations. The duties of the supervisory councils are the study of various problems and submission of proposals to the Ministry of National Economy.

Supervisory councils do not participate in the everyday administration of the enterprise but exercise supervision in such matters as production, exportation, productivity, environmental protection, conditions of work, and technology. They have an advisory or mediating role in the above matters to aid the realization of national economic goals at the level of the enterprise. In those enterprises that belong to the jurisdiction of a supervisory council, one worker representative is assigned by the syndicate and one representative of the employer is appointed, both for a two-year period; each is responsible to the supervisory council for providing the necessary information.

According to Law 1385/83, supervisory councils have 1) the right of receiving information, an elementary degree of participation; 2) an advisory task in every matter that relates to the enterprises under supervision; and 3) the right to exercise control over the enterprise.

At least every three months, the boards of the mines must submit to their supervisory council a report on the course of business of the company. The council can request whenever considered advisable a special report on the operations of the company. Also, the supervisory council or one-third of its members have the right to ask for information and relevant documents about problems that the enterprise faces. The exercise of such authority can be entrusted to one or more members or to experts. Every member of a supervisory council can be informed of the content of the report, the documents, or the information provided.

The boards of the mining enterprises are also obligated to ask the permission of the supervisory council for decisions referring to 1) the supervision or the transfer of the enterprise, 2) the substantial decrease or growth of its activity, and 3) the establishment of permanent cooperation with other enterprises or the interruption of such cooperation. The reference to these cases in Article 12 is only indicative. Based on other arrangements or the charter of the company, it is possible for the business activities to expand, an activity for which the board must ask the permission of the supervisory council.

Participation in Higher Education

In contrast to the United States, the process of self-governance in Greece is extended significantly into higher education, where students are involved in participation as well as workers. New structural arrangements for graduate schools provide for worker (staff) participation as well as

for student participation in decision making. Student
participation is not of the same order as worker participation, but it parallels the spirit of self-governance.
Activity in higher education shows the spirit of involvement or participation that permeates the socialist-oriented
government.

Law 1268/82, referring to the structure and operation
of schools of higher education, introduced new types of
student participation. All those working, including the
students, in schools of higher education (AEI) are free to
create syndicalist organs to represent them and push forward their rights and authorities. The AEI must facilitate
the representatives of the students in exercising their
right of participation in the organs of decision making as
provided by the law. Student representatives are elected
by the student syndicalist organ, which operates as a
legal entity of private law in every academic section within
a university. Representatives of the National Student
Union of Greece (EFEE) participate in the National Council
of Higher Education (ESAP).[16] A representative of EFEE
also participates in the Secretariat, which is responsible
for the operation of the ESAP.

In the elections of administrative officers within universities (presidents, rectors, deans, chairpersons, and
their deputies), the students have an equal number of
votes as the faculty, a parity that gives them real power
and voice in administrative matters. Representatives of
the students and the special postgraduate scholars (Ph.D.
candidates) participate also in university organs, the general assembly, and the board of directors, the senate, and
the deanship.

It should be mentioned that in the procedure of
evaluating a candidate for a position in Teaching and
Scientific Personnel (DEP), the students' evaluation of
teaching abilities, democratic ethos, personalities, and
social contributions of candidates are all seriously considered. Particularly the teaching ability of the members
of the DEP is evaluated every semester by the students in
their courses.

These innovative arrangements for the representation
and participation of students as provided by Law 1268,
lack of experience, the role played by political parties in
certain cases, and other existing structural and administrative problems are criticized as the cause of certain
malfunctions in the system.

Syndicalist Freedoms

Besides the legal consolidation of worker participation, it was important to secure the necessary conditions for the promotion and substantial implementation of this institution. The protection of the worker representatives from any kind of persecution or pressure and the obligation of the employer to discuss with the workers their problems stand as examples of this need. Law 1264/82 regarding syndicalist freedoms and Law 1387/83 regarding group firings were drafted to ensure the above conditions.

According to Article 16 of Law 1264, the employer or his representative is obligated to meet the representatives of the syndicates (if they so wish) at least once a month in order to consider the problems of the workers and the enterprise and to offer solutions. This law establishes the need for wage and salary negotiations between employer and employees. Article 14 forbids relocations of members of the syndicate without the consent of the syndicate itself. In this case, the form of worker participation is very effective and almost equal to the exercise of veto, since the consent of the syndicate constitutes a precondition for the validity of the relocation. This law also recognizes the control of the syndicates over terminations of employment as well as Law 1387.

Law 1387 also binds the employer to proceed to negotiations with the representatives of the workers in order to examine the possibility of avoiding or limiting group terminations. If consensus between employer and workers is not reached, the prefect or the Ministry of Labor will take part in the discussions. The right of the workers to participate in such joint discussions is of critical importance, because in case of disagreement the decision about firings is carried over from the sphere of employer authority to the jurisdiction of the government.

PARTICIPATION AND SELF-MANAGEMENT:
PRACTICAL APPLICATIONS AT THE MICRO LEVEL

The substantial application of worker participation in Greece is far behind the development of related institutions in Western European countries. Up to the 1970s, participation was very limited, especially in the private sector, and was confined practically within the narrow limits provided by the collective agreements and, in certain cases of legal entities of public law, mainly at the advisory level. With the political change of 1974, when democracy was again restored to Greece, some steps were made toward participation. But only recently, with the laws of 1983, which have been considered landmarks for the development of the new institution, has participation been generalized in the public sector.[17] In the private sector (industry) some efforts are also moving forward for the application of some form of participation in the problematic enterprises.

Participation in the Public Sector

Worker participation in the administration of legal entities (corporate bodies) or enterprises controlled by the state has been applied sporadically in Greece up to the 1980s, as for example, participation in administrative organs of decision making of certain legal entities of public law, like the Harbor Coffers and the Harbor Authorities in the decade of the 1940s.[18] Law 3752, passed in 1929, requires in advance "the opinion of those concerned" before ratification by the state of personnel regulations for legal entities of public law, certain legal entities of private law, or physical persons who are linked by contract with the state.

Recently, representation of workers has been introduced into consultative or advisory organs of newly established public enterprises, which have the character of legal entities of private law, like the Public Corporation for Housing and Urban Planning (DEPOS) and Athens Airport S.A.[19] Until 1983, participation in management was limited to a few legal entities of public law. The legislature was rather distrustful of public utilities but did trust the participation of producer representatives in the administration of organizations dealing with the disposal, development, financing, and protection of agricultural production, like the Autonomous Currant Organization (ASO), the National Tobacco Organization,[20] the Cotton Organization, the Organization of Kopais, the General Organizations of Land Improvements, the Coffers for the Protection of Olive-Oil Producers, and the Agricultural Bank of Greece.[21]

Legislation in 1983 (Laws 1365, 1385, and 1386) introduced and generalized the institution of worker partici-

pation, together with representatives of other social constituencies, in the administration of enterprises in the
public sector and the administration of private enterprises
that are under the control of the state. In large organizations that are in the process of socialization (like
banks, Olympic Airways, etc.), advisory committees are
established by Law 1365/83 for the study of the whole issue of worker participation in administration and for helping these organizations introduce and implement socialization. Thirty such advisory committees have been created
in various branches of the economy. Some advisory committees have already started operating, and some of the
subjects studied and proposals made refer to the clarification of areas in which the government makes decisions,
those areas in which the workers councils make decisions,
and the jurisdictions of the regional councils.

Various social constituencies participate in these advisory committees as well. For example, the Advisory
Committee of Commercial Banks has 13 members: one representative each of the Administration of the National Bank
of Greece and the Commercial Bank of Greece, one representative of the Association of Greek Industries, one representative of the shareholders of commercial banks, one
representative of the Commercial Chamber of Greece, one
mayor of municipality (elected), one representative of
the General Confederation of Workers of Greece, three
bank employees from all commercial banks (elected by
universal vote), one representative of the Commercial and
Industrial Chamber of Athens, one representative of the
Ministry of National Economy, and one representative of
the Ministry of Commerce.

Worker Participation in the Private Sector

A first implementation of democratic relations between
labor and management in Greek industry were the factory
councils in the period 1928–36 in the tobacco industry.[22]
Also, some short-lived factory councils operated before
World War II in some large factories and especially in
the shoe industry. These councils were informal; no law
provided for them and their responsibilities were very limited. Several laws during the 1936–40 period of Metaxas's
dictatorship made collective work agreements compulsory,
but worker participation in the procedures of problem

solving on personnel matters and work conditions at the workplace was limited.

Collective work agreements refer as a rule to allowances and to salary and wage increases. Collective agreements in Greece do not generally cover work arrangements and internal regulations of enterprises, and as a result work contracts are enacted without the participation and cooperation of the workers concerned.[23] Collective agreement legislation is poor in regard to the institution of worker participation, the only exception being the Collective Work Agreement of May 12, 1981, "for the implementation of the institution of bi-partite committees for hygiene and security of the workers in the mines, quarries, industry and electricity production," which provides for the compulsory institution of bipartite "Worker Hygiene and Security Committees" in units that employ more than 500 salaried workers, the extension of this institution in every unit employing more than 30 salaried workers, and the establishment of one bipartite "Central Hygiene and Security Committee."

According to the above Collective Work Agreement, in every establishment that directly or indirectly is involved in excavations, industrial manufacturing, or electricity production employing more than 500 salaried workers, a worker hygiene and security committee is established in which four elected representatives of the workers and four representatives of the employer participate. The chairman of the committee is the senior member of those appointed by the employer. "In the Committee participate also, as speakers without voting rights, the person responsible for issues of hygiene and security in the unit, the technician in charge and the doctor of the unit, if such exist." The establishment of a worker hygiene and security committee is optional for the employer who employs more than 30 and up to 500 salaried workers.

The worker hygiene and security committee constitutes, according to Article 3 of the 1981 Collective Work Agreement, "a consultative organ for the creation and continuation of healthy and safe work conditions."

With Laws 1365/83 and 1386/83, forms of worker participation are established in the private sector only in the mines-quarries branch of industry and "problematic enterprises."[24] In the introductory statement of Law 1386/83 for problematic enterprises, it is stated that an indispensable prerequisite for promoting development is a policy for the social control of means of production, which up to then had been expressed in law either through state intervention in the structure and operation of the enterprise or through participation of workers and other social consituencies in the administration of the business. This law provided for the establishment of a société anonyme under the title Industrial Reconstruction Organization (OAE), which operates under the supervision of the state, to rescue any problematic enterprises that are judged as viable. When the OAE decides to undertake the administration of an enterprise, a representative of the workers participates in its administrative board. The law provides for worker participation also at the stage of converting debts into capital.

Law 1316/83 for the National Drug Organization, the National Drug Warehouse, and the State Drug Warehouse also establishes the operation of a five-member supervisory council responsible for the rules for proper product manufacturing (product quality), security of personnel and installations, protection of the environment, the increase of productivity, necessary investments, and the improvement of working conditions in drug-production units. A workers' representative of the unit participates in the supervisory council, elected from the general assembly of personnel.

Finally, the implementation of the institution of worker participation is possible in the private sector with special individual agreements between the factory unions and the administration of the enterprises, as happened in the AMIANTIT company in 1982.

Cases of worker participation in the boards of directors in the private sector are still very limited. The reasons for the delay in having such institutions established in industry include first the political polarization that characterizes Greek labor relations. This polarization has had an especially negative impact on chances for direct communication and reconciliation between the representatives of workers and the representatives of employers within the workplace. The businessmen looked with reservation upon the labor movement, whereas the leftist parties and the unions had an intense suspicion of worker participation in management. A second reason was the tardy development of industry and particularly the very limited size of most economic units.

Below are some examples of companies that sought to implement worker participation in their decision-making bodies.[25]

AMIANTIT, S.A.

AMIANTIT produces different types of lime cement and employs 200 people. In the past, the workers were often in conflict with the administration, as typified by a four-month strike related to the issue of compensation for unhealthy work that ended in January 1979. The labor-relations climate started to improve in March 1981, owing to the new administration, which took over and applied modern ideas in labor relations. There were improvements in production methods, especially the cutting of lime under water to avoid the creation of dust.

Since 1982, in a private work arrangement between the legal representatives of the administration and personnel, it was agreed to promote a collective work agreement to regulate (1) such issues of collective work differences as hours of weekly employment, allowances, additional leaves and vacations, and changes in the status of worker-technicians to employees; and (2) such institutional issues of the enterprises as certain discharges of union representatives from official duties in order to carry out their syndicalist tasks, management auditing of the enterprise by a union representative, participation of a union representative in the administration of the enterprise (initially without voting rights), worker participation in the net profits of the enterprise, and additional insurance of personnel with a Greek insurance company.

Since 1982, a profit-sharing program was introduced under which workers with the company for more than three years share 12 percent of the net profits proportionate to the years of their employment. Workers who leave the company after ten years of employment can also participate in the profits for the next two years. Since 1978 the company has been in the black, but it is expected that in 1987 it will be in a position to distribute profits for the first time.

The accounting books of the company can be checked at any time by the representative appointed by the workers. AMIANTIT is the only private enterprise in Greece that since 1982 has accepted workers on its board of directors. In the seven-member board, there are two worker representatives with one-year authorization, which can be renewed. High rotation of workers in these two seats exists because union and administration agree that representation is a way to involve more workers in the decision-making process.

VELKA, S.A.

VELKA, established in 1927, is one of the largest spinning and weaving industries in Greece. Until the summer of 1981, its board of directors was composed of family members of the owners. In September 1981, the administration called a general assembly of the 1,000 personnel from its two plants and announced that because the enterprise was overindebted, it was forced to cease operation. Up to that time, the administration had followed a strict policy preventing the formation of a factory union. The workers had no involvement whatsoever in decision making, and they had not been apprised of the faltering economic situation of the enterprise.

The workers elected a 15-member committee in order to fight for the retention of their jobs. After long discussions and negotiations, the company was taken over by the OAE, in December 1983. The seven-member executive committee included the chairmen of the two factory unions. Since 1983 the agreement of the workers' representatives is necessary for production plans, firings, productivity, and supplies.

The relations between the union and the managers (the latter being considered devoted to the owners) are tense and conflicts often occur, but the climate of suspicion existing between management executives of the enterprise and the workers does not seem to affect production negatively. Both the new administration and the union agree that the productivity of the workers has increased since the owners left and the company was taken over.

Hellenic Shipyards Company, S.A.

Hellenic Shipyards, which employs 5,000 people, was badly afflicted by low demand for shipbuilding and repair and was considered for rehabilitation in April 1985. Before the end of 1986, efforts were made to evaluate the real economic condition of the company and estimate its value.

This case has a unique characteristic: for the first time in Greece, workers agreed to be compensated only partially by salary. In October 1985, the new administration agreed with the union that each worker would be paid in cash up to 145,000 drachmas (approximately U.S. $1,000) and the rest in shares of the company. The whole portfolio of the company was bought by the state from the previous owner, and the price of a share was determined after the end of the economic auditing. According to estimates, 12 percent of the portfolio would come under the workers' control. The agreement included a provision that compelled the company to buy at the original price the shares of those workers who wish to sell them.

COULISTANIDIS-COUTSAKIS & CO., S.A.

COULISTANIDIS-COUTSAKIS & CO., S.A. (a spinning and weaving industry) employed 250 workers in 1980. By that time, the debts of the enterprise had reached 220 million drachmas. In February 1980, payments were ceased, and in October 1980 the remaining 117 workers invited Michael Coulistanidis to take over the duties of the compulsory administrator. He agreed to undertake the management of the company, and the operation of the enterprise was ensured until the end of 1983 when a closedown became inevitable, since the interest of the debts was increasing more quickly than the company could afford. When the OAE declined to take over the administration, the enterprise closed down in 1985.

During the period 1981-85, the workers showed considerable initiative in the administration of production (actually there was not any supervision in the factory) as well as in submitting suggestions and negotiating with the various banks, the Social Insurance Foundation (IKA), and the ministries. It should be noted that most of the workers were older than 50 or 60 years of age and had been with the company for more than 25 years.

It is notable that the workers, out of fear of being involved in any political party, refused to form a union. The fact that they were able to organize and to operate the factory without any formal structure for some years can be considered evidence of the untapped forces that may exist in production manpower.

PYR. KAL.

This is a weapons-production industry employing 3,500 workers in three plants. The debts of the enterprise reached 1 billion drachmas. After several efforts at survival that proved unfruitful, the company was taken over by the OAE in April 1984.

In the new executive board there were three worker representatives elected by the personnel through an election procedure for a two-year tenure, with their membership renewable or cancelled at that time. The General Assembly of the Workers' Union ruled that these representatives cannot serve concurrent terms as members of the union council and that they must report twice a year to the union council.

Because of the large number of votes, a proportional representative system was established for the election of factory representatives for the union council. One representative is elected among 30 to 70 workers employed in the same department. The representatives meet in order to exchange views with the members of the union council and with the representatives of the workers in the board of directors of the company. The general assemblies turned out to be impractical and were replaced by the department assemblies, where issues of industrial relations and production were discussed and proposals were submitted to the union or to the administration. Members of the union participate in a hygiene and safety committee as well as in two supplies committees. A union representative attends the meetings of the board of directors, where important decisions are taken and are subsequently submitted to the executive council.

Self-Management

We can say that degrees of worker self-governance, along with citizen participation, have been developing significantly in what is called the social sector. We have noted degrees of worker participation at all levels--including the board of directors--in certain problematic enterprises. Significant levels of worker self-governance are also evident in the cooperative system, although such a system is clearly under significant supervision and protection by the government. Companies of popular base are characterized by community ownership, that is, local citizens and not the government are the main stockholders.[26]

The concept of self-management in Greece is understood as a special case in which the workers fully own and manage the firm. We noted in the United States that about 1,000 firms have this status, even though many more thousands seem to be moving toward this prototype because of the significant subtrends of worker ownership and worker participation that, with public support, are on the increase.

Our concept of worker self-governance was designed to cover degrees of development in worker authority that could be observed from a factual as well as a normative standpoint. In the context of Greece, self-management carries strong ideological overtones as characterizing only those firms fully managed and owned by all workers with one vote per person. There are a few prototypes in existence. While various cooperatives in the social sector meet this standard, only one firm, the Pantelemidis factory, meets this norm in the private sector.

The Pantelemidis enterprise employs only 14 people, a fact that must be contrasted with U.S. cases. After its owner's death in 1981, and because the heirs refused to accept ownership because of the high debts of the business, the workers themselves undertook the operation of the factory. A nephew of the previous owner, a shipbuilding engineer with a good background in business administration and experience in worker participation and self-management, had brought up the idea of self-management to the workers of the factory, who were facing the problem of unemployment.

The autonomous operation of the enterprise by the workers, however, seemed to face certain problems. Self-management as a form of organization was not easily understood by the workers, and the responsible institutions (such as the banks) with which the enterprise was dealing were questioning its very existence, since legally there is no separation of ownership and gain derived from the product.

An informal scheme of self-management and a feasibility study were made with a view toward putting the ownership of the enterprise into the hands of the municipality of Evosmon, where the seat of the enterprise is located.

The organizational structure of the new scheme is now as follows:

1. a general assembly of the workers as a main organ of decision making,

2. a coordinating committee consisting of eight workers elected by the assembly, responsible for exercising control over the works, and
3. an executive committee consisting of four members-workers elected by the coordinating committee, which handles the economic issues of the factory.

During the initial period that the factory operated without supervision, the general assembly was held at least once a week because of the many issues that had to be discussed and the frequent disagreements among personnel. Today the general assembly meets once a month outside working hours, only to inform the members of activities.

In spite of the problems, the enterprise is considered profitable. Such progress is owing to several factors, including

The competitiveness of the products. Although the demand is high, there are few units that produce parts of machinery in Greece.

The emphasis given to public relations. From the beginning, the workers themselves tried to promote their case in all possible directions. Some suppliers were persuaded to reduce the prices of raw materials, while the customers agreed to buy larger quantities in advance. Through such agreements, they managed to gain the sympathy of the public, and local branches of the Social Insurance Foundation (IKA) and the Revenue Department helped them—hesitatingly and only after indecisiveness—because this productive unit without an owner was not legally recognized.

The solidarity of the workers. A deep spirit of interest and solidarity made possible the full use of human resources. The most conscientious among the workers are in constant readiness to maintain internal unity and to bring their attempt to success.

It should be noted that the workers are in their 50s and 60s, and almost all of them have been working in this factory since its establishment. They are not involved in political parties, and they did not want to create a union. The workers distribute 10 percent of the profits among themselves, allocate 70 percent for expansions, and offer the remaining 20 percent to the municipality for works useful to the public.

THE POSITIONS OF INTERESTED AND POLITICAL PARTIES IN PARTICIPATION AND SELF-MANAGEMENT AT THE MICRO LEVEL

The Labor Unions (Syndicates)

Mainly because of the weaknesses of the syndicalist movement (problems of organization, conflicts, subjection to government control, and the like), the role of the labor unions in the social development of Greece after World War II was limited. Their course toward models of social development was influenced by the leaders of the middle class.[27] The choices of the content of social change were also determined by the governments. Put in another way, the management of labor relations was left largely to the initiative of the government each time, whereas the syndicates were defining their position according to the political orientation of the party that supported them. The predominance of the political trends in the syndicalist movement, however, did not allow the autonomous development of certain positions on the basis of labor criteria about desired and attainable developments in labor relations.

The attitude and the position of each labor union depend on the policy and the directives of its supporting political party. Some labor leaders see participation as a choice deriving from their political affiliation with the party and support participation as a policy of this party (for example, the labor unions that are supported by PASOK), while others see participation as a means to self-management and a gradual lessening of state control.

At this stge (early 1980s), a majority of the boards of the major syndicalist organizations are affiliated with PASOK, and therefore their general political tendency is to support the governmental measures that promote participation. Many labor leaders, however, recognize certain problems in accepting the limitations that Article 4 of the law regarding socialization imposes on the right to strike and consider this article as misleading in the unrealistic preconditions it sets for striking in the public sector.[28] As an example, we mention the Hellenic Federation of Bank Employees' Unions, which, disregarding the above article, proceeded to a mobilization and strike.

We can notice a mobilization of workers for more participation, for there are a number of conferences and seminars organized for training syndicalists in responsible participation at the Center for Study, Documentation, and Training (KEMETE) of the General Confederation of Workers of Greece as well as elsewhere. In seeking worker participation, the GSEE and labor unions recognize the necessity for this training in anticipation of the future introduction of legal worker participation in the private sector.

A number of conferences and meetings have been organized in the last few years at the local, regional, national, and international level by various labor unions where matters related to participation, self-management, and socialization have been discussed by syndicalists, employees, employers, members of the political parties, and scholars. These conferences and meetings face at the theoretical level the subject of participation and self-management, but the discussions refer to the Greek reality.[29]

Generally speaking, the demand for realizing participation within enterprises is prominent among the labor unions, and policies for collective bargaining, collective agreements, arbitration, and strikes are often examined to create mechanisms for worker participation in the formulation of terms of work. Also, the participation of worker councils and committees in management decisions or economic policy provides the means for workers to affect the leadership, production, and general operation of the enterprise.

The possible forms of change and democratization of labor relations that are discussed by various groups are differentiated on the basis of political ideology. On the one hand, the members who represent PASOK support a more-autonomous managerial model; on the other, those members who represent the Communist party leave room for state intervention in the future. Another problem being discussed is the limitation of worker and labor-unions power. There is confusion about the limits of these two groups' influence, some scholars even arguing that these parameters may cause the institution of participation in Greece to fail.[30] It is important that these discussions be enriched with opinions and pure labor criteria rather than political criteria to permit both syndicalists and managers to make decisions on the basis of work and to consider the positions of all political parties in order to advance the social view.[31]

The Employers (Industrialists)

In most cases ownership and management coincide in the same persons in Greece. Some Greek industrialist-owners, either because they are not well informed or are following antiquated entrepreneurial philosophy and ideology, react negatively to worker participation in management; they are afraid that their own rights will be somehow limited and their property will be affected. Other Greek industrialists are more open minded and socially oriented and have more updated information about how recent developments in other countries of the EEC provide for optional worker participation in European sociétés anonymes.

We should point out that Greek entrepreneurs are rather conservative and in most cases prefer the "sure and easy" profit. The majority of them are specialized in the production of consumption goods, semi-processed goods, and light-industrial goods. For this reason, Greece does not have a solid industrial background.

Greek industrialist-owners have certain fears and negative feelings based partly on a rather confused perception of worker participation in the management of their enterprises and partly on the fact that workers' unions are directed by political parties and may react negatively to the imposition of participation by law.

The Association of Greek Industries (SEB) considers, more generally, that the economic policy of the government and the new institutional measures have had a negative influence on productivity and industrial development. The SEB feels that government policy until October 1985 brought the economy and Greek industry to a state of crisis that resulted in (1) the stagnation of production during 1985; (2) the high cost of labor accompanied by a decrease in productivity and a decline of the competitiveness of Greek industrial products; (3) the administrative controls that froze prices, reduced profits, increased losses, closed down an increased number of enterprises, and decreased the number of new industries; and (4) the decrease of industrial investments.[32]

The SEB believes that the economy is already entering a phase of deindustrialization and that development can be achieved even under the present negative conditions if the private sector will be encouraged in a positive way.[33]

This sector should seek a reduction of the public sector's restoration of free competition (liberation of prices), improved conditions for financing production, the correlation again of work compensation to productivity, and an immediate solution to the issue of problematic enterprises. Worker participation and/or self-governance is not discussed as an issue.

Recognizing an obvious change in the attitude of the government concerning the problems of the economy and industry, the chairman of the board of the SEB has recently called for a creative dialogue between the "social partners" (government, industrialists, and workers) and for the government to end its experimentation and testing of participation, socialization, self-management, and so forth and proceed to a consistent policy.[34]

The Political Parties

The political parties in Greece have various ideological approaches to worker participation and self-management. Their position toward measures and legislation that promote worker participation depends on their own philosophical perspective and ideological goals.[35]

The Panhellenic Socialist Movement, at present in power, appears positive about worker participation and self-management. Although during the last decade it introduced and used the terms socialization and self-management as critical responses to the terms nationalization and worker participation, it has not clarified sufficiently their meanings. This has created confusion around the nature and characteristics of the two concepts. After 1981, when PASOK became the government of Greece, the "immediate objective of socialization" has been defined through related concepts that, for some people, were viewed as deviations from the original goal, like "gradual socialization of strategic sectors of the economy," "sector of social experimentation," "socialization of overindebted but viable enterprises," and so forth. The president of PASOK, Andreas Papandreou, stated that the sector of social experimentation includes (1) socialization of overindebted but viable enterprises; (2) companies of popular base;[36] (3) municipal and community enterprises; (4) cooperation in the sectors of production, transportation, consumption, housing, and the like; and (5) self-managed enterprises.

Despite the efforts made during the last five-year period to promote worker participation as a means of obtaining economic rehabilitation for problematic enterprises and reformation of public administration, problems remain about the possible forms the new institutions should have. The issues seem to continue to be discussed at a theoretical and idealized level and remain quite confused (e.g., the cooperative organization, the plan for promoting self-management, and others). There is lack of experience, a lack of concrete and tested models, and a lack of the necessary infrastructure, all of which create serious reservations about worker participation at its initial steps in the Greek economy.

The New Democracy Party (ND) does not discuss participation and self-management. It appears to be skeptical about the entire issue, which it considers a political device of the governing party. From official and unofficial statements, it is clear that New Democracy views negatively such institutions as self-management, socialization, factory syndicalism, and even worker participation or supervisory councils, which are today so extensively and indiscriminately used. According to its recent ideological manifesto, under the title "Liberalist Road to Post-Socialist Society," New Democracy is a party of radical liberalism, contrary to the variety of socialisms, and "does not attempt to take away property from those who have it, but to offer property to those who have not." The manifesto of New Democracy conceptually groups together and denies the viability of such institutions as socialization, self-management, and planning. The syndicalist movement is not mentioned in the manifesto, but the position of New Democracy, as defined by syndicalist organizations ideologically close to it, is for a syndicalism free and without interferences of any kind.

The Communist Party of Greece sees the issue sympathetically as a helpful tool toward transformation and state organization of society. The KKE is influenced by the idea of state intervention and planning; it was from the beginning in favor of nationalization and worker participation in management and against socialization and self-management, which it considered myths of the petty bourgeoisie and inventions of capitalism. Later, it accepted these new institutions as socialistic and leading to debureaucratization and a humanely centered society. It now uses the terms nationalization, worker participation,

and socialization, but it eschews the term self-management.
Supporting centralized planning, the Communist party op-
poses theories dealing with decentralization, self-management, self-government, and autonomy at the regional and
local level, but accepts favorably worker participation in
the first supervisory council in the mines of northern Evoia.

The Communist Party of Interior (KKE esoterikou),
the majority of its members having established in 1987 the
Greek Left, is clearly in favor of socialization, self-management, and workplace syndicalism. It has made several
proposals and a serious effort to define the above concepts
within the context of the present Greek reality. It considers worker representation and participation necessary and
important institutions for overcoming the capitalist crisis.
It believes that through a procedure of structural transformation and the participation of labor it is possible to
move into a more rational economic development. It favors
the establishment of special organs of participation and
representation within the private-capitalist enterprises and
supports worker participation in the decision-making process in public enterprises at the board level. It supports
presidential decrees that make it possible to implement
Law 1365/83 regarding socialization within the public sector and provide for a supreme worker role in the administration of public enterprises. This party also maintains
that industrial syndicalism must participate at the enterprise level by complementing the profit-making (capitalist)
mechanisms with certain social criteria. It holds that the
labor movement must contribute to the shaping of the plans
for the rational organization, rehabilitation, and development of the organizations of public utilities as well as
promote within private enterprises plans for development,
employment, and prices with a strategy for dealing with a
crisis of worker control and participation. The KKE esoterikou was the first political party to discuss the issue of
works councils within private enterprises, in 1979. A proposal for appropriate legislation was made by Parliament
members V. Drakopoulos and L. Kyrkos, former leader of
the party.

Finally, the liberal party Democratic Renovation (DA),
through the declarations of its leader Kostis Stefanopoulos,
appears to favor worker participation in the management
and the profits of the enterprises. In his speech to the
syndicalist members of his party, Stefanopoulos declared
that the workers constitute "a major promoter of a rational

and socially just economic development." He also emphasized, although merely in broad and general terms, the
position of his party, which favors worker participation
in the management and the profits of private enterprises,
and held that only a syndicalist movement free from political influence can consolidate participative democracy.

SELF-MANAGEMENT AT THE MACRO LEVEL

Although the actual degree to which workers are
self-determining and autonomous has improved in a formal
sense to some degree, at the level of the enterprise it is
still rather low. At the same time, the role of labor in
controlling the market forces at the macro level is increasing. The long tradition (since the early 1900s) of labor
participation in high-level councils for labor problems and
social policy and more recently in councils of economic
and social policy has been greatly extended with the advent of the socialist-oriented government. Worker participation and self-management are essential parts of the
ideology of the government to be implemented in the development process, as are the new structural arrangements
instituted by the government for the socialist transformation of society.

Representatives of labor participate at all levels
of planning committees (national, regional, sectoral)
and high-level consultative committees such as the National Council of Development and Planning, the National
Council of Higher Education, and the Central Council
of Health. This development has greatly extended the
duties of labor representatives in many participatory
bodies to which they have been elected or appointed
and enhanced their needs for skill and knowledge as
well as for expert advice, research, and special studies.
An insistent effort is made to monitor them so that labor
can meet its new obligations.

Participation at the macro level has not created conflicts or raised reservations. The cooperative tradition in
the fields of labor problems and social policy seems to
have a favorable influence on the attitudes of employers
and other groups. Labor participation at that level is
met with favor. Of importance also are the favorable attitudes of the nation-members of the European Economic
Community, with which both Greek labor and management

cooperate and have contacts, and the actual implementations of such participatory practices in greater arenas.

Broadening of the participatory activities of labor is
expected to give a more-active role to labor in shaping
policies and implementations. The legislative and institutional reforms introduced since 1981 are enabling labor to
play that role and follow the progressive mainstream of
Western Europe. Labor's role in the social development of
Greece is expected to increase in the future.

CONCLUDING REMARKS

The evolution of the role of labor in the production
process is a continuous procedure that is related to political and economic ideas and institutional arrangements as
well as the specific characteristics of the industry in each
country. The political and economic conditions and the
fact that Greece is a developing country with a large number of self-employed in its economy, a rather expanded
public sector, and a limited number of important industrial
establishments with more than 500 workers did not favor
the establishment of modern labor institutions. Furthermore, industrial development until the 1980s emphasized
expansion rather than employment and neglected qualitative
changes in capital and labor relations that occurred in
other parts of Europe during the 1950s and 1960s. However, following the 1981 elections, when the Panhellenic
Socialist Movement came into power claiming to bring socialist transformation, several innovative practices concerning the advancement of the role of workers began to
be implemented.

The foregoing analysis gives us an idea both of the
social experimentation toward advancing the role of workers in the production process in Greece and of the outcome
up to the middle 1980s. The effort to implement new ideas
faced a number of problems deriving from lack of previous
experience, insufficient clarity of new roles for management and labor, and the complex nature of the area of
experimentation, that is, socialized enterprise. Furthermore, the period of experimentation coincided with a general decline in the performance of the economy, which
limited the impact of these innovative arrangements. New
ideas, however, have been introduced in the field of worker self-governance, and these ideas might in the future

lead to a new equilibrium and perhaps the increased involvement of workers in shaping the future of their working establishments.

NOTES

1. N. Zagouras, "The Introduction in Greece of the
Institution of 'Worker Participation' in Management,"
Review of Labor Law 43 (1984):681–97, in Greek. Litsa
Nicolaou-Smokoviti, New Institutions of Labor Relations,
Participation and Self-Management (Athens: Papazissis,
1988), in Greek, Ch. 7, "Self-Management in Greece in
the 1980s," 149–99.

2. Nicholas G. Zagouras and Chrisostomos G. Ioannidis, "Autonomous Work Groups at the Emery Mines of Naxos"
paper presented at the Conference on Self-Management: Experiences and Perspectives, Center of Planning and Economic
Research, Athens, May 28–30, 1986, in Greek.

3. For discussion, see Chris Jecchinis, Trade Unionism in Greece: A Study in Political Paternalism (Chicago:
Roosevelt University, 1967); Theodoros Catsanevas, Trade
Unions in Greece (Athens: National Center of Social Research, 1984), in Greek.

4. Center of Planning and Economic Research, Plan
for Economic and Social Development, 1983–87: Preliminary
(Athens: KEPE, 1983), in Greek.

5. See Chapter 7 of this volume, "Development toward Community Self-Governance in Greece."

6. Government Gazette, A, No. 80, June 22, 1983, in
Greek. See Ioannis Vavouzas, "The Social Character of
the Public Enterprise," Review of Social Research, No. 64
(1987):43–55. Athens: National Center of Social Research,
EKKE, in Greek.

7. Olympic Airways (OA), Hellenic Post Office (ELTA),
Water Supply and Sewerage Systems Company of Athens
(EYDAP), Piraeus Port Authority (OLP), Port Authority of
Thessaloníki (OLTh.), Water Supply Organization of Thessa-
loníki (OYTh.), and Sewage Organization of Thessaloníki
(OATh.). Profit, December 18, 1985, in Greek.

8. As stated by Antonis Tsirigos, former syndicalist
and present worker representative in the board of the DEH.
During the Eleventh Conference of the GENOP/DEH, it was
discussed that ASKE does not function effectively.

9. See D. Stergiou and G. Papanicolaou, "Where
Socialization of Public Enterprises Has Ended." Large

research study conducted by D. Stergiou and G. Papanico-laou, Economic Herald, No. 2 (1601), January 10, 1985, pp. 29-32, in Greek.

10. P. Linardo-Rilmon, "Where Is Socialization Going in the Public Enterprises?", Economic Herald, No. 19 (1670), May 8, 1986, pp. 54-56, in Greek.

11. Alexis Mitropoulos, Labor Institutions in Greece (Athens: Sakkoulas, 1985), p. 123, in Greek.

12. T. Skylakis, in his article published in Marketing Newsletter, January 14, 1984, in Greek, supports that socialization and its effects upon certain sectors and the whole economy must be carefully examined (as, for example, the influence of socialization upon unemployment, inflation, economic development, social justice, and free competition).

13. Antonis Tsirigos, "The Socialization of DEH: Problems and Prospects," Public Sector, No. 5 (May 1987): 22-27 (Athens: Special Publishing Co.), in Greek.

14. See Antonis Tsirigos, "In the Public Sector, Management Varies from Nonexistent to Unessential: The Role of Socialization in DEH as A. Tsirigos Sees It," Express Daily, No. 6897, March 23, 1986, p. 6, in Greek.

15. The first supervisory council was established by Law 1385/83 in the mines and quarries of the Prefecture of Evoia. It consists of 13 regular members and an equal number of deputies, that is, four representatives of the state, three representatives of the workers in the supervised enterprises who do not hold a key position in their organization, three representatives of the employer who participate in the board of the supervised enterprise and have key positions in it, and three representatives of the local government of the Prefecture of Evoia (i.e., the municipalities and communities that are influenced by the activity of the supervised enterprises). See Zagouras, "Introduction in Greece," p. 686.

16. ESAP is a collective organ that makes proposals to the government on issues of higher education. In ESAP participate representatives of the competent ministries, the Technical Chamber of Greece, the Coordinating Committee of the Legal Associations of Greece, the Panhellenic Medical Association, the General Confederation of Workers of Greece (GSEE), the local government, the deans of all the institutions of higher education, and other scientific and trade organizations.

17. Zagouras, "Introduction in Greece," pp. 682-85, nn. 1-4.

18. Codification of legislation of 1939 regarding the Harbor Coffers and Law 1630/51 regarding the Piraeus Port Authority (OLP) provide for a 12-member board with one representative from each of the following: the municipality of Piraeus, the permanent dock workers, the permanent personnel, the Hellenic Chamber of Shipping (NEE), the Commercial and Industrial Chamber of Piraeus (EBEM), the International Maritime Union of Greece (DNE), and the Panhellenic Association of Shipping Agents (PENP) alternatively. The chairman of the Piraeus Labor Center (EKP) also participates.

19. According to the law regarding Public Corporation for Housing and Urban Planning (DEPOS) (Presidential Decrees 811/1980 and 12/1981), the 11-member advisory council is comprised of one representative from each of the following: the GSEE, the PASEGES, the Supreme Executive Committee of Public Servants (ADEDY), the Central Union of Municipalities and Communities of Greece (KEDKE) the SEB, and the Technical Chamber of Greece (TEE). The advisory council is responsible for drafting advisory reports for the planning of policy goals, long-term DEPOS planning on the budget, the balance sheet, and the performance statement and for drafting sentences or written comments on issues relative to the goals and the activities of an enterprise.

20. On the 12-member board of the National Tobacco Organization sit three professional tobacco producers elected by their respective cooperative organizations and one tobacco trader elected by the Hellenic Tobacco Trade Federation (Legal Decree 3758/1957). The Supervisory Council, consisting of four members, holds one representative of producers who is appointed by the Ministry of Agriculture.

21. Five of the 12 members of the bank board are representatives of the producers who participate in the cooperatives (Legal Decree of May 8, 1946 regarding modification of Agricultural Bank of Greece legislation). In order to elect their representatives, the respective federations and cooperatives are classified into five agricultural districts. In every district the cooperative organizations elect two representatives. Finally, the Ministry of Agriculture appoints one member from each district.

22. Theodoros Catsanevas, "Participation of Workers and Employees in the Management of Enterprises in Greece," Economic Herald, No. 23 (1361), June 5, 1980, pp. 3-4, in Greek.

23. Stavros Voutiras, Social Policy (Athens: Anastasiou, 1980), p. 159, in Greek.

24. Problematic enterprises are companies of special importance to the Greek economy that face financial difficulties and are in a state of overindebtedness (see Chapter 7).

25. Litsa Nicolaou-Smokoviti and Severyn T. Bruyn, "The Social Structure of Self-Managed Firms in Greece: Guidelines to Policy Studies," Studies no. 1, Piraeus Graduate School of Business Studies, 1984, pp. 73–108; Zagouras, "Introduction in Greece"; and Alkis Raftis and Dimitrios Stavroulakis, "Workers Cooperatives as Self-Managed Enterprises: The Case of Greece" (Paper presented at the XI World Congress of Sociology, International Sociological Association, New Delhi, August 1986).

26. See Chapter 7 of this volume, "Development toward Community Self-Governance in Greece."

27. Chris Jecchinis, Labor Relations and Development (Athens: Papazissis, 1984), in Greek.

28. Article 4 specifies that in order to make a decision to strike, a general assembly of 51 percent of all employees registered is needed.

29. Conferences and seminars have been organized by GENOP/DEH, GSEE, OVES, the OTOE, the OSE, the Institute for Study of the Greek Economy (IMEO), the Center of Planning and Economic Research (KEPE), and others.

30. The European experience has shown that labor unions must play the first and decisive role, while workers' representatives must have secondary jurisdictions. See Mitropoulos, Labor Institutions, pp. 133–43, in Greek.

31. Jecchinis, Trade Unionism in Greece, pp. 38–39.

32. Theodoros Papalexopoulos, Speech of the President, Association of Greek Industries (SEB), Annual General Assembly, May 16, 1985; see Industrial Review, no. 607/608, op. cit. S. Mantzavinos, op. cit.

33. S. Mantzavinos, Speech of the Treasurer, Association of Greek Industries (SEB), Annual General Assembly, May 14, 1986; see Industrial Review, no. 617, op. cit.

34. Theodoros Papalexopoulos, Speech of the President, Association of Greek Industries (SEB), Annual General Assembly, May 14, 1986; see Industrial Review, no. 617, op. cit.

35.   Mitropoulos, Labor Institutions, pp. 184-97,
202-10, 214-17, 217-19; M. Androulakis, Socialist Self-
Government--Self-Management (Athens: Synchroni Epochi,
1983), p. 137, in Greek; I. Dragasakis, "Myths and So-
cialization," Rizospastis Daily, December 3, 1982, in Greek;
George Rousis, "Socialization of Means of Production from
the Marxist Perspective," Rizospastis Daily, April 7, 1983;
T. Tolios, "Substantial Participation in the Supervisory
Council," Rizospastis Daily, July 12, 1983; George Rousis,
Worker Participation: A Field of Class Conflict or Class
Cooperation? (Athens: Synchroni Epochi, 1983), p. 137, in
Greek; "Supervisory Councils and Class Conflict," Avgi
Daily, June 12, 1983, in Greek; "Worker Participation in
the Public Sector," Avgi Daily, October 17, 1984; Central
Committee of KKE Esoterikou, "For a New Course of Labor-
Syndicalist Movement in Front of Crisis," Avgi Daily,
April 24, 1983; "Seven Organizations of the Public Sector
Are in the Process of Socialization," Profit, December 18,
1985, in Greek.

36.   See Chapter 7, "Development toward Community
Self-Governance in Greece," Section "Companies of Popular
Base."

PART II

ISSUES
IN
COMMUNITY
SELF-GOVERNANCE

5. The Concept of Community Self-Governance

Scholars have said that the local community in modern nations is close to extinction. Many studies describe its decline and even its eclipse. Some observers interpret the phenomenon as an inevitable and irreversible part of modern development. The idea that a residential group could develop a fair degree of economic self-determination is perceived as a fiction of contemporary society.

The loss of economic self-determination at the local level is mirrored now by the disappearance of community studies in the professions. The local community was a major focus of sociological research in the first half of this century but today it has lost its appeal. Because the locality has declined in its power of self-direction, it no longer has the same significance. Similarly, community planning was a major interest of city planners and architects, but the concept is no longer discussed in their journals. The idea of constructing autonomous communities is regarded by many planners today as hopelessly utopian. The notion of community self-determination may have little appeal for those in a position to encourage it in post-industrial society.

The concept of developing self-reliant communities was first questioned by city planners facing urban sprawl, but now it is wholly the domain of planners looking at the megalopolis. The rise of the metropolis has coincided with the decline in power of the local community and has been accompanied by both progress and destructiveness in human organization. The organization of the city is thus a source of confusion as well as concern for social planners who must make decisions about its future. The causes of the decline of community life and the basis of envisioning a new direction for community development are therefore central issues for social planners today. We are interested in new models of planning for community self-governance as we discuss whether or not people in a modern locality can become genuinely self-determining in their economic life. Are local people capable of governing their own lives in the midst of a metropolitan society?

THE HISTORICAL PICTURE

The decline in power of the local community is a complex process, but one causative factor is clearly the competitive-market economy. If we can understand the loss of local self-determination as being a function of the competitive market, we can perhaps better judge the focal points for the purposeful redesign of community life.

The causes behind the relentless and seemingly uncontrollable urban growth may well be summarized in Max Weber's definition of the city as essentially a settlement with a market. It was the market, much more than its size, its degree of impersonality, or its intense social problems, that characterized the city. The city was basically created by the need to exchange goods and money within a limited geographical area in order for people to make a livelihood together. Other sociologists have examined the characteristics of the city, but none has so strongly advanced the market as its defining feature.[1]

Weber's definition is important because it explains the cause of both the city's progressive development and its destructive direction. The market is the creative force in the city's evolution and simultaneously a basis for its loss of humanity and self-determination. The expansion of the small village into town, city, metropolis, and finally megalopolis with its multiple commercial centers is largely a function of the market. Our hypothesis is that the shape of the city is significantly determined by the market forces of commerce and capital exchange. The market is not the only determinant of city size and direction, but it is such a critical factor that it is essential for us to understand it as the basis for investing in the future of human settlements.

The expansion of the village into the metropolis has also been determined significantly by the new technology of transport and communications. It was in part the invention of the automobile and telephone that helped city populations explode into suburbia and the invention of passenger airlines and television that helped stretch cities farther into the hinterland. But technology is socially determined and remains basically a function of the market. It acts on the market system in certain ways but is also determined by market forces. Our hypothesis is that the competitive market has been responsible for not only the direction of city growth but also the imminent extinction of the community as a way of life. Restoration of the community, then, means acting directly on the market.

Peter Bender argues that all the scholarly concern for the loss of community is misplaced and that we must instead look positively at the historical forces that have reshaped the landscape. He says that the "small, unique and particularistic units of life that make for the experience of community have been sentenced to death by historical necessity." He notes how many people have sought to recapture a sense of community in large-scale organizations and also by imputing it to locality-based social activity 'regardless of the quality of human relationships that characterize these contexts." But it cannot be done. In fact, he supports the argument of Sheldon Wolin that people have sought to "engraft elements of community onto the main stem of organization without success." What we know about American history, Bender says, is that the community has not collapsed. It has simply been transformed into new spheres of life. It may exist in enduring and intimate relationships that people have apart from the small town or the village, but it cannot be claimed superficially in the corporation or the marketplace. He concludes by saying that "community, as a social form and as an experience, is distinct from organizational life or gesellschaft."[2]

While Bender disclaims the idea that community must be associated with a locality, he admits that the experience of community has diminished in recent times and has to be rediscovered in modern life. The essence of community is found in "a social network characterized by a distinctive kind of human interaction." It differs from market competition in that it is mediated by emotional bonds. He continues to say that "a market orientation . . . dominates too much of our lives and that the experience of community does not comprise enough of them." A new concept of community is needed that is different from that of the small town, but the question is how it may be recreated in the midst of this historical transition of contemporary society.[3]

We agree on the importance of finding a new concept of community based on the quality of human interaction and not only on the basis of locality. We also agree that it requires rediscovery in the midst of progressive market forces. The meaning of community needs redefinition, but we would argue that it can also have a reference in space. An essential feature of community rests in the quality of human life experienced together in a place, as well as in national organizations and networks. Important communal experiences can be found typically among people identified in physical locations. We are arguing that the rediscovery of community life means re-examining the competitive market as a system destroying the community and that the community can be found in localities as well as in other social networks. The resolution of local problems such as drug addiction, crime, and delinquency are in part dependent upon the organization of local communities.

The theme of our work is that the competitive market was socially created and that it can also be socially changed, that we are not simply objects of the historical forces of business, at the mercy of the winds of the competitive market. We can act back on the market system; changing the modern market can give back life to the local community as quickly as it could take it away. But the new local community can never be the same as the old towns and villages of the past.

THE MARKET AS A CAUSE OF SOCIAL PROBLEMS

Data on how the market creates social and economic problems are too extensive and diverse to introduce here, but we want to illustrate the point because our argument is that people in localities cannot be in command of their own lives until the market system is altered. The data show that key decisions affecting local life are increasingly made in distant places, sometimes thousands of miles away. The subject of plant dislocation illuminates the loss in local self-determination.

In the past decade, for example, plant shutdowns have severely disrupted local economies in both the United States and Greece. In the United States, we can observe the extensive impact of decisions made elsewhere. In Ohio

alone, for example, the statistics are depressing. In
Youngstown, the shutdown of a sheet and tube company
put 5,000 employees out of work, and Libby-Owens-Ford's
Aeroquip closed out 390. In Akron, Goodyear Tire termi-
nated 1,384 workers; Firestone, 1,000. In Cleveland, 2,000
jobs were lost when White Motor moved truck production to
Virginia, and 230 jobs went in a Westinghouse shutdown.
In Dayton, Sherwin-Williams closed out 110 workers. In
Canton, Ferro-Allos shut down 210 jobs. The pattern re-
peated itself throughout the country, devastating community
life. It is easy to see why planners have lost hope for
self-determination in the locality.

In Greece, factory shutdowns have also had a negative impact on community life. There are the cases of
Samos island, Drama, and other areas where tobacco factories closed down and Soufli, where silk factories also
closed. As a result, many people, especially younger
workers, had to leave their towns and villages to seek
employment in Athens, Thessaloníki, or abroad.

In the decades of the 1950s and 1960s, there was a
major displacement of the axis of tobacco processing and
export, which was traditionally located in eastern Macedonia (in the four large cities of Xanthy, Kavala, Drama,
and Serres), due to the lack of demand for the high-quality
tobacco that was produced in this area. The varieties of
expensive aromatic tobacco were in great demand in Germany, but the sale was stopped with the spreading of
blenders (filter cigarettes), which do not need high-quality
tobacco. As a consequence, the big centers of processing,
warehousing, and exporting high-quality tobacco were
transferred to Thessaloníki. The three centers of Xanthy,
Drama, and Serres declined dramatically, and only Kavala
maintained some activity.

It is important to note that other cities have benefited from the changes in the market. Thessaloníki benefited from the transfer of factories, since new work positions were created in the city. Small quantities of high-
quality tobacco, which continued being cultivated in the
area of eastern Macedonia, and the quantities of secondary-
quality and low-price tobacco cultivated in western and
central Macedonia were now carried over to Thessaloníki
for processing. The tobacco was bought by the industrialists from the producers and was processed in larger industrial units in Thessaloníki and exported. Despite the
development of new economic activities, the problem of

insufficient absorption of labor supply in eastern Macedonia was further intensified. A large number of young workers emigrated from that area to Germany in search of jobs.[4]

The exodus of hundreds of thousands of members of the active labor force, from their local communities to the big urban centers in Greece and abroad, to Germany and other European countries, characterizes the decades of the 1950s and 1960s in Greece. These intensive population movements in Greece, the main cause of which was high unemployment, have disrupted local community life at the national level.

Here we see how the seemingly small Greek economy is not unlike the U.S. economy insofar as it is part of a large market system operating across European nation states. The movement of displaced workers in the United States from the northern states to southern states is not unlike the movement of workers in Greece to Germany and other European states. But the suffering of workers is the same. Our argument is that change can take place through an alternative process of planning so that whole communities are not destroyed in the process. The market system operating as a competitive process by itself has become too destructive of community life.

The consequences of capital flight are disastrous for local communities in social, economic, political, and personal terms. Sidney Cobb and Stanislav Kasl have conducted longitudinal research on the health and behavioral effects of job loss from plant closures. Among the workers studied over a 13-year period, they found a suicide rate about 30 times the national average. They also found higher incidences of heart disease, hypertension, diabetes, peptic ulcer, gout, joint swelling, dyspepsia, and alopecia in the displaced workers than among control groups of employed workers. They found too that the closings had serious psychological effects: extreme depression, anxiety, tension, insecurity, and loss of self-esteem.[5]

Workers lose their health-insurance benefits in the United States when they lose their jobs. Fewer than 30 percent of the unemployed have any health insurance at all; those who do must spend 20 to 35 percent of unemployment benefits merely to continue their former coverage. But generally the unemployed go without. The displaced worker has greater medical needs than the employed worker but the answer to those needs is no longer available.[6]

In Greece, the negative impacts of factory shutdowns and corporate impacts on the environment are also plainly visible as a result of firms competing in the market. The effect of shutdowns and the impact of environmental pollution on communities are exemplified by Elefsina, a municipality located 22 kilometers away from Athens with a population of 30,000 people and 70 to 80 percent of its active labor force in heavy industry. Elefsina is a classic example of the hydrocephalic expansion and centralization of the Attica plain. The concentration of heavy industry in this town (steel, oil, blast-furnace, etc.) has created great environmental pollution and suffocating living conditions for people living there.

In 1978 and 1979, a study was conducted by a physician, George Polydorou, regarding the effects of environmental pollution on respiratory diseases of children and workers in Elefsina as compared to the rural area of Sperchiada. The results of the study showed that respiratory diseases were up to seven times higher in Elefsina than in Sperchiada. In the period from 1981 to 1985, another study was conducted by the World Health Organization and the Children's Health Institute regarding respiratory diseases, skin diseases, and eye diseases in Elefsina as compared to the semirural areas of Mesogia. The results showed that such diseases were four to eight times higher in Elefsina.

The blast furnace of Halivourgiki in Elefsina was finally closed in order to eliminate environmental pollution, but 1,200 workers lost their jobs. The Shipyards Yfestos closed down also, and 1,050 workers remained jobless. Two distilleries (Votrys and Kronos) closed down, and 200 more workers lost their jobs. Several industries in the area face bankruptcy and must close down or severely limit their operation due to the restrictions imposed by national and international health standards.

It is important again to note that some new industries have developed, too. In Elefsina, 36 new industries were established in the last five years while 37 old industries were expanding. This process is sometimes described by the Schumpeterian phrase, "creative destruction." The process of losing jobs and creating new jobs is conceived as part of the natural forces of the market. In the capitalist belief of the twentieth century, periodic unemployment is a short-term necessity to achieve progress and high levels of economic development. But we are

raising the question of whether the destruction of community life is essential to maintain progressive economies.
The issue rests on whether the transformation of economic
life can take place without such destructive consequences
to workers and the life of communities.

One part of the dislocated workers were absorbed by
the local industries, old and new, but a big unemployment
problem was created in the area for the workers, the
majority of whom were unskilled. This problem is exacer-
bated by attraction to the area of newcomers in search of
industrial jobs. Despite high unemployment and environmental pollution and its detrimental effects on the health
of the workers and their families, Elefsina seems to drive
a relatively large number of newcomers. The unemployment
problem in this case, therefore, appears to be more important than the pollution problem.[7] This constitutes a fundamental dilemma and a difficult problem to solve. Other
factors also causing community decline (crime, divorce,
mental disorder) have to be faced, too.

A complex process is required to deal with the devastation of such communities as Elefsina by the corporate
impacts on its economy, its environment, and quality of
life. The community problems are extensive enough to
warrant consideration of a serious alternative. Can a new
system of exchange become a basis for the redevelopment
of community life?

THE MARKET AS A CONTRIBUTOR TO PROGRESS

It is important to understand that the competitive
market that destroys the community has also been the progressive force in the development of society. The proponents of city life are no less in number than the community sociologists who criticize it. Their argument must be
presented here because their points are also critical to an
alternative.

Celebrants of city life argue that without the rise of
the metropolis we would have no cultural progress: no
symphonies, no great universities, no great theater or
opera, and none of the great corporations that have given
us the technological advances we enjoy today. They say
that great museums and ballet companies do not come into
being in the small town. The city has brought us culture
as well as wealth. We now have a new consciousness of
who we can be as civilized human beings.[8]

The proponents of the competitive market as it now exists go still further. The city has made possible our social progress. It has broken down the provinciality of rural life and the smothering prejudice, boredom, and backwardness of the small town. The sense of community may have declined, but the city has helped destroy the moral repressiveness and local elitism of the small town and village.

Others declare that the city is the economic engine of the nation. Jane Jacobs claims that cities consistently generate new economic growth and have been the source of economic renewal in modern nations. Cities become stronger and larger because they are able to replace imports with their own modes of production through improvisation and innovation, which in turn generates new exports. In effect, the city grows on the basis of reciprocating systems of work.[9] We will return to this point, but the question remains as to whether all these good things need be lost in the reconstruction of community life.

SOCIOLOGICAL APPROACHES TO THE PROBLEM

Community sociologists portrayed the developing problem in case studies begun before the midcentury, like Democracy in Jonesville, Middletown and the Yankee City series in the United States. In 1947 Lloyd Warner described labor unrest and disruption in Newburyport, Massachusetts (Yankee City) when the local owners of a shoe factory sold out to owners in New York.

> Two fundamental changes have been occurring concomitantly, in recent years, in the social organization of Yankee City shoe factories. The first is the expansion of the hierarchy upward, out of Yankee City, through the expansion of individual enterprises and the establishment by them of central offices in distant large cities. The second is the expansion of the structure outward from Yankee City through the growth of manufacturers associations and labor unions, also with headquarters outside Yankee City and with units in many other shoemaking communities in New England and elsewhere. Both . . .

decrease Yankee City's control over its own
factories by subjecting the factories or segments of them, to more and more control ex-
erted from outside Yankee City.[10]

The case studies were representative of what was
described as the "great change" in community life across
the nation. Various sociologists have sought to conceptualize its meaning. Roland Warren, for example, has
been a leading interpreter of the change in terms of
"vertical-horizontal relationships" in the locality. Vertical
relationships are formal links between local organizations
and their parent organizations outside the community.
U.S. examples would be the connections of the local YMCA
or Girl Scout Troop to their national offices. Horizontal
relationships are formal links in the locality, such as between the Scouts and the YMCA in the local "community
welfare council." Similarly, the local subsidiaries of
General Motors and Xerox have a vertical relationship to
their national headquarters and trade associations and a
horizontal relationship with the local Chamber of Commerce.
The same vertical and horizontal relationships exist with
churches, trade unions, and other voluntary organizations.[11]
The "great change" is in the power of external linkages to shape the direction of community life. The basic
decisions regarding each local unit are made in the national headquarters. The power of local horizontal relations has thereby been weakened, and thus there is a
decline in real community life. The locality can no longer
function as a planning unit with true self-direction; it is
no longer a community.
Other sociologists have described the problems of the
city as stemming from neighborhood disorganization. The
problems of crime, delinquency, and drug addiction have
been laid to the lack of neighborhood controls. Many attempts have been made to recultivate neighborhood life so
as to solve these problems, but again this is difficult or
impossible as long as the neighborhood is disrupted by
changing market forces.[12]
Sociologist Robert Nisbet has taken a more global
view of the decline of community life in modern nations,
describing it in terms of a breakdown in primary groups
and the institutions of communal life. The enduring face-
to-face group has disappeared from the life of the factory,
the church, the neighborhood, and the family itself. The

primary groups, once characterized by Charles Cooley as the nursery of human nature, was where original values of integrity, honesty, and social responsibility were developed. Without primary groups functioning in the basic institutions of the locality, the values are placed in jeopardy and sometimes distorted or lost in the process of socialization. They might be rediscovered in the "integrity" of the street gang, but they are not integrated into the round of institutional life. They can be lost in the organization of a factory's assembly line, the bureaucratic church, and people moving in and out of the neighborhood. The enduring primary relationships cannot be rediscovered through government welfare agencies and the divorce courts.[13]

These important analyses of the "modern problem" did not normally root themselves in the market system itself. The market was rarely connected to the rising rates of crime, suicide, drug addiction, divorce, and mental disorders. A severe neurosis in the adult would be traced psychologically to family instability or the absence of a father during childhood but not to the market system that caused the family breakup in the first place. Nor was the question of why people had to keep moving out of the neighborhood really addressed at its root. The market system was not examined in connection with personal problems. The time has come to make these connections, to answer these questions, and to take a new look at the importance of community life. This means that we must first look at the market as a political creation, not as a natural phenomenon outside human control and beyond our management.

THE MARKET MYTH

Karl Polanyi wrote a classic treatise on the "great transformation" from feudalism to capitalism that took place centuries ago. His study is most applicable to our understanding of the "great change" taking place today, because he demonstrates that the market system was not a spontaneous creation but was brought into existence by government laws and policies. It was not a purely natural phenomenon conceived by nineteenth-century economists as operating outside the legal domain but had come into being by alteration of the legal framework of the medieval period.

It was a creature of the new democratic state that wanted
to destroy the bondage of serfdom and replace the estate
system by changing the feudal laws governing the use of
land, capital, and labor.[14]

The myth of the Middle Ages was destroyed and a
new myth of the modern period was created. The new myth
brought forth new values and selectively ignored other
values; it celebrated freedom and individuality in the economy but said nothing about social justice and equality in
the economy. It provided for the right of workers to quit
their jobs but provided no right to a job; it offered people
the right to buy corporations but offered no protection to
consumers who came to be dominated by corporations in the
marketplace; it gave the right to owners to produce unsafe
products but no right to consumers to obtain redress for
injury; it gave employers the right to speak harshly to
employees but no right to employees to speak back without
being fired. The myth of the market gave rights to people
with capital but gave no heed to its impact on people in
the local community.

We are today in another transition. We have gained
the freedom of the market but have lost the base of our
communities, gained the values of individualism and competition in the economy but lost the values of fellowship
and mutual aid. We are now proceeding to redress the
imbalance. Polanyi has told us that to make such a
transition effectively we must pay attention to the "laws"
undergirding the market economy.

If we take the laws of the market as the primary
cause of rapid change in residence, domination in work
life, and many other problems to be discussed later, we
begin to find ways of altering the market. The question
is: What are the legal methods for reversing community decline? How can we begin to provide a legal basis for
overcoming the market forces? Put another way, how can
we regain control over local land, capital, and labor
without involving government ownership? How can we restore life to the community without state controls over the
market? How can we provide a social foundation to the
private economy? And how can we invest in new patterns
of community development that will increase opportunities
not only for individuality and freedom but also for social
justice?

Let us think of the solution in terms of three attributes of community life: autonomy, viability, and polity.

We cannot engage in all the legal arguments on social policy but we can look at this special market pattern of community development so that the details can be debated and discussed as part of the decisions of social investment.[15]

Some social theorists believe that the return of power to the local community can be accomplished by taking charge of the market mechanisms. It is conceivable today for local people to control the adverse effects of the market economy without recourse to government ownership and regulation. The government can help facilitate the process but the objective is to gain social (not state) control and reduce the necessity for the formal government to intervene. It means altering the social structure of the private sector so that local people become more important in determining their future than the larger competitive market or the regulatory state.

THE CONCEPTUAL FRAMEWORK: AUTONOMY, VIABILITY, AND POLITY

If we conceptualize this problem of decentralization into measures of local autonomy, viability, and polity, we can examine the degrees of governing capability in the communities of any nation. These terms provide the conceptual framework by which we can interpret vastly different developments in the United States and in Greece as both nations face the destructive tendencies of the competitive market and metropolitan dominance.

By autonomy we mean the capacity for people in a locality to be relatively independent of outside controls. All communities have some degree of autonomy but the autonomy of all communities varies in some measure. Dependency on outside institutions includes some degree of state control or private corporate control. The information about the degree of local autonomy offers a basis for social planning but it is not sufficient by itself to measure a capacity for local self-governance.

By viability we mean the degree to which people can handle their own economic problems with local leadership, skills, and material resources. Viability is different from autonomy in the sense that it is one task to be formally independent and another task to be able to solve one's own economic problems without needing outside skills and financial assistance. Here we need local resources such as capital and knowledge to operate the local economy. We are not talking about achieving self-sufficiency in this criterion but rather achieving higher levels of self-reliance. This can mean such things as developing greater economic diversity and creating ecological loops that allow for local consumption of local production.

By polity we mean the degree to which the local political economy has become democratized. The process of democratization includes the local corporate system as well as the municipality. The basic idea in planning is to find ways to reduce the necessity of government control over the economy by introducing self-controls within the private sector. This means introducing systems of social accountability and democratization into the corporate life of the market economy without loss of productivity. These steps of course lead toward a totally different kind of political economy than can be typified by state capitalism or state socialism.

These criteria help us evaluate the degree of community self-governance in a locality. Each criterion can be separately examined while observing the interconnections of data from other criteria. For example, we know that a local economy can become autonomous without developing viability. That is, it can become independent from outside controls without the local resources needed to manage the enterprise system. This loss of viability has happened with a number of Third World nations that nationalized the subsidiaries of multinational corporations but then did not have the management skills and the local capital to keep them in operation. We also know that a local economy can be viable and not autonomous. That is, a local community can have a vital industrial life while fully managed and owned from the outside. Finally, we know that a community can be autonomous and viable at the same time and still not have a democratic polity. That is, the local economy can be independent of outside controls, be resourceful, and still be autocratically managed by a local power elite.

Thus, each variable is relatively independent from the others. A local economy can be autonomous without being viable, viable without being autonomous, autonomous and viable without being democratic, and formally democratic without being viable and autonomous. The latter case of being democratic without being autonomous can exist even though these two categories are closely related. Being democratic suggests a strong measure of autonomy, but even in this case there is a certain independence of measures. A system of local producer cooperatives may be democratically organized, but all their markets can be tied up with outside corporations that control the direction of their production. Or, a local government agency may have some worker participation (a degree of polity) in the context of a decentralized government, but in the final analysis the control over certain key policy questions is maintained from the outside.

We are interested in methods of increasing community self-governance measured by these criteria. To comprehend the complex development of these community norms, we must look at the meaning of social governance, social ownership, social property, the social sector, the social market, and social decentralization in relation to the local economic order.

Social Governance

The concept of community self-governance broadens our framework of what constitutes worker self-governance and social control over production in society. Social governance involves more jurisdiction than worker self-governance in the context of the community. Relatedly, the concept of social ownership is more generic than the concept of worker ownership. Let us begin with reference to the meaning of the term social, since it represents the overall concept for our subject.

The scientific meaning of being social can be different than popular and ideological meanings. The scientific meaning refers to the probability that people are interdependent and oriented toward one another in determining their action. Put another way, people are social insofar as their actions affect one another and they take each other into account symbolically in deciding on their form of action.

Social action has both a subjective and an objective meaning. Its subjective meaning refers to the degree to which people are conscious and take each other into account while the objective meaning refers to the fact that they are interdependent and affect each other by their actions regardless of whether or not they act with each other

in mind. These two meanings both bear on our analysis
of social governance. Workers in a self-managed firm, for
example, may be socially conscious of their interdependence
and act accordingly in their own interest within the firm
but may not be fully conscious of how they are socially
interdependent with other firms. Thus, they may act independently (and competitively) and destroy the basis by
which they can act together as a system. They may destroy their industrial community by their self-seeking behavior in the marketplace. They may not know how to
market products cooperatively and in ways that avoid
self-injury and eventually government supervision in the
public interest. This problem of competitive markets is
the most critical question of development in Yugoslavia
today. The Yugoslav market continues to participate in
the self-destructive forces of the capitalist system. And
the government continues to grow as an outside monitor of
the economic system.

The producer cooperative has become self-accountable
to its workers, but in the organization of the industry--as
a social system--it can become competitively self-destructive. Cooperatives usually operate on a small scale within
a capitalist system and therefore lack structures of cooperation outside themselves in their market area. A system of cooperatives, like conventional firms, can lack
externally determined rules of cooperation. Producer cooperatives operating in a business system often lack norms
of fair play within their trade associations.

Unlike self-managed firms in Yugoslavia that are
designed to compete with one another, cooperatives are
normally designed to cooperate in the marketplace. According to the sixth international cooperative principle,
"cooperatives should cooperate between themselves at the
local, national and international levels." In the cooperative sector of Greece this is generally sought in practice.
Local cooperatives cooperate horizontally at the local level
and they form federations at the national level.[16]

Establishing a pattern of cooperative businesses is
not sufficient by itself to lead toward the revitalization
of community life, but we take the principles on which
they are founded as part of the scheme of social development leading in this direction. The implementation of cooperative practices in the marketplace is part of what we
are describing as social governance within the economy.

Social governance requires cooperation between competing firms within an entire industry. In business systems, cooperation among firms often requires legislation or social jurisprudence to avoid collusive practices. The kind of cooperation that is legitimate works in the public interest rather than merely the self-interest of the firms. The new practices must be clarified and defined in the law. Historical experience has shown that businesses can (and do) cooperate in the public interest. Indeed, the market is most effective when the productivity and the well being of people in the system of enterprises is advanced cooperatively by firms in the context of the larger society.[17]

The concept of social governance does not mean eliminating competition but rather directing it properly in the interest of the industry and the society. This means that firms must cooperate in a way that integrates their own interests with the public interest. We will look at modes of cooperation in the local economies of the United States and Greece, but the issues of industrial cooperation are sufficiently complex and important to illustrate that we have added an appendix to further clarify the process. The appendix discusses the cases in which democratic firms cooperated through federations in Israel (kibbutzim), Mondragón, Spain, and Yugoslavia to advance their purposes in the context of largely capitalist environments.

Again, firms can be objectively interdependent without managers being conscious of how their action may eventually lead to monopoly, inflation, and government regulations. In a self-managed system of enterprises, workers may come to "own" their firm but not yet to "own" (collectively) their industry. Thus, the effective governance of industry is connected to a form of social ownership. Social ownership is dependent, in turn, on a concept of social property that leads to the readiness of people to act together to treat destructive tendencies in the market system.

Social Ownership and Property

The concept of social ownership is closely related to the concept of property in the context of the community. Property ownership refers to the fact that people possess and have the right to control things. Ownership refers mainly to a sense of rightful possession of things, while

property refers more directly to the things themselves.
<u>Property</u> is an object of value that a person may right-
fully acquire, while ownership is the appropriation of
property to people who recognize the things as belonging
to them. A social concept of ownership and property has
evolved interdependently with the development of democratic institutions in modern society.

Hannah Arendt notes that the function of laws in the
seventeenth, eighteenth, and into the nineteenth century
was not primarily to guarantee liberties but to protect
property. It was property, and not the law as such, that
guaranteed freedom.

> Not before the 20th century were people ex-
> posed directly and without any personal pro-
> tection to the pressures of either state or
> society; and only when people emerged who
> were free without owning property to protect
> their liberties, were laws necessary to protect
> persons and personal freedom directly, instead
> of merely protecting their properties. In the
> 18th century, however, and especially in the
> English-speaking countries, property and free-
> dom still coincided; who said property, said
> freedom, and to recover or defend one's prop-
> erty right was the same as to fight for free-
> dom. It was precisely in their attempt to
> recover such "ancient liberties" that the
> American Revolution and the French Revolution
> had their most conspicuous similarities.[18]

Arendt saw respect for private property as the age-
old remedy against government abuse of the person. The
framing of laws through which the rights of privacy were
guaranteed was the dividing line between what came to be
defined as "public" and "private." "The Bill of Rights in
the American constitution forms the last, and the most ex-
haustive, legal bulwark for the private realm against
public power."[19] But there was a still deeper meaning to
this evolution of property law.

George Friedrich Hegel saw private (bourgeois) property as interfering with the ultimate harmony of people
throughout history. He noted how people labor to create
things in society and then struggle against each other to
possess them. All historical struggles, he said, become

struggles between property-owning people. With the ancient advent of property-owning family units, there began a struggle for mutual recognition of family rights to property. He saw that people fought one another to possess property in part because it was looked upon as an essential element of individuality; people believe that they must preserve and defend their private property in order to maintain their own identity and integrity as individuals. But Hegel saw a way out of this alienating condition. The introduction of social (not private) property was a method for reducing this alienation between individuals.[20]

This was of course an idealization of what was happening in history. For Hegel, the institutionalization of private property signified that the objects of this world were becoming incorporated into the subjective world, that is, the objects were no longer dead things but belonged in their totality to the sphere of self-realization. In effect, he was saying that people appropriate property to themselves symbolically through institutions and thus gain greater social (versus merely individual) control over them. At the same time, the remaining institutions supporting private property separated people. As long as property was separately possessed, it continued to be a basis for violent struggle. Hegel believed that the consequent life-and-death struggle based on private property could come to an end only when the opposed individuals were integrated into the community of the nation.

Here we see the seeds of a theory of social law as opposed to theory based solely on individual rights. In this Hegelian picture, private property makes individuals oppose the "universal" and unwisely follow the ties of individual self-interest. Hegel thus goes beyond Locke in the liberalist doctrine of the social contract insofar as he sees the rule of law embodying the "abstract right" of property.[21]

Locke assumed that property had an individual character and that people should be free to defend it.[22] People owned property in their own person and thus it was implied they should even have rights to the fruits of their own labor, a point of interest to Karl Marx. The freedom to own private property and the right to its fruits was an implicit part of the Lockean notion and part of the arguments behind the writing of the U.S. Constitution. But Hegel assumed that property had a broader social meaning in the development of self-realization. The function of the state's judicial administration for Hegel was to actualize into necessity the abstract (social) side of personal liberty in civil society. This of course required exercising the powers of the state to safeguard the property that belonged to the whole. It was on this point that Marx differed from Hegel in his concept of property as a function of society rather than the state.

Following Hegel, Karl Marx saw property as a major source of modern alienation, separating people from their life in community.[23] But Marx did not relegate the final jurisdiction of property to the state. Instead, he saw the society as the ultimate arbiter of objects greatly valued, primarily the modes of production in society. The modes of production were common property to be socially managed by people without the necessity of direct state control. In a revolutionary situation, Marx recognized that the state would need to take control temporarily, but the socialization of the economy would eventually reduce the necessity of the state to maintain outside control over it.

The problem of both capitalist and socialist states today is in determining the next step in socializing productive property while keeping that important distinction between the state and the society. The socialization process has seldom been understood in post-Marxian thought, and it remains a central issue of development today. It is a critical part of our theory assessing the direction of policy research in modern society.

Social ownership refers to the right to control property in conjunction with others at different levels of governance in society. We see the analysis of this control beginning with society in both the socialist and capitalist traditions. The society provides the foundation for the state to operate with legitimacy. Today that legitimacy is normally given to a democratic state. This state, in turn, dispenses the right to control property at various levels of hierarchy in the public and private sectors. The legal right to control property among different groups changes over time, but it is always legitimated by the government and the society, which together give property its legitimacy.

This means that all property is social in an abstract sense in both capitalist and socialist states, but critical questions remain on the kinds of control granted by the government. The properties of production in socialist countries have usually been appropriated by the state for its own governance, but we have suggested that without social planning to deconcentrate and socialize these properties, this action remains in tension with Marx's concept of development. The state cannot serve as a permanent substitute for the authority of the society or the community. It cannot be conceived as the ultimate authority over the economy. Marx foresaw the society as the ultimate authority and in one sense it was the future community (communism), following from the historical development of socialism, that would be the final arbiter of power in the economy.

The concept of social property is complex, but clearly part of the normative definition requires that all productive assets have legal, social, and economic characteristics that make exploitation impossible. The concept of socializing property means reducing or eliminating exploitation associated with its use. Our argument is that this begins to happen through the creation of a social sector in the economy. This is the problem of our inquiry into the nature of community self-governance.

The Social Sector

Today we are seeing the development of democratic corporations organized to represent broad constituencies outside the state. They are creating what we may call the social sector, that domain of economic life that is designed to operate in the interest of the people who are affected by it in the context of the whole community. It is not constituted by traditional state governance or by oligopolistic capitalist governance. It is constituted as a nonstatist system of exchange composed of democratic institutions accountable to their constituencies.

The social sector is an evolving phenomenon and not defined by a single piece of legislation. In our framework, we see corporations emerging in modern nations that show increasing signs of fitting into and shaping a new social sector. These include community development corporations, community land trusts, community-based banks, cooperatives, and self-managed firms. Various traditional corporations and public agencies that undergo reformative processes of democratization begin to enter into the social sector. Government corporations do not qualify until they are fully removed from government control. Traditional

corporations fo not fully qualify until they are entirely
worker owned and self-managed.

This means that certain semi-autonomous government
agencies can take steps toward becoming part of the social
sector by meeting certain criteria, like high degrees of
worker participation in management and easy public access to agency information for citizens wishing to obtain
it. Similarly, private businesses take steps toward becoming a part of the social sector when they maintain
certain systems of social accountability to their constituencies: workers, suppliers, creditors, customers, and the
local community. Corporations that maintain social audits,
social charters, and democratic practices begin to approach
the criteria demanded of the social sector. These examples
represent progressive steps toward entering into the social
sector. The social sector is a democratically constituted
economy designed to be independent of direct state control
and structured to operate in the interest of the people it
affects in a system of exchange.[24]

Social ownership is a function of this social (nonstatist) sector and can be understood at different levels
of control. The major levels of control begin theoretically
with the society. This would seem ambiguous at first,
because society is not itself an organization that can act
with a goal. It is rather a social entity that contains
organizations and is in part an extrainstitutional order of
relationships through which people retain the power to
create and change institutions. It is the source of social
movements and revolutions. In effect, we have said that
this social body of people with a common territory and
identity "authorize" the state to act with its own administrative levels of governance that, in turn, authorize the
existence of organizations for collective action like corporations and, finally, the local municipality.

The local municipality (or city government), however,
does not represent the final arbiter of authority. It is
supported by another local body of people with a common
identity and territory. This body is also partly noninsti-
tutional and nonorganizational and is called the community.
Thus, the legitimacy of certain groups to exercise control
over property begins with the larger territory of common
identity called society and ends with the local territory of
identity called the community.

In other words, the beginning and the end of the
legitimizing source of property control is nonstatist. The

society authorizes the state, which, in turn, authorizes corporations. At the local level, corporations are given appropriate jurisdiction to control things in the context of a city government, which, in turn, is authorized ultimately by a noncorporate body of people called the community.[25]

Social governance thus means the management of economic affairs in the context of the society and ultimately the local community. Social ownership finds its ultimate reference in the nonformal and goalless framework of the society. The society, in turn, finds its ultimate reference in the emergent community.

This abstract discussion of the social sector has direct relevance to our study of development in the United States and Greece. We argue that a social sector is developing quietly in the United States without the conscious intent of formal legislation. It is being initiated in the form of worker and community-oriented enterprises in the private system, as we shall see. In Greece, the social sector is formally defined by law. Despite similarities of our own conceptualization of the social sector with the Greek one, as defined by law, the extent of government involvement provided by the Greek law differentiates substantially the two models.[26]

The social sector is significant to our analysis of development of autonomy, viability, and polity in both countries. The development of relatively self-reliant communities is therefore not accomplished simply by government legislation--as important as that may be. It does not consist simply of decentralizing authority to city governments. It is a much more complex process of cultivating a socially self-governing economy.

The development of this sector means that systems of free enterprise remain open to fair competition while becoming primarily designed to cooperate in the public interest. The enterprises develop within the nonstatist sector of the community.

The Social Federation

The process of socializing the private economy is so complex that it is best conceived as experimental. There are no clear formulas on how to do it. Furthermore, the process should be recognized as taking place differently in every nation. Broadly stated, it involves on the one hand decentralizing and "destatifying" government corporations without losing their public purpose. On the other hand, it can mean creating a social constitution for private firms so that they can operate more formally in the public interest. In other words, the process of creating a social sector involves replacing the conventional private and the state sectors with a new sector of publicly oriented business.

This may be done in some cases through the establishment of publicly oriented charters for private corporations, backed by legislation. It can be done by encouraging firms to train employees for participation in management and ownership. It can be advanced by establishing social audits in corporations. It may be further advanced by creating formal constitutions for firms designed to protect their constituencies. These actions begin to define enterprises as social entities without resulting in their demise as economic entities.

Creating a social sector also means establishing social constitutions for federations such as trade associations and trade unions. Trade associations especially need a legal basis for controlling selected aspects of corporate competition in the public interest. The social federation is an intercorporate agent acting democratically and selectively as a substitution for government controls. As it evolves in its capacity to be accountable, it becomes a part of the social sector.

The socialization of the enterprise system at the level of the community then involves not only policies on worker self-governance but also policies on the practice of interfirm relationships, that is, on the practice of cooperation in the marketplace. This means finding modes of cooperation that are not collusive in the private interests of firms. The practice of cooperation in the public interest (along with competition) becomes a defining feature of the social economy. This is not a remote ideal for business practice. We are talking about the extension of an ideal practice that seems to have already begun to take place in Greece and in the United States.

While interfirm competition is often controlled through government agencies that seek to protect the public from exploitive practices, modest social controls have also begun through trade associations to lead firms to function effectively in the larger public domain. These practices of business federations remain to be studied as part of an economy that reduces the need for state controls.

Trade associations in the United States have acted in their own self-interest to increase government regulations, but they have also acted against government intervention in ways that are in the public interest. They have established ethical codes and private tribunals to adjudicate conflict between corporations and to settle problems between their member corporations and consumers. They have established public standards for manufacturing products (e.g., grading lumber for construction and providing safety guidelines for orthopedic appliances) in the interest of the public without state regulations. They have established uniformity in the structure of products (e.g., the size of shoes and the size of light bulbs) that are in the public interest.

The secret to finding a basis for interfirm collaboration in the public interest is in discovering how every corporation benefits by the new rules. In this social-federational control over production in the enterprise system, actions have been taken because business leaders have recognized that traditional competitive practices would have caused destructive corporate warfare. A common recognition has emerged among corporate leaders that all firms (and the public) together would lose. Interfirm cooperation in some cases is essential to the survival of the industry as well as the firms within it.

Thus, leaders in business federations have begun to socialize business themselves in select ways within the private sector. These select ways include the adjudication of interfirm disputes, product standardization, the creation of formalized ethical standards, and trade agreements on consumer warranties, which have served to reduce the need for government administration. In Marxist terms, a social consciousness has been seeding itself within the womb of capitalism. It is a consciousness among business leaders about the delicate interdependence of firms in the context of the marketplace and society.

These self-regulatory efforts are the result of almost a century of struggle among firms attempting to survive the competitive market. These actions represent a slow transformation of the market itself. Further action along these important lines of cooperation among firms becomes critical to examine. Much research is still needed to determine answers on how these federations can help socialize market behavior so that firms can operate in both their own interest and the public interest. More research is needed on the proper legal foundation for encouraging firms to exercise controls in the public interest.

The problem is to determine how specific types of collaboration can take place without resulting in subtle collusion in the interest of the industry or big corporate members of the federation. The solution requires a new concept of the market as a social system. It involves seeing the market as a private system of exchange that can begin functioning by itself in the interest of society.

The Social Market

All markets are social in the sense that firms take other people into account and are interdependent in buying and selling goods. The "social market" thus has a factual dimension. But it also has a normative dimension insofar as its sociality can be increased. This may sound rather odd, but it is true that the character of the market can begin to change as it becomes constituted by socially oriented firms and trade associations that take more serious account of the people they affect in the community.

The market is a system of exchange that begins to function differently when socially constituted firms cooperate together in the social sector. In the United States, community corporations are developing quietly to exercise controls over the marketing of land, labor, and capital in the public interest. As we shall see, they are small in proportion to conventional corporations, but they represent a new basis for building a social foundation to the market. In these cases, the whole community is formally represented in overseeing the purchase and sale of property. The sale of property is made in the interest of the community. Property in these instances is owned by the community.

The community land trust is a type of real estate in the United States that buys land not for speculation and private profit but for the advantage of everyone in the locality. The community credit union is a type of bank that uses capital not for making profits overseas for big bankers but for local people to build a better shopping center and a playground for kids in their neighborhood. Employee pension funds, managed by some labor unions, have been designed to invest with human values. They invest not in South African business but in housing construction on behalf of workers getting jobs and for planning their own future homes. These types of firms operate in a market, but they add value to local community life. These types of firms and their market transactions help develop the social sector.

These community-oriented enterprises are creating a new legal foundation for the marketplace. Their system of exchange is based more on a process of cooperation for social and economic returns in the interest of the community than on competition for economic returns in the interest of managers, executives, and wealthy shareholders.

In Greece, popular support is being mobilized to decentralize metropolitan government controls to community controls. The present government is seeking to develop new local powers for municipalities that in the past have been exercised solely from the metropolis. This involves a whole new concept of social authority and legal jurisdiction in the market economy of Greek life.

The term decentralization is used in Greece with a special meaning under the PASOK administration. It means that the central government transfers jurisdictions to the local government. This term differs slightly from deconcentration, which means that the central government transfers jurisdictions to the state organs, that is, the prefects. The present government is thus making an effort to (1) decentralize jurisdictions at the first and second level of local government and (2) deconcentrate jurisdictions from the central ministries to the regional state organs (the prefectures), to develop the country as a whole and not only regions like greater Athens and Thessaloníki.

The task of decentralization in our conceptual framework is theoretically twofold. It involves increasing the authority of local governments while also increasing the democratic authority of local economy, including the subsidiaries of corporations whose offices are in the central city. The main task involves establishing a social market in which firms operate in the interest of the community as well as in the interests of their parent corporations. Thus, decentralization is not conceived solely as a government operation. Indeed, the primary task is the cultivation of a local economy that is socially organized to reduce the need for government operations.

Social Decentralization

The cultivation of greater local control in the economy does not mean social isolation. It means a greater recognition of the importance of a social-economic interdependence with distant cities. But the type of interdependence we are discussing accents local autonomy. This is the paradox that must be understood in making new approaches to community development.

There are both social and economic advantages for localities to stay in touch with the outside world through trade and commerce. Social advantages come from outside contacts that help avoid local elitism. If the local enterprises are socially structured in the sense that we are suggesting, big property owners no longer come to rule the municipality. But it is also true that democratizing the local economy is not easy to do effectively; there is often a subtle continuance of the old power structure even as democratic institutions in the economy are developed. In this slow process of democratization, local elitism is best challenged by contact with people from other countries and the big city. We believe these contacts can be maintained even while advancing the development of community life.

In the United States, we have noted that Roland Warren describes the shift from local control toward national control in terms of changing relationships among local organizations, which have moved from horizontal relationships at the local level to vertical relationships at the national level, involving them in new alignments and commitments. Local organizations have been forced to adjust themselves to new lines of power and communication developing from federal programs. The negative result has been a loss of community and a disruption of horizontal integration held by organizations in the local community, but the positive result has been that it has been accompanied by a reduction in local elitism and an increase in local competitiveness among nationally oriented local businesses. Local power structures are fragmented while local autonomy is lost. These vertical relations to the big city have been a major cause for community decline, but hidden within this loss is a social gain in the sense that former patterns of local elitism were destroyed.

Commerce with cities outside the locality is therefore critical to social development. Local power structures need to be challenged by new enterprises and business practices periodically introduced into the local economy. Our argument is that the structures of the community-oriented businesses we discuss in the next two chapters allow this to happen without a total loss of community. The process of rediscovering a new economic basis for local community life then involves solving a paradox. It involves creating structures that remain open to outside commerce while maintaining a social coherence with local community life. Put in the classic terms of Ferdinand Toennies, it involves integrating the values of both gemein-schaft and gesellschaft. Put in the terms of Max Weber, it means finding a way to be both subjectively communal and deliberately rational at the same time. It is the challenge of the postmodern period.

Economic advantages come with the introduction of new technology and capital from metropolitan firms and multinational corporations. This keeps the local economy progressive and productive. The introduction of outside products also increases the possibilities for import replace-ment, in turn increasing the capacity for the community to be self-governing.

The subsidiaries of multinational corporations can be introduced into a locality without major forms of domi-nance. Socialist nations like the Soviet Union and China have taken the lead in negotiating joint controls with mul-tinationals, which have been notorious in the past for their exploitation of foreign environments. Likewise, citi-zens in a locality can negotiate contracts (usually with national support) to maintain corporate oversight into the local administration of foreign subsidiaries. These con-tracts can mean optimally sharing ownership--at best or-ganized as worker-managed subsidiaries. Full local control need not happen all at once but can be planned to develop over a period of time.[27]

Yugoslavia's multinational firm Energoinvest set the pattern for this practice of decentralization over a decade ago.[28] We can now observe multinational cooperatives be-ginning to organize themselves as decentralized corpora-tions. These examples suggest that sufficient local con-trol can be maintained in the field of international trade to guarantee an adequate amount of self-governance of the local economy.

The history of multinational corporations shows a tendency toward decentralization. They have gradually divested from total control over all management and owner-ship and have increased their level of shared control with local leaders. There is every reason to believe that care-ful negotiations with corporate executives can continue this trend in the direction of becoming organized more fully as a multinational cooperative. The multinational cooperative emphasizes bottom-up control and increases its authorization of control at higher levels of organization as it moves from a confederation to a federation. The multinational corporation deemphasizes top-down control and increases its authorization of control at lower levels of organization as it moves from a command system to a federation.[29]

IN SUMMARY

In sum, the concept of community self-governance can be studied in terms of local autonomy, viability, and polity. New democratic corporations are emerging to strengthen the local economy to become more self-reliant, and new legislation is being created to decentralize authority from central-government controls to local controls. It follows that the promotion of democratic firms on a significant scale suggests that new cooperative norms of the market can be realized to overcome the destructive forces of the competitive market. In other words, economic alternatives are developing (and can be further promoted) that are oriented toward the development of community life. These alternatives require new concepts to explain the development of a new system of exchange, concepts that include social governance, social property, social federations, the social sector, and social decentralization in the economic life of nations. These concepts become a part of the language of development in the cultivation of a socially governed economy.

In the following two chapters we will examine how innovative processes of community development are beginning in the United States and Greece. The discussion of developments in the United States is highly selective in describing social changes on a small scale, keeping in mind especially our criteria of autonomy, viability, and polity. There are no current efforts in the United States focusing on the development of community life on larger scale in the manner of Greece. The discussion in Greece follows our conceptual framework, but the political factor is emphasized, as the developments we trace are promoted by governmental policy. We will compare the larger political contexts of both nations in our final analysis when we evaluate the different patterns of development taking place in these two nations.

NOTES

1. Max Weber, The City (New York: Free Press, 1958).

2. Thomas Bender, Community and Social Change in America (New Brunswick, N.J.: Rutgers University Press, 1978); Seldon Wolin, Politics and Vision (Boston: Little, Brown, 1960), pp. 366, 376.

3. Bender, Community and Social Change.

4. Information was collected by personal interview with Mr. Kolymvas, former Chairman of the Board of PASEGES, December 10, 1986.

5. Sidney Cobb and Stanislau Kasl, Termination: The Consequences of Job Loss (Research report no. 77-224, National Institute of Occupational Safety and Health, June 1977).

6. Paula Rayman and Barry Bluestone, Out of Work (Boston College: Social Welfare Research Institute, 1982).

7. Information collected by personal interview with the elected mayor of Elefsina, Mr. Leventis.

8. Lewis Mumford, The Culture of Cities (New York: Harcourt, Brace, 1938).

9. Jane Jacobs, The Economy of Cities (New York: Harcourt, Brace, 1938).

10. Lloyd Warner, The Social System of the Modern Factory (New Haven, Conn.: Yale University Press, 1947), p. 108.

11. Roland Warren, The Community in America (Chicago: Rand McNally, 1963).

12. Robert E. L. Faris, Social Disorganization (New York: Ronald Press, 1948); Martin Neumeyer, Juvenile Delinquency in Modern Society (New York: Nostrand, 1961). Many of the studies of the Chicago School were in this tradition: The Hobo, The Gold Coast and the Slum, The Ghetto, and The Gang. Cf. Robert Ezra Park, Human Communities (Glencoe, Ill.: Free Press, 1952).

13. Robert Nisbet, The Quest for Community (New York: Oxford University Press, 1953).

14. Karl Polanyi, The Great Transformation (Boston: Beacon Press, 1965).

15. Roland Warren, ed., Perspectives on the American Community (Chicago: Rand McNally, 1973); cf. Severyn T. Bruyn and Paula Rayman, Nonviolent Action and Social Change (New York: Irvington Press, 1979), pp. 53ff.

16. Furthermore, there are international cooperatives operating for various business purposes: intercooperative

trade, banking, insurance, purchase of fertilizers, etc. All of these cooperative businesses transfer representative power to the higher organs for decision making. The higher organs are composed of representatives of the lower ones whose interests they represent. This observation on the "sixth international and Greek cooperatives" is based upon discussions with an expert on cooperatives in Greece, Dr. C. Papageorgiou.

17. Maple Flooring Manufacturing Association v United States, 268 U.S. 563, 586 (1925). The seeds of this development can be seen in the capitalist system. In the United States, the Supreme Court acknowledged that trade associations could openly and fairly gather and disseminate information as to the costs of their product, the volume of production, the price of the product, and the approximate cost of transportation from the point of shipment as long as members of the association did not attempt to reach any agreement with respect to prices or production that would restrain competition.

18. Hannah Arendt, On Revolution (New York: Viking Press, 1963), p. 180.

19. Ibid., p. 256.

20. One of Hegel's historical fragments, written after 1797, declares that "security of property is the pivot on which the whole of modern legislation turns," and in the first draft to his pamphlet on Die Verfassung Deutschland (1798-99), he states that the historical form of "bourgeois property" is responsible for the prevailing political disintegration. Hegel maintained that the prevailing social institutions had distorted even the most private and personal relations between people. George Friedrich Hegel, Theologische Jugendschriften, p. 223, and Documente zu Hegels Entwicklung, p. 268. This interpretation is noted in Herbert Marcuse, Reason and Revolution (Boston: Beacon Press, 1960), p. 34.

21. For more on Hegel's concept of property, see Leo Rauch, Hegel and the Human Spirit (Detroit, Mich.: Wayne State University Press, 1983), p. 138ff. Hegel did not consider the peasant nor the proletariat capable of self-government. He lived in the ethos of his own day in which they were left without a franchise. See Charles Taylor, Hegel and Modern Society (Cambridge, England: Cambridge University Press, 1979).

22. Locke believed that "every man has 'property' in his own 'person.' This nobody has the right to but

himself. The 'labour' of his body and the 'work' of his hands, we must say, are properly his." John Locke, Two Treatises on Civil Government (New York: Dutton, 1924), p. 130.

23. Marx claimed, "Private property has made us so stupid and partial that an object is only ours when we have it, when it exists for us as capital, or when it is . . . utilized in some way." Karl Marx, Early Writings, trans. and ed. T. B. Bottomore (London: 1964), pp. 43-44.

24. The mandate from Marx to develop a social sector can be seen in many sources of his work, but it can be briefly noted here in his response to Lassalle's proposal to develop a "free state" as part of a socialist plan in 1875 in Germany. Marx will have nothing of it. "It is by no means the aim of the workers, who have got rid of the narrow mentality of humble subjects, to set the state free. . . . Freedom consists in converting the state from an organ superimposed upon society into one completely subordinate to it." Marx took pains to note that "Right can never be higher than the economic structure of society and its cultural development conditioned thereby." The structure of the economy needed to be altered fundamentally, he said, in order to achieve "a higher phase of communist society." Karl Marx, "Critique of the Gotha Programme," in Selected Works, ed. Karl Marx and Frederick Engels (New York: International, 1968), pp. 330, 332.

25. George Gurvitch was concerned about the extent to which modern law was based on a concept of individualism as opposed to a communal concept. He believed that a new philosophy of law was needed to counteract this tendency. The realm of nonstatist law surrounding corporate behavior we are discussing here is included in what he calls "social law." For a careful examination of his work, see Richard Swedberg, Sociology as Disenchantment: The Evolution of the Work of George Gurvitch (Atlantic Highlands, N.J.: Humanities Press, 1982).

26. We discuss the meaning of social sector in the last chapter of this volume, where we compare our experiences. In the United States, legal battles in the private sector over social issues such as human rights of employees in corporations continue to take place. Free speech is a special concern because corporations often have more rights to control behavior than employees have rights to act freely. Today it is against the law for corporations to fire employees because of race, religion,

or gender in the United States, but employees are still not adequately protected against their attempts to "blow the whistle" when they see the corporation endangering the environment or exploiting the consumer. Bosses still have the right to search the papers of employees on corporate property, while employees do not have the right to their security in this regard. An employee cannot be discriminated against in hiring because of belonging to an association (e.g., the Communist party) but the process of firing is not so clearly designated in the law. Being fired for any reason--including accidents--is not backed up clearly in the law by "due process."

27. The gradual decentralization of the authority of multinational corporations is discussed in Severyn Bruyn, The Social Economy: People Transforming Business (New York: John Wiley & Sons, 1977), chaps. 8, 9. For examples of democratic federations of business at the world level, see J. G. Craig, Multinational Co-operatives: An Alternative to World Development (Saskatchewan, Canada: Western Producer Prairie Books, 1976).

28. Based on a conversation with an executive of Energoinvest in Yugoslavia and a reading of company documents.

29. For further elaboration on this point, see Severyn T. Bruyn, The Field of Social Investment (Cambridge, England: Cambridge University Press, 1987).

6. Development toward Community Self-Governance in the United States

Taking the concepts of autonomy, viability, and democratic polity as criteria for assessing steps toward building a social foundation for local self-governance in the United States, we can observe areas of the economy moving in this direction for the last two decades. These changes have occurred in part through enabling legislation providing incentives for the development of democratic corporations and also through social movements and the voluntary actions of people motivated to treat the problems of the market economy.

If we take the competitive market as the central element to be controlled in land, capital, and labor, we have a starting place for optimizing local autonomy. We shall see that legal devices are already in place for changing the system and that the main problem is how they are best put together in a national plan for community development.

AUTONOMY (LOCAL SOCIAL OWNERSHIP)

Land: The Community Land Trust

When local land is on the competitive market, all sorts of problems arise leading to community decline. We mention only one problem here because our task is describing alternatives.

Speculation in city land is in part a function of the competitive market and leads to the fostering of slums. Slums have often been created on the edges of a central business district because landlords speculate on rising market values. When city businesses decide to construct new buildings, adjacent land rapidly increases in value and can become more valuable than the buildings on it. Buildings on land with such potential appreciation are allowed to deteriorate. Absentee landlords do not care about tenants or maintenance because anticipated future profits outweigh such considerations. The city government then tries to solve the problem with housing codes, safety regulations, zoning ordinances, and enforcement agencies. The cost of government goes up, but essentially the problem is usually unresolved.

There is a solution to this problem that has begun to do away with both the competitive market and the need for government controls in selected cases. Communities have begun experimenting with what is called a community land trust (CLT) as an alternative to land speculation (Leesburg, Georgia; Clairfield, Tennessee; Hancock County, Maine; Columbia Heights, Washington, D.C.; Cincinnati, Ohio; Minneapolis, Minnesota; and various other locations). The CLT is a nonprofit cooperative that buys land and holds it in the community interest and the wider public interest. It is designed not only to avoid speculation and the rapid turnover of land, which destroys its productive capacity, but also to create a democratic foundation to the local economy.[1]

The CLT owns land through a trusteeship whose democratically selected board (one-third representatives of lessees, one-third representatives of the local community, and one-third representatives of the public interest [often professional people]) oversees the use of the land in the interest of the community. Local people are given the opportunity to lease the land for life as long as they maintain it in the public interest; lessee representatives defend their interests in policy making on the board. The CLT differs from the land conservation trust, which is primarily concerned with the retention of natural resources. The U.S. tax structure provides a framework for promoting the conservation of natural assets for the common good, and in the latter kind of trust, land is held by an organization that is not necessarily representative of the locality.

The charter of the CLT states principles of general use rather than specific uses, so lessees have a great deal of freedom. Free enterprise is encouraged. The charter may state that the land is not to lie fallow, that it must be kept in productive use. In rural areas, land-trust charters may emphasize the prevention of soil erosion; in cities, charters may state that a tract of land is not to remain unused (as a lot collecting trash dangerous to children), that it must be put to some recreational or productive use. The lessee therefore can utilize the land in many ways to make profits that do not violate the public interest and may keep their profits as long as they pay the fees. The CLT encourages individual incentive within a broad framework of community interest.

The lease fee can be used for the purchase of more land, hence the trust must have its own mechanism for self-expansion. Ideally, as CLTs broaden their ownership bases, they federate in order that one board does not gain control over too large an area. A board consists of people who live in a city neighborhood or a rural community who are not there to build land empires. Thus, a CLT expands on the basis of creating new trusts through a democratic federation. The central board of the federation has very limited powers in respect to local use of land. It functions very much on the principle of subsidiarity: the larger body should not govern any activity that cannot be governed better by the local community.

CLT experts believe that not all land uses should be locally controlled. Certain land resources require the oversight of a regional trust board. For example, it is more appropriate to assign control over natural resources like rivers to regional or federal organizations than to a local community. In the northeast, water might be a resource under purely local control but in the west, where water can be a scarce commodity, allocation of water rights should be determined by a democratic federation operating on a wider geographical basis. And certain regions are more subject to outside exploitation and control than others. For example, land in Appalachia is largely owned by a few dozen gigantic corporations in fuel, transportation, and lumber. A study of land ownership in 80 rural West Virginia counties found that the corporations owned 40 percent of the land and 70 percent of the mineral rights. The study also found that 75 percent of the land and 80 percent of the mineral rights were held by outside people or corporations. Further, the property taxes paid by the owners were extremely low. The resource wealth has been slowly drained out to absentee corporations while the communities themselves have remained poor.[2]

The CLT is designed to eliminate these inequities. It can act more effectively than the local government in many cases, because local officials often refrain from interfering with the "free market." The CLT can lease the land to local developers and require its proper use and a fair return. The board sees to it that the land is not destroyed by outside corporations, that the land continues to make a contribution to local development. It could recommend that outsiders contract with a local corporation for resource extraction, which then makes a fair return profit that along with fees paid to the land trust, means capital in the local community.

If the leaseholder terminates a lease, owned improvements (e.g., buildings) may be sold or remanded. The CLT typically retains a first option to buy the improvements at the owner's original cost adjusted for inflation, depreciation, and damage during the ownership period. Such property can be sold to the next leaseholder. Thus, the first leaseholder is guaranteed equity in the improvements and the succeeding leaseholder is able to buy the improvements at a fair price. Nobody profits from unearned increases in market value; no buyer is priced out of the market by such increases. Any increase in value not owing to a leaseholder's efforts remains with the CLT. Neither the CLT nor the leaseholder holds the land itself as a commodity.

Lease fees represent a fair return to the community for use of the land and resources. They are similar in principle to local property taxes but with a special difference: they are based on the value of the land alone. Many municipalities not only tax improvements but tax them at a higher rate and tax undeveloped land and extracted natural resources at considerably less than their full value. The CLT corrects these injustices.

The CLT is still experimental. Its first U.S. use occurred about 20 years ago, and only in the past few years has the model begun to achieve public recognition. It has a longer tradition in other countries. The Jewish National Fund of Israel was founded in 1901 as a land trust and operates today on a national scale, but it is not a fully nongovernmental institution. Furthermore, it is more centralized than in the United States; the fund owns most of the productive land and considerable additional land in both rural and urban areas. Land is held in the public interest and leased out for use, with improvements owned by leaseholders.

Land trusts have also been developed in Mexico and Tanzania, where the governments are more closely associated with the land-trust movement than is so in the United States. The central governments have given land trusteeships to village communities that in turn grant use rights to individuals. Leaders in the United States celebrate the fact that the land-trust movement is independent of government controls.

Capital: Community Development Finance Institution

We have noted the deleterious impact of capital flight on communities, but this is only part of the story. The capital market has been harmful to communities in other ways. Indeed, the need to find methods for gaining control over local capital did not grow out of the runaway plants but rather out of the struggle of people in neighborhoods discriminated against by city banks. The competitive capital market has not been any more favorable to the poor than the land market has been, and people have found it necessary to devise an alternative system for democratizing capital. They have organized community development credit unions and other types of community development finance institutions (CDFIs).

One of the reasons for setting up CDFIs was the conventional banks' "redlining," that is, their refusal to invest in certain neighborhoods because of perceived credit risks. (The term redlining originated in the custom of drawing red lines on maps around ethnic, racial, or low-income neighborhoods deemed off-limits.) Redlining leads to deterioration and eventually abandonment of the neighborhood. The slow decay is of course attended by crime and other social ills. The residents who are branded credit risks have to turn to loan sharks for personal loans, which costs them far more than they would have paid to the banks and more than borrowers with better addresses. The local community deteriorates while the banks improve their credit status. In other words, lending institutions use the savings of local depositors to make loans elsewhere. The money is diverted to build up other areas (e.g., new suburbs) instead of applied to local mortgages, home improvements, and personal and business loans. The residents are hence doubly victimized:

their neighborhoods decline and they are deprived of the rightful use of their savings.

The first step toward what has become known as "greenlining" was taken by older residents of an Italian neighborhood in Chicago in the early 1970s, when they discovered that they could not obtain mortgages but that their children in the suburbs could. The group had very little capital power--combined assets of only $36,000 compared with the bank's $88 million. Because it requires approximately 5 percent of an institution's assets to wipe out its liquid assets, withdrawal of the $36,000 would be unavailing as a protest. The group decided on a "bank-in"; people lined up at all the tellers' windows to make minor transactions during the bank's busiest hours. These irritations eventually pressured the bank into committing $4 million to the community for mortgage loans.

The real greenline alternative was discovered later when residents found that they could establish their own banking system, a community bank organized under credit union legislation. A credit union is a nonprofit cooperative incorporated under state or federal law for people with common affiliation, such as a profession or an occupation. It was only a step further to a credit union based on the common bond of residence in a particular community. This new type of credit union was to be based on locality.

The community development credit union (CDCU) is a nonprofit cooperative incorporated under state or federal law for low-income people living in one locality. Its purpose is to promote thrift among its members and to make loans to its members at reasonable interest rates for community development. The CDCU is controlled by the member-residents, each of whom has one vote regardless of amount of savings. Although it may accept deposits by nonmembers outside the locality, loans may be made only to members. Money not currently on loan may be invested in federal and state government securities and other CDCUs. The earnings of the CDCU are not federally taxed. Some earnings are retained as a reserve for loans; the remainder are returned to members in services, dividends on savings, or interest rebates. The money that the CDCU keeps within the community can in turn be mobilized as capital for cooperatives and other locally owned businesses.

The CDCU is defined simultaneously as a financial institution, a neighborhood institution, and an institution of learning. As an institution of learning, it deepens its members' understanding of finance and community economics; inspires members to see how it can expand its influence; and develops members' skills in keeping records, conducting meetings, contracting, financing, collecting data, hiring and firing, and relating with other CDCUs.[3]

The CDCU is legally designed for low-income neighborhoods, but other types of community-oriented finance institutions have also developed. For example, the Institute for Community Economics in Greenfield, Massachusetts, has a revolving loan fund (RLF) available to finance community land trusts. The capital volume increased by almost 200 percent in 1982 and is now over $1 million. The RLF has placed 45 loans with community land trusts, worker-owned businesses, and community service groups in 11 states.[4]

The South Shore Bank is a prominent example of how local people can turn around neighborhood deterioration. The South Shore is an area eight miles south of Chicago's Loop whose residents were determined to pull themselves out of a local depression. They created a bank that in ten years is a standard in socially responsible investment. By mid-1984, it had reached $50 million in development loans and had developed affiliated companies to carry on its work independently. These affiliates include the City Lands Corporation, a real estate development company managing the investment of $24 million in the rehabilitation of 340 units in five multifamily housing projects; the Neighborhood Institute, a not-for-profit firm packaging loans for energy retrofitting, with its own housing center, that is currently managing a $1.4 million project developing 137 low-income housing units; and the Neighborhood Fund, with investments of $761,000 in minority-owned businesses.

Some communities are too small to sustain a local bank and therefore pool capital and coordinate efforts with other communities. In Birmingham, Alabama, Neighborhood Services, a coalition of more than a dozen neighborhood organizations, has established a revolving loan fund to finance the acquisition and development of local housing. The coalition has been developing cooperative housing in the city and has recently become interested in land trusts as a part of its method for increasing local control over capital.

All such financial institutions localize and democratize capital, taking capital out of the traditional market system. We shall note later how community finance institutions can create the basis for their investees (enterprises) to own them. Newly capitalized enterprises may come to own the bank that created them in the first place.

Labor: Worker Cooperatives

We have discussed the trends toward worker self-governance, but we now want to see how it becomes a part of the larger picture of community self-governance. The labor market has been the subject of critical study since Karl Marx's first interpretation of alienation under capitalism and is still under study because of its complexity. In Marx's view, labor had been reduced to a commodity like capital and land in the economic system. In the original meaning used by Hegel, alienation referred to a divergence between human existence and human essence; existence referred to the actual reality of people living in the world; and essence was the human potential of the individual. The problem was to overcome the privatization of property insofar as it played such a critical role in generating alienation. Marx saw the potential for the socialization of property and for human beings to become creative, free, and self-determining in their labor. People could not realize this potential when treated as objects for hire within the market system.

Marx foresaw the worker cooperative as a stage in the process of eliminating the alienating forms of capitalism, but he did not foresee other stages of worker participation that would develop within capitalism. Today we can observe a slow reformation of business enterprises through quality-of-work-life projects, labor-management committees, and increasing degrees of worker ownership, with labor participating at new levels of corporate governance. Recent cases of worker buyouts and labor-management agreements in the United States are reshaping the traditional role of labor. With labor representation on the boards of directors of Weirton Steel, Seymour Specialty Wire, the former A&P stores in Philadelphia, and other U.S. corporations, the possibility exists for a gradual shift toward the worker-cooperative model. We have noted how employee stock ownership plans have led to an increase in worker ownership to over 9,000 corporations, of which about 10 percent are majority owned by employees. These trends show a direction developing in U.S. enterprise that is taking more account of workers as a human part of the enterprise. The trends reduce tendencies in the capitalist system to treat labor as a commodity, but the movement has a very long way to go.

The major point to be made here is that employee ownership means very little unless the stock is arranged in such a way that it cannot be purchased by outsiders. To maintain local control over the corporation, the stock must be taken out of the market. If not, the worker-owned business may be purchased by a conglomerate and once again become subject to capital flight, unnecessary layoffs, and the attendant problems of community decline.

Studies show that it is important for worker cooperatives to separate membership rights from ownership rights. Membership rights give employees the opportunity to vote for the board of directors and to receive a portion of the net income from the company, but ownership of the company is located in the company as a whole. The workers simply have collective rights to the final disposition of property. This important arrangement then removes labor from the marketplace and localizes control over the corporation.

We can now see more significance in Polanyi's interpretation of the "great transformation" from feudalism in land, capital, and labor. Just as the market system was slowly divested from the feudal system by a series of legal and political changes we are talking now about divesting legally from the market system and developing a social economy out of local community life (see Figure 6.1).

Our point is that the creation of local autonomy is a feasible goal for social investment. There are many social and economic advantages in shifting from absentee ownership to local controls. First, jobs become more stabilized and income is more secure in the locality. People do not need to worry about plant relocation. Second, the community is in a better position to negotiate for the provision of services such as schools, churches, and public utilities. It can assume that companies will remain part of their future. Third, the local government can be more certain of tax revenues. Fourth, local control contributes to a better cash flow for localities and a stable commercial base; the income of local employees can be counted upon

Figure 6.1

Community Autonomy

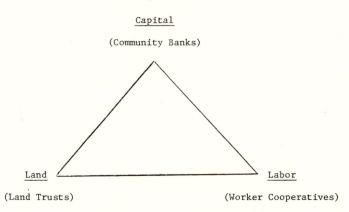

to circulate through local banks and businesses. Local control thus increases the probability that a company's retained earnings and distributed profits will also be held and spent within the community. Employee ownership and control advances the possibility that local profits will remain within the locality. Fifth, local ownership increases the opportunities for workers to lead and thus to experience personal development in the firm. Also, employees can feel more pride in their work. The ultimate advantage is that social problems and the devastation left in the wake of market forces—unemployment, crime, delinquency, family instability, mental illness—can now be more effectively treated in the context of the community. For all these advantages it is feasible and important to take steps toward increasing local autonomy. The question remains whether such steps can be viable in the face of market forces still operating on local communities.

VIABILITY: LOCAL SELF-RELIANCE

We have said that the degree to which a community can become economically viable and self-reliant is no longer a matter of serious interest to planners. We define viability as the degree to which people can handle their own economic problems without excessive dependency on outside institutions. Viability is different from autonomy

in the sense that it is one thing to be formally independent and another thing to be able to solve one's own economic problems. The idea that localities can solve their
own economic problems has become so far removed from
reality that planners do not take it into consideration.
New England, for example, is dependent on other regions
for 80 percent of its food, and it seems impossible that a
community here could approach any self-reliant capability
for producing its own food, much less other major areas
of industry.

Yet self-reliance is not wholly irrelevant, because
localities can become overly dependent upon outside entities and thus lose their capacity for problem solving.
Company towns, one-industry cities, and sleeper suburbs
illustrate such dependency. They have legal autonomy
yet can be quickly destroyed by their need for outside
sustenance and support. People living there do not have
the knowledge, skills, resources, and industry to sustain
the life of the locality. It is important therefore to invest
in some degree of economic viability as part of the goal of
restoring community life.

We shall speak here of economic viability and self-
reliance as more realistic than the radical concept of self-
sufficiency. Economic viability is concerned with issues of
community survival and is best conceived on a continuum
from high to low degrees of capability for a community to
solve its economic problems. Self-sufficiency may develop
in the future, with the aid of new technology, but the
practical concern today is to restore a new degree of local
viability in the face of the market forces that destroy it.

Detroit has been a city with a limited degree of viability. It was so dependent upon the automobile industry
that when that industry declined in 1975, the city declined.
The unemployment rate went up dramatically as did crime,
delinquency, and drug addiction. The city almost went
bankrupt and is still attempting to restore itself. Some
Detroit leaders argue that the process of gaining economic
viability should not be dependent upon the comback of the
auto industry.

Dan Luria and Jack Russell have described a new
plan of economic self-governance for Detroit through a
more diversified economy and new structures of local autonomy similar to those we have been describing. They believe that new enterprises should be organized to maximize
social accountability to employees and the community, which

means organizing companies in which workers participate in ownership and management and creating a nonprofit, tax-exempt community corporation structured for local accountability to provide capital for new worker enterprises. Individual investors would be offered stock but without disturbing local control. New capital investment would include the use of local pension funds. Michigan-headquartered private pension funds include five of the 100 largest, with nearly $20 billion in assets. Luria and Russell say that unions must win joint control over area-wide investment banks that guarantee a minimum rate of return to pension funds while targeting a portion of the funds to city enterprises. They also project a new conception of the land-assemblage process in which public-worker-community authority dominates. These recommendations are close to what we have described as creating local autonomy, and they go a step further toward what we now want to describe as local viability.[5]

The self-directed steps of a locality toward establishing greater viability involve what we call a series of contractions and expansions. The term contraction means here a movement to bring economic resources closer to home, which requires developing (1) ecological loops and (2) economic diversity. Expansion means getting in touch with a wider scope of resources outside the locality in the region, the nation, and the world at large, which requires developing (1) export-import trade and (2) institutions of research and development. Finally, we will discuss social inventions in business that make possible the simultaneous action of these opposing tendencies.

Contraction (Centripetal Action)

Ecological Loops

Ecologists have a theory of closed-loop systems wherein the wastes of one production system become the raw materials for another. For example, the carbon dioxide that human beings breathe out as waste is needed by plants and trees. Green plants combine the carbon dioxide with water and light energy to make food. All our food comes eventually from this important activity: animals eat the plants and humans eat the animals; in turn, humans and other animals give off their waste, which is taken by plants as food to survive. This is a closed loop.

Some cities are beginning to invest in closed-loop systems. To illustrate, garbage is a waste material that is also a mix of raw materials that have value. Discarded aluminum is worth about 17 cents a pound to community recycling centers, and recycling has the indirect benefit of reducing garbage-disposal costs. Compressing the aluminum lowers the shipping cost to the central manufacturing plant, raising the value by 25 percent. Smelted and formed into ingots, the value rises again to more than 50 cents a pound. If the ingot becomes, say, bicycle handlebars, the value of the aluminum is more than a dollar a pound. A city that invests in this type of loop takes a step toward economic self-reliance.[6]

Careful investors can look for innovations in technology that lead to loop systems. One instance is the increased use of steel-belted radial tires, which has made it uneconomical to use conventional mechanical shredding processes for worn-out tires. Instead, new techniques are using liquid nitrogen to freeze the tires to hundreds of degrees below zero, and the rubber is then pulverized. The rubber is converted into a wide variety of products, from shoe soles to floorboard or road-surfacing agents. Again, a waste product becomes the supply for a production process. Another instance of innovative technology involves city sewage being turned into useful products. The city of Hercules, California, chose to build a sewage plant called Aquacell. The system consists of an inflated polyethylene greenhouse cover built over three lagoons where city waste is treated. Duckweed and water hyacinths grow on each lagoon's surface, existing on nutrients in the waste water. The sun is screened out to inhibit algae growth. The plants can then be harvested or composted by themselves or along with the sludge to produce fertilizer. Harvested alone, the plants, high in protein, can become animal feed. Methane is also generated during the transformation process and is used to fulfill some of the electrical requirements of the system itself. Here again, a scientific innovation is applied to the creation of a loop system for the locality.

Certain communities are exploiting their special environments. Oceanside and Davis, California, require solar hot water systems for all new homes. Springfield, Vermont, is completing a hydroelectric facility that will allow it to sell power to the utility from which it had been purchasing power for 30 years. Clayton, New Mexico,

gets 15 percent of its electricity from a wind turbine;
Burlington, Vermont, gets about the same percentage from
wood. The Harbor School District in Erie, Pennsylvania,
developed two wells of natural gas between 1978 and 1980
and converted 34 vehicles, including 25 buses, to com-
pressed natural gas. The wells paid for themselves in 17
months, and because the gas burns cleaner than gasoline,
vehicle maintenance has been much reduced.

All communities can make better use of their environment. Buildings can tap the warmth of the soil and
groundwater by means of heat pumps. The heat lost in
burning oil and gas is usually wasted, from 30 percent in
most residential burners to over 55 percent in some industrial processes. An alternative exists in cogeneration systems that halve electricity bills. Massive cogenerators
provide virtually all the heat and power needs of multi-
plant industrial complexes, but the smallest units look
like small compression engines for cars. For example, Fiat
introduced the Total Energy Module System (TOTEM) that
sells for $15,000 and generates heat and electricity for up
to eight houses. The household power plant is almost here.

In sum, investment in closed-loop systems helps to
increase the economic viability of the community. It reduces local dependency on outside technology and it gives
support to people seeking to maintain local autonomy.

Economic Diversity

Cities are like developing nations in that they can
become dominated by one industry. When the industry
fails, the whole city declines. This has been the fate of
hundreds of cities as well as Detroit. People in Weirton,
West Virginia, have experienced a successful worker takeover of their steel plant, which gives them more autonomy;
but it does not give them viability. Their single industry
is still dependent upon the market for steel; in spite of a
major step toward worker control, they could be destroyed
as a community by a change in steel prices on the national
or world market.

It is important, therefore, for social planners to
take a careful look at the economic diversity of a community, including the structure of the economy relative to
basic human needs. The summary below covers what an-
thropologists generally consider to be the physical needs
of people. We are interested in how economic activities
develop around these needs as well as how they are taken

out of the market system. The community may gain in local autonomy but investment in these products and services is a mark of its viability.

1. food: local access to varied food supplies starting with agricultural production and moving through distribution to retail outlets,
2. housing: availability of diverse construction firms to build housing for everyone in the community,
3. clothing: local access to textiles and seasonal garments from production to distribution,
4. transportation: local access to different sources for production and delivery of transport vehicles,
5. communications: availability of adequate media technology for everyone in the locality, and
6. health: local provision of sufficient care for mind and body.

There are other important human needs in religious life, recreation, and so on, but the above activities supply physical needs related to survival. A small community concerned with achieving relative self-reliance should be concerned with optimizing the local production of these goods and services.

Most communities and large cities are simply concerned with maintaining a minimum degree of viability. It is rare to aim for relative self-sufficiency in the production of housing, clothing, food, and transportation. To do so means avoiding overdependency on one type of business as the foundation of the community and rather emphasizing a broad production base and not becoming a "retail city" or a "recreation city" or a "government city." It means creating more diverse production. At the very least, it means providing adequate housing, water, sewerage, and electrical facilities. Each step that a community takes to develop diverse production increases its viability. In this way it underwrites an interest in maintaining local autonomy.

A community can gain in legal autonomy and lose its economic viability. The aim of community development, therefore, is to increase economic viability so that the locality will become less subject to the destructive forces of a national market.

Expansion (Centrifugal Action)

Import-Export Trade

Jane Jacobs looks at the city as a settlement that consistently generates economic growth from its own local production. The city begins with its own production and then develops a "reciprocal dynamic" through trade with other cities.[7]

Detroit began as a settlement in the early 1800s with a small flour trade. Then small shipyards developed to enable a flour trade with other lake cities. By the 1840s, the yards had found customers for their ships in other lake ports and even along the coast. Machinists from the flour mills were transferring their skills to create some of the first steamships. The export work grew and the yards were supporting a collection of engine manufacturers, parts makers, and suppliers of fittings and materials. By the 1860s, marine engines were a major export, and some were being sold in Europe. This basic mode of production had a multiplier effect in the economy. There were also refineries and smelters that supplied copper alloys made from local ores to manufacturers of valves and engine brightwork. Between about 1860 and 1880, copper was Detroit's biggest export.

Jacobs says that a city like Detroit develops by two mechanisms. The first is import replacement. As imports are received and become known, consumers demand that they be produced locally. Local people devise their own techniques of production and are often able to supplant imports because of the saving in transport cost. The second mechanism is innovation. Continuing effort to develop new products for export means that their production can generate a new multiplier effect and bring in new imports that are eventually supplanted by local products. When this creative cycle is broken, the city begins to decay. This is what happened in Detroit.

The Detroit study by Luria and Russell (Rational Reindustrialization) aims at the re-creation of this cycle of import replacement and innovation. Without having read the recent work of Jacobs, they write,

> A rational economic development agenda must
> be centered on replacing the declining private
> activities of the city--auto assembly, parts and
> machining--with new activities that take maximum

advantage of the existing industrial linkages. There are many activities that produce desirable goods and services for a national as well as a local market that fail to exploit these linkages. For example, a bakery may produce bread for the Midwest market, but it doesn't salvage the tool and die shops whose auto industry orders are drying up.[8]

They then advance a new set of social criteria for determining the direction for Detroit's community development and find four types of products that meet all the criteria: 1) deep natural gas and heavy oil production and upgrading equipment, 2) residential and industrial steam/electric cogeneration units, 3) large and diesel fuel-fired industrial process engines, and 4) mine-mouth coal gasifiers. The authors are recommending principles that would help restore the economic viability of Detroit.

Detroit has begun to follow some of these principles in its attempts at recovery, but it is not the only city that is vulnerable to the forces of a national market and capable of recovery. Any city could institute periodic self-studies of the local economy in this manner and then establish agencies to encourage product innovation and import replacement. The city government could do this through its own agencies but at best it should sponsor community corporations in the private sector to assume this responsibility. We will discuss later the role of such corporations in the polity of community development.

A city should institute self-studies not simply for the city at large but also for its neighborhoods. If neighborhoods themselves are not innovating and engaging in import-export trade, they will suffer their own decline. The history of the city then repeats itself as depressed neighborhoods produce crime instead of commerce. The challenge of investment today is to restore neighborhood viability. It can be part of the larger plan of city development designed to revitalize community life. When cities invest in community development, they support the needed transformation toward local autonomy and help reduce the power that the national market has gained over their fate.

Research and Development

Another way in which a U.S. community develops is by expanding its knowledge base. Knowledge is a critical factor in the development of a postindustrial society and is increasingly important with the rise of new technology frontiers. It is no less important an economic factor today than are land, labor, and capital. Knowledge is a marketable item. It can also be localized and socialized in order for a community to maintain its viability.

A program in community development that seeks to restore local viability requires an educational and scientific foundation to keep in touch with the latest developments in technology and product research. For this reason, it is vital that communities expand their connections with institutes of technology and universities that can maintain ongoing studies of the development process.

A model strategy in this direction is the Greenhouse Compact devised in Rhode Island. Even though the plan was voted down largely on tax issues, it remains useful as a design for community economic development. The Compact includes creation of programs to enhance the contribution made by institutions of higher education to social and economic development in Rhode Island communities. If implemented, it would have involved the creation of a general research institute at the state university to assist companies in special areas of research, product development, and product testing; the creation of an academy of science and engineering, for industrial development; and the authorization of the use of public pension funds for venture capital. The goals of the Compact were to reduce unemployment to levels 25 to 30 percent below the national unemployment rate and to raise the average wage to within 12 to 13 percent of the national level.

The "greenhouses" were planned as independent nonprofit institutions for conducting research and consulting with government and industry; they would have helped to identify products and services, locate entrepreneurs, and finance new companies or product-development efforts. The Compact recommended that a customized training program be established for an expanding market in knowledge that would be localized through contracts with the institutions of higher education and thus create a more viable base for community development.[9]

Social Inventions: Decentralizing Business

The expansion of the local economy toward national and world trade is essential at the same time that local

people contract their control over land, labor, and capital.
This appears to be a contradiction under the present system of business, but it becomes possible through business
management based on decentralized systems of authority.

The decentralizing process in business has already
begun by economic necessity. Many executives today have
found that sheer bigness does not pay off. This was first
observed in the wreck of the Penn Central and the cost-
overrun catastrophes of Lockheed and Douglas Aircraft.
It was seen to be still more serious in the decline of the
A&P and many other conglomerate failures. W. T. Grant
was once the third largest variety store in the United
States, but it had to file for bankruptcy after amassing
debts of $1.8 billion, largely from overexpansion. The co-
founders of the Daylin retailing empire found that their
huge bureaucracy could not respond adequately to new
technology and the changing world market, and their for-
tunes waned. The big airline companies--TWA, Eastern,
and Pan American--became victims of overordering costly
jumbo jets. The reality is that corporations can become
too big to be managed effectively in a command system.
Although the Reagan administration has encouraged con-
glomeration, every industry has also been in process of
adjusting to overbigness by dismantling or decentralizing.

Some industry decentralization has taken place
through increased worker participation. We have mentioned that employees in the Philadelphia stores of the
ailing A&P purchased and are now managing the stores.
Employees in the subsidiary of General Motors in Hyatt,
New Jersey, have purchased the local plant and contracted
for production with their former Detroit employer. Worker
management in a big firm is good for decentralizing authority but not sufficient in itself unless it becomes more
locality based.

Peter Drucker's concept of "federal decentralization"
is a process of altering the management system so that the
corporation becomes a number of autonomous businesses.
Each has responsibility for its own performance, its own
results, and its own contribution to the total company.
Each unit has its own management and can have its own
board of directors: "Federal decentralization has great
clarity and considerable economy. It makes it easy for
each member of the autonomous business to understand his
own task and to understand the task of the whole business.
It has high stability and yet is adaptable."10

One of federal decentralization's greatest strengths is "manager development." Each manager is close enough to business performance to get immediate feedback on his own task. This humanizes the work force, increases employee authority, and at the same time is more efficient. Drucker says,

> The federal principle therefore enables us to divide large and complex organizations into a number of businesses that are small and simple enough so that managers can know what they are doing and can direct themselves toward the performance of the whole instead of becoming prisoners of their own work, effort, and skill.[11]

Drucker points to some of the efficiencies of decentralized systems. He describes how Alfred Sloan first experimented with decentralizing within General Motors; a new level of autonomy and efficiency developed in the management of its car manufacturing divisions. He notes that a bigger step toward decentralization occurred in Sears, Roebuck that eliminated the need for middle management. A Sears vice-president oversees 300 stores, each an autonomous unit responsible for marketing and profits. Each store manager may have 30 section managers, each running an autonomous unit and responsible for meeting marketing and profit goals. Hence there are only two levels between the lowest management job (section manager in a store) and the president: the store manager and the regional vice-president.

Johnson & Johnson, a mammoth multinational producer of health-care products, has taken still one more step in federal decentralization. For many years it has limited the size of autonomous local businesses to 250 employees. Each has its own complete mangement and board of directors, and local business reports directly to a small, parent-company top-management team. Even with sales of over a billion dollars and more than 40,000 employees, Johnson & Johnson states there is a need to operate in such fashion.

The Milwaukee Journal is not mentioned by Drucker, but it has taken the next qualitative leap toward federal decentralization. It developed as a worker-owned company in the 1950s when the original owners sold their stock to the employees. As the company expanded and bought other companies, it used the conventional form of command management. Employees in the new subsidiaries have now been given the right to purchase stock and can place representatives on the central board of directors. This is development toward a true federation of autonomous businesses.

The overall direction of management decentralization can be schematized on a gradient of increasing controls for local businesses (see Figure 6.2).

Figure 6.2

Decentralizing Authority

Command system – – – – – Federation – – – – – Confederation

(G.M.) (Sears) (Johnson & Johnson) (Milwaukee Journal) (NAM)

General Motors is on the far left of the gradient; it was decentralized significantly under Sloan but still retains a relatively strong central command system. Sears is more decentralized than G.M. in regard to local outlets and marketing functions. Johnson & Johnson is still more decentralized, with local boards of directors. All these firms, nonetheless, remain within the category of a command system. It is a qualitative leap from this system to the Milwaukee Journal, where local firms have representatives on a central board of directors. This would be the next logical step for Johnson & Johnson if it wished to decentralize into a true federation.

The next qualitative step in decentralization involves the confederation, in which local corporations are given full power to operate independently without any top-down controls, as in a trade association. This does not necessarily make the organization weak. Modern methods of communication make the confederation in many ways more effective and efficient than the more-centralized forms of control. For example, the National Association of Manufacturers (NAM) can quickly communicate with the 14,000 plants owned by its member companies through computerized mailing. It seems that NAM mobilizes political and economic information rapidly on issues of common concern in the manufacturing field. All trade associations are confederations of independent yet cooperating businesses.

Many of them are, in their own way, more powerful nationally than large businesses operating under a command system. Indeed, computer networks manifest the enhanced
power that loose alliances acquire in an information
economy.

Federal decentralization is a social invention in the
private sector that encourages the simultaneous forces of
contraction and expansion for local communities. A local
business can expand its market through franchises and
autonomous businesses in other cities and nations. A national business may decentralize its subsidiaries into federated local units. Experience has shown that the decentralized enterprise can often be a more-efficient and
-effective way of doing business.

If Johnson & Johnson were to develop a national
board of directors on which representatives of its local
boards would participate, the local firms would gain in
power and reduce the likelihood of shutdowns. They would
increase their local viability by virtue of their representation at the national level and also increase their moti-
vation to succeed as profit centers within the federation.

The democratic federation is a common form of management in the nonprofit sector of the economy and has
served well in the economic affairs of such varied organizations as the Presbyterian Church, the YWCA, the Rotary
Club, trade unions, and the Chamber of Commerce. It
could be the next step in the organization of the profit
sector, giving local people greater control over the locality
while maintaining access to national and international
trade. This may become an important direction for social-
sector development in the years ahead.

POLITY: LOCAL SOCIAL ACCOUNTABILITY

The concept of polity refers to the way power is distributed in the community, not simply the formal distribution of power through the local government but rather
through the total community with its various organizations
and variegated class structure. Creating a democratic
polity in this larger sense is more difficult than creating
a democratic government. It means undoing the class inequities in the local economy while maximizing the overall
community income; it involves overcoming the destructive
forces of the market without succumbing to an economic
decline.

We are interested in the issues of polity in the local system of enterprises in part because we think it is connected to the resolution of social problems. The creation of greater equity in the economic organization of the locality should offer a better opportunity to treat the problems of slums, crime, delinquency, divorce, mental disorders, and so on.

This new step in community development will require investing in a system of local corporations so that people can share power more responsibly in the round of local life and will require as well supporting structures of social accountability in the business sector within the context of the whole community. The social mechanisms for achieving the objective of sharing power have already been legally created but have not yet been implemented as part of a coordinated plan. We have already discussed some of these mechanisms, such as community corporations and worker-owned firms. A new planning strategy requires imagination on this legal and social frontier. The question is whether we are ready today for a coordinated plan of development.

The local government is in a central position to help advance this mode of self-development. No other institution could assume the leadership role as well. Of course, doing so would place government in a paradoxical position. It would be authorizing and encouraging a method of planning that would reduce its own power; that is, it would be setting up the organizations in the economy that would take government out of solving the problems of the city and initiating a method of nonmarket development that could stabilize growth and local self-management. The municipal government must look outside itself for community groups to perform this task. It cannot act entirely on its own or it becomes self-defeating. It must support private corporations in a position to promote cooperative processes in the market system.

A corporation created by law to encourage cooperation and represent the whole community outside the government is the community development corporation (CDC). The government would do well to examine the grounds for supporting this structure to act on its behalf as an agent of social development.

The Community Development Corporation

The community development corporation is a democratically organized corporation designed to operate in the interest of the locality. All citizens in its geographic area are given, by means of their purchase of a low-cost share (e.g., $5), the right to vote for a board of directors that sets corporation policy. The board is in a unique position to provide a coordinating plan for establishing a more-equitable economy in the locality.

The CDC was created as a legal structure in 1967 by the Ninetieth Congress as a method for overcoming pockets of poverty in communities across the nation. Congress was responding to city riots that were reactions to the destructive forces of the market. CDCs began to organize slowly with marginal support from the Office of Economic Opportunity in various cities. A few CDCs, such as those in Bedford-Stuyvesant in New York City and the Hough area of Cleveland, Ohio, have become known nationally for some of their efforts, but CDCs never reached a point of take-off. About 1,000 have been created in the nation. They have been evaluated at different times for effectiveness and have been given moderate marks of success, but they have never been notable for making revolutionary changes in the local market economy.

Our argument is that CDCs never had a methodology for overcoming the excesses of the market. A few people envisioned them with the single purpose of overcoming the destructive effects of the market, but the vision had no overall plan. Consequently, the CDC has always been considered a relatively insignificant entity for treating local problems associated with poverty. It operates within the competitive market to create jobs, with no larger purpose of economic conversion. Many CDCs have at times been embroiled in local politics, which slows them down, but their growth has been checked by the national markets' acting against the social development of city neighborhoods.

Nevertheless, the CDC has taken helpful steps toward initiating a wide variety of local enterprises, including shopping plazas, housing construction, electronics plants, supermarkets, restaurants, factories, and job training programs. The enterprises admittedly have been established largely within the competitive-market framework of land, capital, and labor and hence are unable to always overcome the damaging process of community decline. And CDCs

have not systematically acted to introduce the legal frameworks we have been discussing: land trusts, community
banks, and worker cooperatives. But the opportunity is
increasingly seen by community leaders as these other innovative firms grow in number.

The next step in the development of the CDC, therefore, involves a new plan of social development. It also
involves providing broader support nationally through
long-term planning, equity capital, debt financing, and
technical assistance. These CDCs are in a position to
provide the thrust for forming a system of local corporations operating outside the market forces. They represent
the functional equivalent to formal government operating
in the private sector of the local economy (see Figure 6.3).

Figure 6.3

The Local Economy: An Alternative Model

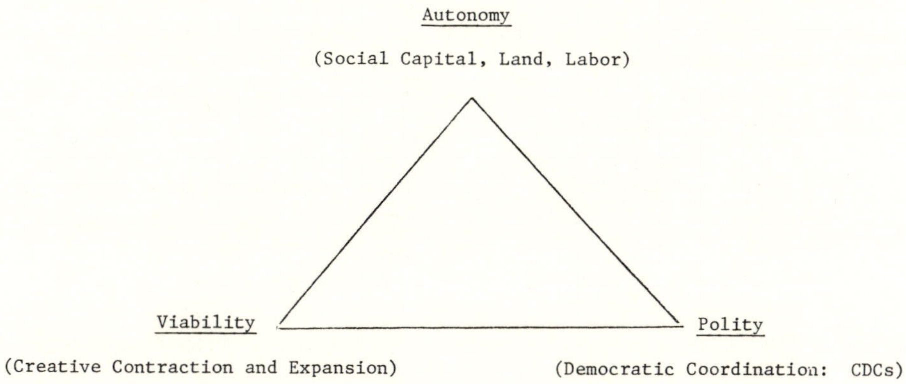

Autonomy

(Social Capital, Land, Labor)

Viability

(Creative Contraction and Expansion)

Polity

(Democratic Coordination: CDCs)

A Coordinated Plan: CDCs

The new direction for the CDC in the United States
involves planning for the simultaneous contraction and expansion of the community economy. It does this on the
one hand by localizing controls through community land
trusts, community finance institutions, and worker-owned
firms and by developing ecological loops and a greater
diversity for the local economy, while on the other hand
helping to broaden local resources through import-export
trade and forging a new link with higher education.

Finally, it negotiates both the expansion of local firms becoming globally connected and the contraction process by which global firms develop local controls through corporate federations.

We have spoken about how knowledge must be added as an economic factor along with land, labor, and capital. Knowledge has always been a latent factor in the market system, but today it has become a significant force as the professions become a central part of the service economy and essential to the development of new technology.

The CDC is a channel through which communities localize and democratize knowledge. The Greenhouse Compact plan is one example of how this new force of knowledge might become harnessed for local advantage. The CDC is the logical agency to help implement it, with the aid of university faculties in its region. This becomes part of its central role in reconstructing the foundations of the local economy.

There are innovative experiments underway today for investors to examine. The city of Burlington, Vermont, has initiated a program of investment that combines community land trusts and employee ownership along the lines we have been suggesting. It has begun to implement a model plan for developing new private ventures based on the following criteria:

1. market viability: judging the capacity of new businesses on traditional standards of market needs and business skills of the principals;
2. quality local employment: creating jobs having better than median regional wages, potential for skill enhancement, and for employee participation in company decision making;
3. traded or exported goods or services: giving preference to ventures that export their products in outside markets to encourage an inflow of new dollars;
4. local ownership: assuming that the more "equitably held the local ownership structure--with full employee ownership as the ideal--the more likely the firm will maintain local roots, and the more equitable will be the sharing of rewards and responsibilities"; and
5. diversity of economic base: spreading investments "across diverse industrial or service groups."

Especially noteworthy is the creation of a "nonprofit Local Ownership Development Corporation" (LODC). The function of the LODC is to receive funds for investment in employee-owned firms and to stimulate the development of such enterprises. Social investors will learn by investigating the Burlington venture.[12]

The innovative enterprises we have been discussing are not normally part of any concerted plan for community development. The members of local cooperatives, land trusts, and community development finance institutions are not commonly aware that together they are a legal system for overcoming the destructive forces of the market. There is no central agency to consult with them about their common purpose, to build the locality into a more self-governing community. The CDC could help develop local autonomy and viability by organizing these firms in business and commerce. It could help create worker-owned businesses and promote their products in a national and international market without losing autonomy and viability. The new role for the CDC could be to promote the development of the locally oriented enterprises in the context of an overall community plan. The CDC is in a special position to assume this role because of its democratic base and overall purpose for development outside city government. In fact, it could help to unite these seedling enterprises into a local movement. The CDC could call together representatives of the enterprises to explore their common goals and policies in the locality, and together they could implement policies having statewide and national implications.

Let us look at what a CDC might do as a model experiment for social investors. When employees purchase shut-down plants, the CDC staff talk to employees about how a community land trust is important to develop because it can keep the property from becoming a marketable item. It preserves local control over land use in case future employees decide to sell to an outside corporation. A land trust board would give the employees the right to use the land in perpetuity.

Let us follow the model experiment further. The new worker cooperative may need capital to start the enterprise, and the CDC would tell them about community finance institutions. A CDCU may be available locally for capital, or there may be a special revolving loan fund such as the ones created by the Industrial Cooperative Association and the Institute for Community Economics in Massachusetts. When the workers get their enterprise going, they may want to provide a percentage of their profits as a charitable (tax exempt) contribution to a land trust or CDCU. In these ways they contribute to the larger local movement to build community-oriented enterprises.[13]

The CDC itself may have a way to go in accommodating to the new plan because it has not been oriented in this direction. The CDC and the CDCU have both lent money regularly to traditional capitalist enterprises, which then become part of the national market. They have not capitalized shopping centers with a land trust charter or normally funded new enterprises such as worker cooperatives. Their capital has been simply an instrument of the market system. The CDC has often been separate from the cooperative movement at both the local and the national level.

One of the tasks of the CDC in the new plan is to help community finance institutions localize capital while expanding export-import trade. A key problem of impoverished localities is the outflow of capital without an adequate return to residents. This type of capital outflow could be redirected and localized.

Much rethinking of CDC goals must go into the new more-coordinated plan. The CDC has made mistakes in capitalizing the market system and thereby limited its own potential as a force for social development. For example, it occasionally buys conventional enterprises and maintains ownership; this simply plays into the capitalist process of stock ownership and outside control. It is regressive for two reasons. First, purchase of the firms ties up CDC equity so that it cannot continue to utilize its capital for start-ups or other constructive purposes. Second, management in the CDC-owned enterprise is appointed from the outside by the CDC; the CDC thereby can dominate the workers in the same manner as an outside capitalist. It is better for the CDC to capitalize and support independently operated business cooperatives, still aiding as a business consultant but not acting in an outside ownership capacity (see Figure 6.4).

The CDC would inform community banks about the methods for successfully spawning socially owned companies in Mondragón, Spain, where cooperatives have been created effectively for over 40 years. The Mondragón Bank has devised a method for making small business cooperatives succeed. Bank staff utilize a special system of supervision and training in the development of a cooperative, and its success is a part of the bank's highest priority. The

Figure 6.4

Model of Community Development

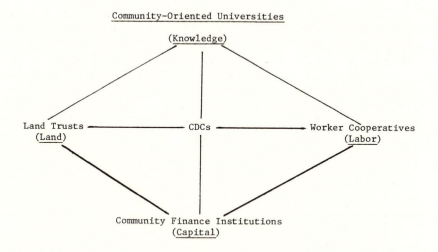

cooperative later becomes involved in the bank's self-management, as part of a federation of cooperatives created by the bank for its governance.

In light of this plan for local development, the CDC should:

1. encourage employees to purchase cooperative equity in the firms they now own;
2. sponsor new businesses on principles of worker owner-ship and self-management;
3. facilitate linkages between cooperatives, land trusts, community banks, and other democratically based groups;
4. establish a center for new entrepreneurship with ven-ture capital directed toward the cooperative movement;
5. support programs combining skill training and coopera-tive education for the unemployed, former convicts, minorities, youth, drug addicts, and delinquents in the neighborhood; and
6. cultivate relationships with local colleges and univer-sities to institute community self-studies directed to-ward the social development of the local economy.

FINAL ARGUMENTS

The Source of Capital Investment

Some community analysts have argued that there are no funds available to risk toward a new direction in community development, but others point out that the real problem is the proper placement of investable funds, that is, redirection of existing capital flows. The greatest potential for socially redirecting capital flows is in the pension funds. Their advantages are their size, their long-term perspective, and their established use of social criteria. State pension laws and the Employee Retirement Income Security Act (ERISA) have relaxed the prudent-investor rule in the past few years, allowing more flexibility in placement of funds. Thirty-one states have undertaken socially targeted pension investment for economic development.[14]

Patrick McVeigh believes that overcoming a capital shortage does not mean seeking easier access to pension-fund capital but rather finding more-efficient vehicles for its deployment.[15] He points to three major movements in the targeting of pension funds to illustrate the potential for redeployment: one involves housing; another, small business development; the third, equity financing. He argues that although social investors have placed their capital in all three directions, they have simply tended to displace private capital and therefore still represent new sources for socially directed capital investment. Let us follow his argument.

First, housing investment has been a high priority for social investors. In June 1983, 31 states held $14.7 billion in housing securities through their state-administered pension funds, but it is doubtful that they have had any effect on increasing the level of affordable housing. The bulk of the investments are in mortgage-backed securities of the Government National Mortgage Association (GNMA, called Ginnie Mae). The GNMA guarantees payment of principal and interest on privately issued securities that are backed by pools of government-issued or government-guaranteed mortgages. Ginnie Maes yield competitive rates, are liquid, and are relatively risk free. They are popular with managers of pension funds seeking to achieve social goals through the development of local housing.

Studies show that by investing in Ginnie Maes, pension funds have merely displaced private investors.[16] The Federal Reserve of Boston has concluded that the purchase of GNMA securities by pension funds apparently does not increase the supply of mortgage money. A withdrawal of pension funds from GNMA would not affect the home mortgage market because private investors would quickly fill this gap. These funds, therefore, could be available for a new cooperatively based plan for community development. There is still a need to investigate further where that replacement funding will come from and what organization might be temporarily short of capital in the transfer process.

Second, managers of public pension funds frequently purchase Small Business Administration loans, partly to support the values of local development but also because 90 percent is guaranteed by the federal government. The loans have a competitive rate with little risk. Again, it is doubtful that the SBA loans are responsible for an infusion of money for economic development. Pension-fund investments simply displace private capital and continue to finance conventional business and perpetuate the problems of the market. But this is an important source of capital because SBA loans permit support for employee-owned businesses and other community-oriented firms while remaining relatively risk free for the investor.

Third, the equity market has been a prominent vehicle for pension funds. Sometimes ERISA regulations have been interpreted so as to restrict equity investments to only the largest and most-successful firms, but a current restructuring of the market is producing a significant change in the rationale for this vehicle. The restructuring began with a movement to restrict investments in companies doing business in South Africa. There are today 28 states, eight cities, and various private pension funds (e.g., the United Auto Workers and the International Ladies Garment Union) that have taken action to divest funds from companies in South Africa. This capital is available to middle-sized, non-blue-chip firms.

In sum, capital is available for investment toward frontiers in community development. First, the funds for GNMA housing can be redirected experimentally toward co-op housing with no higher risk of investment; these investments may also include community land trusts under the guidance of CDCs. Second, funds available for typical

small business loans can be redirected toward employee
ownership and self-management and other community-oriented
corporations without increasing the risk of investment.
Third, the funds for equity investment in big corporations
involved in South Africa can be redirected toward middle-
sized firms taking steps toward employee ownership.   These
steps might be taken through a cooperative-oriented stock-
ownership plan; the equity could also be sold gradually
to the employees under the guidance of the local CDC.   In
general, these funds would then encourage the development
of an economy that is still competitive but increasingly
based on principles of cooperation.

Finally, big corporations that undergo some reduction
in stock prices have the option of decentralizing so that
their subsidiaries gain local autonomy and the entire administration becomes governed more directly on the principles of a federation.   We have noted how this pattern of
administration can be economically beneficial to a company,
but it is also advantageous to investors interested in local
development because the national market helps to ensure
their liquidity.   Also, for social investors it suggests a
greater balance in the flow of funds from overcapitalized
areas to undercapitalized areas.   The administration of a
federation tends to equalize the distribution of internal
capital among its units in wages, investments in new technology, and expansion.   Greater local control increases
the likelihood that capital does indeed flow to necessary
local projects and does not just displace private capital.
The investment does not then lead to more deindustrialization.   For local employees, it increases job security, provides greater control over their own economic resources,
and allows them to gain the benefits of a national market.
Put another way, the decentralized firm can help increase
the viability and the autonomy of the local economy as
well as its own vitality and profit-making ability.   In
sum, if the changes are done effectively, everybody wins.

An Experimental Approach

The pattern of social development recommended here
is a starting place for experiments in overcoming the effects of the competitive market.   This plan is designed to
test the transformability of the market where it leads to
undesirable ends.   It is intended as a way to break the

national markets' stranglehold on the locality, but it should be seen as an investment pattern to be constantly studied and evaluated as the changes are made.

The new policy could mean concentrating investments in neighborhoods or sections of the city without attempting a massive metropolitan change, testing each alternative corporation for its capacity to localize labor, land, capital, and knowledge. It also means testing how these corporations work together effectively in the contexts of particular localities. Dozens of social, legal, and political issues must be settled as these four components of the market are simultaneously introduced in a suburb, a ghetto, or a central business district. If changes are made too rigidly or massively, they could result in more problems than they are intended to resolve.

Altering these four components of the market to any significant degree could also have a major effect on the local power structure and local culture. The plan implies a slow reversal in the "great change" toward vertical power. It means reintroducing a new form of horizontal power through the work of the CDC and other community organizations. Furthermore, under employee ownership and democratic banking, the business sector may begin to change its values. It may begin to look more like the nonprofit sector. The process will require systematic observation so that adjustments can be made from time to time because the social and cultural effect of the structural changes cannot be easily anticipated. Therefore, it is important to have continuing studies conducted with the aid of local colleges and universities.

The Multilevel Community

One argument against increasing the power of the local community in the United States is based on what the community was like a century ago. It was not all friendliness, cooperation, and amity. The early community often contained prejudice, discriminatory practices, and elitism, which could be seen as the danger in returning controls to the locality. The argument has merit, but is countered by two fundamental changes that are introduced in this plan.

First, the old community was under a local market system. Much of the elitism and discriminatory practices came from the fact that a few families controlled the land

and the businesses. The new community suggested here is
based on democratizing patterns of ownership and management; former patterns of elite ownership and control are
less likely to be reproduced.

Second, the expansion of the local community through
business federations reduces the likelihood that the former
conditions of localism will repeat themselves. The top
boards of federations located outside the community (e.g.,
churches, YMCAs) have often taken positive steps in recent
times to reduce discrimination and prejudice at local levels
of their organization. Also, the mass media have had a
positive effect in broadening the local acceptance of ethnic
and racial differences in corporate life. Similarly, transportation today carries people out of their localities frequently enough to reduce tendencies toward the extreme
provincialism that characterized the village in the past
century.

Third, the re-creation of community life in the modern
locality reduces the intense search for community at the
level of the nation. When a sense of community is not
found in the locality, people search for primitive identi-
ties in the nation, so the loss of community at local levels
has its price in an extreme identification with the nation-
state. Erich Fromm in Escape from Freedom noted the
danger of this drive for a national community in the midst
of the changing and collapsing forms of capitalism in Nazi
Germany. Emile Durkheim clarifies the meaning of this
danger in the tribal totemism and intense collective identity that develops in the "sacred community." The sacred
community today is the nation-state.

The danger today is not so much in localism as in
nationalism. In the nuclear age, the risk of continuing
the destructive effect of the market on local life and permitting its course toward centralizing power in the nation-
state is greater than the risk of augmenting power in the
local community. The loss of the local community to the
market forces of modern nations can result in a still more
intense form of national community going beyond patriotism
to idolatry and war.

Our argument for a new plan to restore local autonomy and viability in the United States is really a call
for balance in the search for community. This step toward
a new balance is an attempt to overcome what Durkheim
once called the "egoism" and "altruism" developing in
modern nations. He found these deviant forms of social

relationship pervading especially the life of modern cities. Egoism (weak solidarity) led to suicide, crime, and family instability. At the level of the nation, altruism (intense solidarity) led to war based on self-sacrifice. The socio- logical problem was to find a balance between these two extremes.

Durkheim believed the anomic (normless) forces of the market system to be a central cause of these problems. He was concerned about the chaotic and cyclical nature of capitalism and called for a new balance in community through a movement for solidarity. It may be on this speculative theory of a needed balance through the search for solidarity that the argument for investing in community development must rest its case.

The local community becomes the final arena for de- cision making and of principal consideration in national planning. The question arises as to how planning deci- sions will affect the local community, which is where the philosophy underlying social development is finally judged. The community can be the locale for creating new forms of enterprise that are both profitable and accountable to the people they affect, where free enterprise need not be re- strained but can be enhanced by norms of justice and democracy. It remains for social planners to chart a new path for business in the context of the community. The continued social transformation of business and the market system is a definite part of the future of the U.S. economy.

NOTES

1. Robert Swann and Ted Webster, The Community Land Trust (Cambridge, Mass.: Center for Community Economic Development, 1972). See also Kirby White and Charles Mathei, "Community Land Trusts," in Beyond the Market and the State, ed. Severyn Bruyn and James Meehan (Philadelphia, Pa.: Temple University Press, 1987).

2. Institute for Community Economics, The Community Land Handbook (Emmaus, Pa.: Rodale Press, 1982), p. 4.

3. Brad Caftel, Community Development Credit Unions (Berkeley, Calif.: National Economic Development Law Project, 1978), p. 38.

4. Ian Keith and Chuck Mathei, "New Developments in Social Investments," in Community Economics (Greenfield, Mass.: Institute for Community Economics) No. 1, Summer, 1983.

5. Dan Luria and Jack Russell, Rational Reindustrialization: An Economic Agenda for Detroit (Detroit, Mich.: Widgetripper Press, 1981).

6. David Morris, The New City States (Washington, D.C.: Institute for Local Self Reliance, 1982); examples of ecological loops are drawn from this book.

7. Jane Jacobs, The Economy of Cities (New York: Random House, 1969); Jane Jacobs, "Cities and the Wealth of Nations," Atlantic Monthly (March 1984).

8. Luria and Russell, Rational Reindustrialization, p. 12.

9. The Greenhouse Compact carried a tax plan that was defeated in a referendum by voters, but the plan remains as a model of development for other states and communities ready to undertake it.

10. Peter Drucker, Management (New York: Harper & Row, 1973), p. 574.

11. Ibid., p. 575.

12. Community Economic Development Office, Jobs and People: A Strategic Analysis of the Greater Burlington Economy, December, 1984. On LODCs, see Christopher Mackin, Strategies for Local Ownership and Control, unpublished paper (Somerville, Mass.: Industrial Cooperative Association, 1983). LODCs function like a trade association of producer co-ops and serve as another community-oriented corporation worthy of consideration for social investors.

13. Similarly, other types of community-oriented banks can be devised experimentally with the creation of consumer co-ops, land trusts, and CDCs themselves. The National Consumer Bank was chartered in 1979 to aid consumer co-ops, while 10 percent of its loans were reserved for producer co-ops. The bank was designed to become owned by the business co-ops to whom it gave loans. As the loans were paid off, these businesses participated in the governance of the bank. Also, the CDC itself has need for capital support. National legislation had been proposed in 1967 with the original legislation to create CDCs to also create a community development bank. The bank would become owned by the CDCs it helped to create. That part of the legislation, however, was never enacted into law. Pending the revival of the legislation, the CDC must develop local banks to help capitalize their expansion.

14. Alicia Munnell, "The Pitfalls of Social Investing," New England Economic Review (September/October 1983):20-37.

15. Patrick McVeigh, "Pension Funds and Industrial Policy: Are the Vehicles Worthy?" (Unpublished paper, Program in Social Economy and Social Policy, based on field research with Franklin Research and Development Corporation, Boston College, Boston, Mass.)

16. Michael Clorves, "Social Investing without Any Tears," Pension and Pension Age, May 12, 1980, p. 10. Quoted in McVeigh, "Pension Funds."

7. Development toward Community Self-Governance in Greece

INTRODUCTION

Our purpose in this chapter is to undertake a macro analysis of community self-governance in Greece, beginning with a schematic historical perspective of local self-government. We trace the loss of community power, caused by the competitive market, the centralization of the administrative system, and the general orientation of national policies toward the local communities. Subsequently, we examine in detail the problems as perceived today by the present administration and the strategies for their solution as articulated in its National Plan for Economic and Social Development 1983-87 to reverse present trends and to control the distorting influences of market forces. We then proceed to a description of the key structural arrangements set up by the present administration, which are expected to contribute to development at the local and regional levels and to carry out specific responsibilities for implementing national policies for the communities and the region. Our analysis is, therefore, concentrated on Plan policies and the provision of structures by which action for communities is taking place in Greece. The 1983-87 Plan includes a focus on autonomy, viability, and polity, as it is directed largely toward the cultivation of local

---

This chapter is strictly descriptive of the situation in Greece. We consider its inclusion here as necessary in order to document our thinking and also to inform the reader who is not familiar with developments in the area of communities of small countries in the process of social change.

government authority. This Plan gains significance for
our purposes because it expresses the vision of the government for social change and is, therefore, a document in
which we may trace socializing developments of vital interest to our perspective.

COMMUNITIES IN GREECE:
A HISTORICAL PERSPECTIVE

In terms of cultural heritage, social structure, social
division of labor, and style of life, the community idea and
local self-government can be seen as part of the Greek
tradition and national identity. The institution of local
government has a long tradition in Greece, dating back to
classical times (confederacy, neighborhood), surviving
through the Roman conquest and the Byzantine Empire. It
has been ascertained historically that in Byzantium there
were communal organizations with an independent existence
whose authorities were elected by the people. During the
Ottoman rule, for four centuries there existed centers that
preserved Greek nationality, the spirit of independence,
and the democratic practices of the enslaved people. During the Turkish rule, from the fifteenth to nineteenth centuries, small communities that operated like small and
closed societies (some of which, like Ambelakia, developed
extraordinary commercial and socioeconomic activity and
entrepreneurial spirit), promoted exports to European commercial centers and established a wide network of commercial connections that made them well known outside Greece.[1]
Scholars of social development have documented the
decline of the autonomy of Greek villages and small towns,
which can be traced as far back as the 1820s, when the
French system of administration of provinces was introduced.
The local government was organized on a strict bureaucratic model that gave absolute control to the state. The
decline in power and self-determination refers to the loss
of local authority by local residents to determine the policy of their basic institutions, whose decision-making power
was increasingly centered in the capital city. This process
has been a complex one related to the model adopted for
building a new state; the political factors; trends of modernization, migration, and urbanization; market forces;
and also to the loss of other features of local community
life.

After World War II, Greece faced an intensification of problems and an even more severe decline in power of its communities. Besides political factors, the intensification of market forces and the centralization of administration caused the weakening of the local community and the overgrowth of the capital city and Thessaloníki. Migration to urban areas of the country as well as to foreign countries (especially to Germany) became a significant factor and involved about a third of the Greek rural population. The decline of community life became more and more acute. Urbanism, together with concentration of authorities in the central government (public services), deprived the local community of some basic elements: its population, its economic activity, its authority, and its power. The local community in Greece, therefore, is no longer a self-reliant locality. It is managed from without and deprived of substantial sources of income, resulting in the lack of acceptable levels of development and an inability to participate in the rapid economic and social development of the country.[2]

According to the 1981 census, there are 5,761 communities in Greece; 82.45 percent of the total number of localities have a population of fewer than 1,000 inhabitants. This dispersion of the population has historical, geographic, and cultural derivation. Communities in Greece, being limited in population, activities, and in many cases contact with other towns, are not self-contained; they are considered within a larger area—the region. The region is a broader administrative district (like the tier-level government in England or the tier local government) and was instituted as a planning area.

Attempts to reverse the unfavorable economic conditions prevailing in the localities and the regions were made in the national plans for economic development and specific regional plans. Recently a new political movement, i.e., PASOK, set forth decentralization in its political program and declared social development a pivotal policy target. There seems to be a change in priorities, orientations, and strategies for community development. The government, representing the above political movement, has intended to take steps in community and regional development by founding new structures of local decision making, citizen participation and "social accountability," decentralization, and confederation. Outside government policy, attempts were made to increase self-sufficiency and autonomy, and a few remarkable innovative efforts of local initiative warrant attention. Changes that favor social development are under formulation, but in many cases they are still relatively ambiguous in the specific direction they will be taking and lack the clarity of models observed in other countries.

The proposed programs of social change supported by the above political movement, which set forth selective principles of development, deserve examination. The social mechanisms for achieving the objective of sharing power and delegating authority have already been legally created in Greek communities. Whereas local plans did not really change, more activities of local character are now transferred to the communities and local initiative is encouraged. The National Plan for Economic and Social Development, 1983–87 promotes policies to revitalize local communities and strengthen local government. Decentralization and regional development constitute fundamental targets and are closely linked to the targets of democratic planning and socialist transformation.

Before 1981, the regional issue was brought up in the 1976–80 and 1978–82 five-year plans as well as in the 1981–85 regional development program. The 1981–85 regional program submitted to the European Economic Community authorities mentions the following basic objectives: to reduce internal migration to the minimum necessary and to retain in every region a viable and adequate population, to improve the standard of living in poorer areas and reduce regional economic and social inequalities, to preserve a satisfactory level of employment in all regions that have been growing at comparatively satisfactory rates, and to accelerate development in areas with slow growth. Regional reconstruction as well as decentralization is placed at the center of development policy in the 1983–87 Five-Year Plan for Economic and Social Development. This Plan aims at a revitalization of the periphery and at reversing the process that has led to the breakdown of productive activity and cultural life in the countryside. To this end, local government is actively encouraged to undertake a variety of tasks, and its organizational set-up along regional and subregional lines is to be carefully planned so as to facilitate its large-scale involvement in local affairs.

It must be noted however that under present economic difficulties, the implementation of the Plan seems to be postponed. It remains to be seen whether achievements made so far will be sustained, whether local plans will be successful from the point of view of management, what will be the role of the local initiative in implementing local level plans, and how the activities entrusted to the local government can be realized without sufficient local economic resources. Our scepticism stems from the fact that the rate of overall economic and social development is still very slow and will depend on future economic and political circumstances.

The community and regional problems in Greece; the 1983-87 Five-Year Plan for Economic and Social Development that attempts to meet these problems; and the structural arrangements referring to capital, land, and labor (i.e., social and economic processes by which the transformation of the social and economic environment is attempted) must be understood in terms of implementation at the local level. Our task now is to describe these processes in respect to some typical and innovative examples and thereby provide a basis for evaluating their efficacy.

THE COMMUNITY AND REGIONAL PROBLEMS

Because of the dispersion of Greek population into a great number of communities (5,761 in 1981), the examination of productive and social activities, the social infrastructure, the transportation networks, and so forth are considered within a larger area, the region. The 1983-87 Five-Year Plan for Economic and Social Development states that the problems of the region are basically of a structural character and a result of the choices made by the state in the postwar era. Main weaknesses are the backwardness of the countryside and dependence of the provinces upon Athens, the disorganization of the productive system in the provinces, and a lack of trained manpower.[3]

After the rural destruction during the 1940-49 war period, devastating reduction of the population of local communities and regions through massive internal and foreign emigration constituted one of the most important regional problems. From 1955 to 1971, more than 1,500,000 people of the countryside migrated either abroad (about 900,000 to Germany) or to the urban areas of the country (600,000 approximately). The desertion of the Greek countryside can be estimated at a pace of 87,000 individuals per year, totaling 33 percent of the rural population, during the above period.

The abandonment of local communities in the provinces was also encouraged by the accumulation of capital in those sectors that offered relatively quick and large profits, like housing construction and trade, sectors of activity mainly developed in the urban centers, particularly Athens. Population movement toward Athens combined with remittances from Greeks working abroad (emigrants' remittances, mostly from EEC countries and Greek seamen) increased investments in real estate in urban areas, favored consumer spending especially for luxury goods and services, and further encouraged the migration to Athens. The concentration of the industrial sector, especially of industrial units dependent on market demand and foreign inflows, in the Athens-Thessaloníki axis and its extension also played a decisive role in the regional problems. Tourism played a similar role and contributed to regional development of some parts of Greece.

Great regional imbalances are observed. On the map on page 223, Athens and Thessaloníki are considered developed regions (area A and B); Macedonia, Thessaly, Sterea Hellas (except Attica), Peloponnese, and Crete are considered regions with potential (area C); and Epirus, Thrace, the Islands of the Eastern Aegean Sea, and the Ionian Islands (except Corfu) are underdeveloped (problematic) regions (area D).[4]

The great concentration of population in Athens and Thessaloníki is intensified by the overcentralization of administrative agencies, infrastructure, and services. According to the 1981 census, however, a relative change in this trend can be observed in a slowdown in the rate of increase of population in Athens, the acceleration of population growth in medium-size towns, and the stabilization of the population in many provinces. But although external migration has stopped, problematic regions (area D) continue losing part of their population. There has been a decrease in regional differences and inequalities, but intraregional inequalities are still of great significance. Expansion is usually taking place in the more-dynamic areas, which absorb the benefits, while the problematic areas continue to decline.

Despite some improvements, such as in income per capita, social services (education, health, social welfare), and transportation networks and services, the opportunities for the development of the individual are unequally distributed geographically. Generally, conditions are more

Administrative Divisons, Regional Imbalances, and
Differentiation of Incentives for Community and
Regional Development

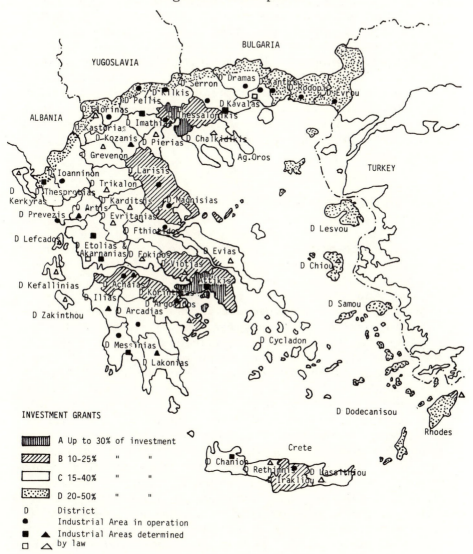

INVESTMENT GRANTS

▥	A	Up to 30% of investment
▨	B	10-25% " "
☐	C	15-40% " "
▦	D	20-50% " "
D		District
●		Industrial Area in operation
■ ▲		Industrial Areas determined
☐ △		by law

favorable in Athens and Thessaloníki, less favorable in
smaller towns, and still less favorable in the agricultural
and mountainous areas and small islands.

As stated in the 1983-87 Plan, the above developments
that led to the disintegration of the social and economic
fabric were further intensified by the lack of effective decentralization and an overcentralized state. The basic
characteristic of local government authorities (OTA) was a

climate of stagnation, caused by the historical tradition of "clientele" politics, centralization, and the perpetuation of the status quo as a result of the combined effect of several negative factors (for example, structural weaknesses like the large number yet small size of communities that do not have facilities to provide necessary services; organizational problems like red tape, bureaucratic mentality, tardiness in decision making, lack of trained personnel, and a lack of the appropriate setting for cooperation and coordination of local government authorities; and economic difficulties like lack of sufficient economic resources allocated by the central government for the provision of local needs).

PROVISION OF THE 1983–87 PLAN FOR DEVELOPMENT
AT THE REGIONAL AND LOCAL LEVEL

The 1983–87 Plan seeks to create the conditions that will allow for an integrated development of Greece, a development that is simultaneously economic, social, technological, and cultural.[5] The former rapid economic improvement is criticized because it was not accompanied by the equivalent cultural progress, the fulfillment of the growing collective needs, but instead ushered in a deterioration of the environment and of the quality of life.

Economic and human resources in the 1983–87 Plan are intended to be organized in the interest of the locality and the entire society and to be accountable to land, labor, and capital in the context of the community. The process of drawing up the Five-Year Plan combined technocratic knowledge with the aspirations of the people by means of organized discussions throughout the country. It also provided for a transition to a democratic planning process. Democratic planning has been applied through the participation of public organizations and local governments in the formulation of the 1983–87 Plan for each prefecture and region of the country. This developmental process, furthermore, is expected to enhance the implementation of projects and infrastructure works determined through democratic planning procedures, in other words, active planning. The 1983–87 Plan is considered the first stage in a political process in which the leading role will be played by the main public and local government organizations, the representatives of the productive sectors, and the state

itself. The institutional reforms; the administrative, economic, social, and cultural decentralization policies; and
the structural changes provided for in the Plan aim at the
creation of conditions for the development of productive
forces. Again, even thought of as overly optimistic, the
Plan points to a desired self-governance. The following
discussion involves the most important provisions of the
Plan pertinent to capital, labor, and land.

Capital

The government seeks through the Plan to direct the
capital-accumulation process of the public sector. The
decision is for a mixed economy in which the public and
private sector and what is called the social sector coexist,
an arrangement that is considered the only alternative that
can lead to the balanced development of the country.

The goal of the social sector is to serve the public
interest and offer a prospect for the profitable development
of the Greek countryside. The term social sector implies
the active participation of local government, cooperatives,
and joint-ownership companies of broad popular base in
economic activity, which is expected to lead to an increase
of local production resulting in reinvestment of the social
surplus in the locality, thereby contributing substantially
to the reduction of regional inequalities. It is furthermore
expected that the socialized enterprises can act as poles of
attraction for private enterprises, which will be directed
toward complementary activities involving reduced entrepreneurial risks.

A new institutional context is expected to encourage
entrepreneurial activity of local government and facilitate
the provision of better social services (water supply and
drainage, transportation, housing, etc.), better development
of local resources, new sources of revenue, and a gradual
introduction of new labor relations. Furthermore, in order
to enhance the role of municipalities and communities in
productive activities, the 1983-87 Plan provides for pro-
grammatic agreements among various ministries, prefectures,
and local self-government organizations whose aim will be
to develop local resources, promote government investment
policy, and reduce unemployment.

A main policy instrument for achieving balanced regional development is the decentralization of the Public

Investment Program. To that end, a collective body at the level of the prefecture is to be vested with powers of decisive importance, which will control the process of formulating and approving the relevant expenditures for regional public-investment programs. Thus, more and more developmental projects are expected to be planned, scheduled, and decided upon by the elected representatives of local self-government and social organizations and be carried out by local administrative and technical staff and by the indigenous labor force (which is mostly under- or unspecialized). This process is expected to result in the transfer to the periphery of powers, resources, and manpower.

Additional monies for financing local self-government are to be raised by issuing special securities as well as through loans to be obtained initially from the Public Consignations and Loans Fund.

Finally, the 1983-87 Plan provides for such support activities as financing services and training personnel through the establishment of a local self-government bank and a technical support agency for local self-government, the development of human resources at the regional and local level through special education and training, and cooperation between the country's scientific personnel and local governments.

Also, special policy measures to be taken in favor of small and medium-sized firms, handicrafts, cottage industry, and the arts industry are expected to contribute to the development of local communities. To that end, sectoral programs for the support of small and medium-sized business that lack the know-how in production organization, management, administration, and marketing and face problems in purchasing raw materials and obtaining loans are to be initiated by the Hellenic Organization of Small and Medium Sized Industries and Handicrafts (EOMMEH).

The special measures for handicrafts and cottage industry envisaged are the creation of handicraft centers in regions that traditionally have specialized in certain crafts, the creation and operation of schools for handicraftsmen, the granting of low-interest loans, the creation of a security capital guarantee for loans, the institutionalization of a special mechanism for loans to small manufacturers, and the securing of all the financing available from the European Investment Bank and the New Community Fund and its dispersal to small enterprises.

We should mention some special incentives for regional and economic development given to private enterprises (industry, tourism) by Law 1262/82 that are designed to encourage rational economic development and productive investment. Such incentives have existed since 1960, before the above law, but they have not had substantial results. Here we must mention also the recent Integrated Mediterranean Programs (MOPs), which are special development programs financed up to 70 percent by EEC sources (and, in some cases, by more than 70%).

Labor

A basic aim of the 1983-87 Plan is to lay the foundations of a strong producer- and marketing-cooperative movement in agriculture and in other sectors of the economy, based on democratic procedures and voluntary participation. With respect to agriculture, the central objective is to link the processes of production, manufacturing, and trade in agricultural products through agroindustrial cooperatives. To support the development of the cooperative movement, the creation of the necessary material, technical, and institutional base is planned as well as the development of a system for the instruction and training of peasants who participate in cooperatives. Sufficient funding is to be secured while a set of incentives for development are to be provided to all cooperatives whether they are involved in production or in trade. An effort is to be made to set up cooperative exporting agencies as well.

Agricultural cooperatives, in cooperation with local self-government and the competent government department, are expected to implement integrated programs for the development of specific branches (e.g., cattle raising, cultivation of feed plants) or regions whose aim will be to maximize benefits from available resources. Such programs will cover the phases of production, marketing, and processing that may possibly be financed by EEC funds.

The Plan also provides enabling institutional framework for the organization of small and medium-sized enterprises into cooperatives as well as for the promotion and strengthening of credit cooperatives. These programs are expected to mobilize the initiative of the rural population for cooperative production, commerce, and manufacturing and create new possibilities for employment.

Land

Systematic planning for land use both in agricultural and urban areas will be introduced through democratic procedures and with public participation. In the agricultural areas, the first target is to control the extension of urban activities (that is, the dispersion of industry and the division of land to create building plots) as well as to ameliorate agricultural uses--protection of highly productive land, definition of agricultural zones, and restructuring of cultivation.

Agricultural development policy is to be based on a more-rational utilization of agricultural land. Land fragmentation will be checked, and the average size of agricultural holdings is expected to be increased. The Plan aims also at government regulation of forest-pasture uses and problems arising from abandoned land as well as at the selective preservation of bordering arable land. The basic goal in agricultural areas is to divide the land into forest zones, cultivation zones, and stock-farming zones and thereby secure both ecological balance and development. The areas that are under environmental protection will be government registered, evaluated, and organized. Provisions are also made so that the forests will offer more recreation and the system concerning their protection and administration will be improved.

To improve the deteriorated town-planning conditions in urban areas, there will be legislative regulations to control land uses. Manufacturing and other operations are most important for the planning of land use, and urban rehabilitation works are also to be undertaken. The establishment of large industrial units in Attica are to be controlled and enterprises of a national scale will be limited by law.

To facilitate the implementation of the above, the government actually introduced legislation that discourages industrial establishments inside the Attica area. It should be noted that this legislation is not permanent: changes occur very often and depend on the person who runs the Ministry of Environment, Physical Planning, and Public Works.

Decentralization and Public Participation

It is explicitly stated in the Plan that the existing structure of local government cannot support the above

mentioned developmental goals. A greater degree of decentralized administrative structure and public participation
is necessary to support the efforts undertaken for regional
development. Utilization of human potential, planning,
and the transfer of initiatives to the local government is
expected to secure social control. A new regional division
and administration will take place according to the 1983-87
Five-Year Plan. The decentralization envisaged in the Plan
consists of the decentralization of administrative authorities, which are to be transferred to the lowest level possible (that is, the functioning of central administration
must devolve to the level of the prefecture), and the
transfer of decision-making powers and financial resources
from the various levels of state administration to the lowest
possible level of local government.

Legal provisions will be made to institutionalize three
levels of local self-government. The distribution of authority among the various levels of local government will
ensure the attainment of the greatest possible decentralization of power. The responsibility for developing each
area's potential will lie with the lowest possible level of
local government. The first steps toward the creation of a
new institutional framework have already been taken
through Laws 1235/82 and 1270/82.

With a new local self-government charter, local governments will be vested first with the authority to make
certain decisions and to implement them directly without
these decisions being subject to prior approval by any
other organ and second with authorities that will enable
them to participate in the planning process.

To enable local governments to meet requirements of
their new development role, funds will be made available
to the Local Government Authorities (OTA) to cover their
operational expenses, to obtain the material-technical infrastructure necessary for them to exercise their powers,
and to undertake entrepreneurial activities.

Public participation is planned to start at the level
of rank-and-file organizations, which, in cooperation with
other planning bodies and through local government authorities at the village and town level, will ensure that
local objectives are given proper emphasis and that people's
views on development are genuinely expressed. With such
a choice, attempts are made for the institutionalization
of actual intervention and participation by people in local
governance.

KEY STRUCTURAL ARRANGEMENTS AND AGENTS
FOR REGIONAL AND LOCAL DEVELOPMENT

Investment Incentives

Law 1262/82, as amended by Law 1360, replaced Law 1116/81 to incorporate the economic philosophy of the new socialist-oriented government. It offers a number of incentives aiming at the country's economic and regional development. The incentives are granted for the realization of productive investments and vary according to the region where the business concern operates (see Map of Greece, p. 223).

The amount of a grant depends on the area in which the enterprise is operating. For area A, no grant is allowed (except in the case of special zones and investments). For area B, the grant covers 10 to 25 percent of the total investment cost; for area C, 15 to 40 percent; and for area D, 20 to 50 percent (except for investments in area D realized in special zones where the minimum rate covered is 35 percent). The exact size of the grant to be given is determined on the basis of socioeconomic and private economic regional-development criteria (export prospects, substitution of imports, energy conservation, use of domestic raw materials and technology, market conditions of the specific industrial branch, productivity, new employment opportunities, prevention of environmental pollution, project viability prospects, etc.), which are designated by ministerial decisions.

Therefore, depending on the region of the country in which a firm is going to be established or to be moved and the particular economic activity that it will be undertaking, and given that some criteria and prerequisites are met, it receives a grant, a donation ranging from 10 percent to 50 percent of the cost of the investment project. Industrial and agricultural activities as well as activities of the service sector (e.g., tourism) are covered by the above law.

The would-be entrepreneur has to contribute a minimum percentage of total cost of the investment project; the remaining cost is expected to be covered by the government and by a long-term bank loan, the interest of which is subsidized. If the investment project does not exceed 400 million drachmas, the government grant is given free. For investment between 450 and 600 million drachmas, 50 percent takes the form of government participation in the equity capital of the enterprise, whereas in projects that exceed 600 million drachmas, the grant takes the form of government participation in the equity capital of the firm. More favorable conditions are provided for cooperatives and local government to proceed to productive investments as well as for Greek emigrants and seamen. Decision as to the applicability of the law regarding investment projects is made by the Ministry of National Economy.

We think that the criteria should specify more details about the kind of new enterprises to be supported. From our own perspective, we feel that according to this law, private enterprises as subsidized tend to reproduce old problems. It is implicit in our theoretical framework that a social foundation should be created for those new enterprises for the promotion of social accountability. There is need for criteria to provide for social audits, ethical codes, and so forth encouraging enterprises to model themselves along these lines to perform their purposes. The main concern should be how to create a social sector and still maintain private enterprises.

Hellenic Organization of Small and Medium Sized Industries and Handicrafts

The EOMMEH is the principal state organization responsible for the support of small and medium-sized enterprises (MME). It was established in 1977, but its responsibilities have been broadened recently to cover a great part of the industrial policy of the 1983–87 Five-Year Plan for small industry and handicraft. Its activities for the support of the small entrepreneurs cover all of Greece in such fields as marketing and product promotion of Greek MME's products in internal and international markets; international relations; financial support of the MME by loans to private enterprises, cooperatives, joint ventures, artisans, and handicrafts; technical assistance; training and educational programs; documentation and information on matters of interest to MME professionals and entrepreneurs; publications; promotion of cooperatives, joint ventures and provision of common services in order to meet the needs of MME for restructuring and modernization; facilities enabling MME access to public-sector procurement programs; promotion of subcontracting by providing the necessary information; and encouraging the development and application of innovations and the improvement of technology within MMEs.

Particular importance is given by EOMMEH to the handicraft and artisan sector. Finally, EOMMEH, through special development activities of affiliated companies, like the Company for Supplies to Small and Medium Sized Industries (PRO.MET.LTD), provides support to various sectors.[6]

Industrial Reconstruction Organization

In Chapter 4 we already discussed some distinctive cases of problematic enterprises that have introduced various forms and degrees of worker participation in decision making, in management, and in profits. Now we bring the discussion at the macro level, and from a broader perspective we consider the significance of these enterprises as they relate to the whole community. This issue has been one which has taken political dimensions and caused much discussion in the past years.

The term problematic enterprises refers to those companies that show problems of viability but play an important role in the economy of the country, either from the point of view of their strategic importance or from the point of view of the number of people employed. Very well-known enterprises, like The Skalistiri Group (Eleusis Bauxite Mines Inc.), The Athens Paper Mill Co., LARKO S.A., E. G. Ladopoulos (EGL Paper Mills, S.A.), VELKA S.A., PYR.KAL. (Greek Powder and Cartridge Company Ltd.), ELINTA S.A., Piraiki-Patraiki (Piraiki-Patraiki Cotton Mfg. Inc.), Fix (Charles Fix Brewery, S.A.), and other industries had to interrupt their operation or face bankruptcy or operation under difficult conditions.[7] Their closing brings severe repercussions upon the community as a whole (increase in unemployment rates, financial losses, etc.) and disruptive effects upon both the life of people connected with them and the local communities that depend upon them.

Problematic enterprises are basically private enterprises operating under private law that are for the time being under government protection and social control. It is not clear whether they will finally remain in the private sector after their restoration or whether they will

belong to the public or the social sector. During the
period of their rehabilitation, under social control with
new boards of a broader social synthesis (without the
participation of the owners but with the participation of
workers), they constitute an experiment in worker participation and are given support for developing some measure
of worker governance and social accountability. By law,
this has been a case for experimentation with new structures of participation, social accountability, and testing
of new ideas.

Taking into consideration the general interest, and
in order to face the problem of unemployment and prevent
bankruptcy of problematic enterprises, it was decided to
release one one-hundredth of the banks' deposits (which
were reserve funds kept in the Bank of Greece) to support
such enterprises and to provide time for finding the best
solution for the problem. Such a measure constituted also
an incentive for the banks themselves, which now had
additional money to use for the problematic enterprises.
Parallel to the above, an informal Secretariat for the
Problematic Enterprises started operating within the Ministry of National Economy, the role of which was to coordinate the relations of the banks and these firms. In 1983,
Law 1386 was voted to address problematic enterprises,
providing for the establishment of the Industrial Reconstruction Organization (OAE) and its functioning as a
société anonyme. Parallel to the establishment of the OAE
was the establishment of the Consortium of Banks that also
participates in the rehabilitation procedures of problematic
enterprises, and of which the OAE is a member.

The OAE aims at 1) the "economic rehabilitation of
problematic or over-indebted enterprises"; 2) the "introduction and application of foreign technology as well as
the development of local technology"; and 3) the "establishment and operation of socialized enterprises or enterprises of mixed economy." In order to attain its goals,
the OAE can, among other steps, "undertake the administration and operation of enterprises in a state of rehabilitation or socialized enterprises" and "participate in the
stock capital of enterprises already existing or to be established."[8]

A basic precondition for the realization of the goals
of the OAE is the exercise of a policy of social control
with worker participation in the collective organs of the
OAE, that is, on the board of directors of the OAE, in the

advisory committee, which declares its opinion for assuming the responsibility of an enterprise according to the regulations of the law; and in the temporary boards of enterprises undertaken by the OAE.

The OAE has an eight-member board, of which the chairman and two members are appointed by the state, one member is appointed by the General Confederation of Workers of Greece, and the other members are appointed by the shareholders.

The advisory committee, composed of five members (one of whom is appointed by the GSEE), recommends to the Ministry of National Economy the application or not of the provision of Law 1386 to the enterprise for which the relative procedure is in process. The temporary administration of an enterprise is formed when the Ministry of National Economy determines the subjection of this enterprise to the OAE and is composed of one or more persons appointed by the OAE and one representative of the workers (Article 8, para. 1).

The new legislation, which attempts to revive problematic enterprises, cannot be considered a socialization procedure--it is more of a rehabilitation procedure. Problematic enterprises present opportunities for experimentation with participation, but there are many other issues involved as well: the restoration of enterprise property, the method of rehabilitation, and the criteria used to define viability. It should be mentioned here that many problematic enterprises belong to industrial branches that are already facing problems of relocation to other countries (like, for example, the spinning mills, the cement companies, and metallic constructions, which flourished during the last 20 years).

Finally, some questions occur about the most appropriate kind of organization and management. Do problematic enterprises belong to the private or to the public sector? Which would make them more effective?[9] As it stands, 45 problematic enterprises have been subjected to the procedures of rehabilitation under Law 1386/83. In 43, a temporary administration in which representatives of the workers participate was appointed until December 1986. More recently, the government has announced that 22 enterprises are considered viable and the rest will be closed down. Special provisions have been announced for workers and employees who will lose their jobs.

The subject of problematic enterprises has been a basic point of friction between the Ministry of National Economy and the banks, particularly the National Bank of Greece, which has a total amount of 170 billion drachmas invested in problematic companies. The basic disagreement is about the problem-solving method rather than the philosophy of the whole subject.[10] Finally, the Ministry of National Economy announced in October, 1985, that the debts to the National Bank of Greece will be converted into common stock. Of the new shares to be issued, 50 percent were to remain with the National Bank of Greece while the other 50 percent would be transferred to the Industrial Reconstruction Organization, which in turn will issue bonds with the guarantee of the state. More recently, it was announced that the debts of the 22 enterprises will be converted to shares, the majority of which will remain with the OAE.[11]

Representatives of the Greek industrialists hold that the subject of the problematic enterprises has taken a political dimension.[12] They suggest that the government "creates" problematic enterprises with the view to proceed to their socialization or that the government "creates" competition between private and public enterprises that undermines private business. Such views are summarized in the following position: Instead of having creative and profit-making enterprises which would produce internationally competitive products and would pay taxes, we will have enterprises subsidized by the entire society. The Ministry of National Economy has denied such assertions, declaring that the aim of the government is not to socialize enterprises of the private sector by identifying them as "problematic."

Integrated Mediterranean Programs

Due to the insistence of the Greek Government for a more balanced development of the EEC countries (northern and southern regions), a special program of action was initiated by EEC. This program provides for specific action in favor of the southern regions of EEC, in order to improve their socioeconomic structure and facilitate the adjustment of these regions to the new conditions created by the Community's enlargement in the best possible way. This action takes the form of a community contribution to

the implementation of Integrated Mediterranean Programs,
extending over a period of seven years, submitted to the
EEC Commission.[13] Greece, as a southern member-state of
the EEC, whose economy is faced with extensive structural
adjustments, may benefit as a whole under the Mediterranean Programs, known in Greece as MOPs.

Integrated Mediterranean Programs consist of multi-
annual operations that are consistent with each other relating in particular to investment in the productive sector,
the creation of infrastructure, and the better use of human
resources. These operations concern the following spheres
of economic activity: agriculture, fisheries, and related
activities (including the agrifood industries); energy;
crafts; industry (including building and public works);
and services (including tourism).

These programs must take account of the particular
handicaps and special possibilities of the various regions
and provide an overall response to the diverse problems
facing the regions in question regarding the objectives of
development, adaptation, and support for employment and
incomes. The measures provided by these programs are
interdependent and cover all sectors of economic activity.
They must be concerned in particular with the development
of small and medium-sized industrial and commercial enterprises and the promotion of new service activities that
could help lessen the unemployment problem; they must
take account of the contributions made by new technologies
and permit an improvement of facilities for energy production, communications, training, environmental protection, and infrastructure in general. Furthermore, these
measures should be linked to measures already taken under
the sociostructural policies, in particular the Community's
regional development policy and specific sectoral policies,
which will continue to cover these regions in the usual
way. The measures envisaged in the MOPs are intended to
boost or complement the measures already covered by the
existing structural funds. These programs are to be
viewed as specific Community action for a maximum period
of seven years, and they are to provide the opportunity
for a further step toward better coordination of all the
structural financial instruments.

All MOPs must be drawn up at the relevant geographical level by the regional authorities or other authorities
designated by each member-state concerned. In determining
the amount of Community assistance for MOPs, account shall

be taken of the actual needs of the various regions and of the economic and social development conditions obtaining in them; priority will be given to the least-favored regions and to the regions most affected by the consequences of enlargement.

The MOPs submitted by Greece qualify for an amount of 2,000 million ECU.[14] The rate of Community participation in financing the operations selected under the MOP may not exceed 70 percent of the total cost of the project or operation, whatever the form such assistance may take. However, in the case of infrastructure projects of special interest that are partly financed by loans, in the context of an MOP presented by Greece, the overall rate of EEC asistance may exceed 75 percent.

The first MOP program for Greece concerns the region of Crete and is already under operation.

The Municipal Enterprises

The enterprises of the local government are considered representative of the social or socialized sector.[15] Because of their size and their public character, these enterprises can contribute to the ecological balance and they can reinvest the surplus locally. They can be established in regions that have been ignored by private initiative. By moving into production, they also motivate private enterprises to improve the quality and reduce the cost of their products and services. Finally, it is envisaged that they can enlarge the planned (social) sector of the economy, socialize gradually the means of production, and pass their ownership not only to institutions of the collective type (like cooperatives and enterprises of popular base), but also to the local government. Municipal enterprises can be considered a practical application of social ownership and property.[16]

The above clarification of the social sector presumes that the enterprises of the local government can gradually extend the social basis of entrepreneurial activities and contribute to the socialization of the means of production and the social transformation of productive relations. From this point of view, the enterprises of local government can be characterized as a dynamic sector for the socialization of the economy and not as a static, socialized sector, able to promote decentralization and regional development.[17]

Such institution of municipal enterprises is not new. In 1857, the Enterprise Municipal Gas of Athens (DEFA) was established in Athens. Later the municipality of Rhodes pioneered in bringing together the local government and the citizens in the municipal enterprise RHODA (which still is active and controls the buses that serve as transportation on the island). The National Tourist Organization (EOT) and the municipality of Ermoupolis, on Syros island, created in 1956 a hotel business. At the same time, the municipality of Lagada undertook the development of a spa. The new Law 1416/84 has contributed even further to the development of municipal enterprises.[18]

There exist remarkable examples of municipalities and communities that have developed activities in certain areas with their own initiative. The community of Agios Giannis (Evoia), in order to solve immediate problems (water supply, road construction, enrichment of cultural life, and the like) encouraged active participation by citizens. The municipality of Kalamata organized the Company of Public Base, a marketing company for selling the products of the new municipal market of the city, in which the citizens were partners. The municipality of Kalamaria established also, in 1983, the Municipal Enterprise of Touristic and Cultural Development, on an experimental basis, which has proved very profitable for the municipality and the citizens as well. The municipality of Athens established three municipal enterprises (a data processing company, an insurance company, and a tourist-advertising company) specifying as main goals the improvement of services offered to its members, an increase in productivity of the municipality, and a decrease of labor costs to allow more social goods to be offered to the citizens. Very recently the procedures have started for the establishment of two other municipal enterprises in Athens, a parking-garage company and a company of decorative and construction materials.

Law 1416/84, Article 11, provides also for the coordination of local government authorities (OTA), cooperatives, and services of the central government for a region so that community action (development, upgrading of services, etc.) may be undertaken. This integrated action by different agencies responsible for the region enhances the mobilization of resources for the solution of local problems and may be financed by the public investment budget or the state budget. Such arrangements are called planning

contracts.[19]   About 40 planning contracts have been signed
that have promoted developmental action in their region.
They address issues of tourism, cultural activities, road
construction, housing, agricultural projects, and others.
Most significant in that field of action is the planning
contract for the integrated development of Amvrakikos Bay.
The draft of the plan for action was undertaken by the
Center of Planning and Economic Research.   The approved
plan was signed by 14 central services and 14 Local Government Authorities (OTA) of the region.   Each service
promotes the activities for which it is responsible on its
own initiative.   They coordinate the activities of all responsible bodies, such as committees and a general assembly.   A developmental company for the Amvrakikos project
(ETANAM) will be also established.

Companies of Popular Base

Companies of popular base constitute a relatively
recent development in the area of shipping in Greece.[20]
The first popular shipping company appeared in 1967.
The main impetus for its development was the reaction of
the inhabitants of Crete to the inefficient transportation
services rendered by private companies.   In order to deal
with this problem, people created a société anonyme with
shares of small value, so that the inhabitants of the
island could participate together and buy a ship.

Up to the present, 11 popular shipping companies
have been created, with 21 ships and a total amount of
capital over 5 billion drachmas.   The companies have a
broad ownership base, and their shares have been bought
by a large number of inhabitants of the region.   Aiming
to service transportation needs efficiently, they gradually
replaced the traditional family shipping companies. ANEK
and Minoic Lines of Crete have been so far the most successful popular shipping companies.

Popular shipping companies have multiple goals,
direct and indirect.   Besides profit, which is considered
important both to their survival and for further investments, other social goals are important as well.   They
are serving the community by providing better services,
reducing transportation costs, offering various social services (to the sick, the old, students, etc.), and creating
new opportunities for employment for people in the commu-

nity. The contribution of these companies to raising funds
from the wider public is very important. It should be
noted that the capital of popular shipping companies comes
94 percent from local funds. They are traditional corporations that lack traditional family control. These companies
have a special character, however, in that there is no
traditional distinction between owners and consumers: the
total number of shareholders make use of the services provided by their ships.

The Greek government attempts to expand popular
companies in other sectors of the economy by encouraging
autonomous regional development that leads to more worker
control and more participation by the inhabitants. The
initial success of popular shipping companies and a general recognition of the possibilities of collective economic
activity for regional socioeconomic development became the
basis for the expansion of broad joint-stock companies in
other sectors as well. Examples are the Development Company of Apokoronou, the purpose of which is the utilization of natural resources in the company's region; the
Cement Industry of Crete, S.A., which has been created in
Herakleion with the participation of shareholders from the
whole island; the Trans-Eurokretan, which has been also
created in Crete by people working in West Germany; and
the agricultural cooperatives of the island, the purpose of
which is to carry out continental international transporta-
tions.

Cooperatives

Cooperatives have a long history in modern Greece.[21]
Greek law is special here insofar as the state maintains a
strong presence in cooperative matters, because the cooperative movement has always been poor and requires state
support and initiative.

The legal protection of the cooperative idea in Greece
was established with Law 602/1915, which was developed
according to the standards of analogous German legislation.[22] This law was not intended only for the agricultural sector but in practice it has affected only this sector. Later in 1979, Law 921 increased the autonomy of the
movement and gave cooperatives the right to promote and
sell their products, but lack of an appropriate financial
framework prevented agricultural cooperatives from taking

advantage of this regulation. A basic disadvantage of Law 921 was that it did not put an end to the middlemen who could act absolutely freely under Law 602/1915. A new law in 1982 referred to the restoration of the democratic operation of cooperative organizations; provided one vote for every representative-member, regardless of the lot he or she possessed; and institutionalized participation of administrative employees on the board. Law 1541/85 extends the activities of agricultural cooperatives.

According to Law 1541/85, Article 21, the general assembly constitutes the highest administrative organ of the cooperative and consists of all the members, each member having one vote. The board of directors consists of at least five members and decides all the administrative and managerial matters as stated by law, the corporation statute, and the decisions of the general assembly. If the number of the employees of the corporation exceeds 20, then there is one representative of the workers on the board of directors, who has all the rights and obligations of the other members but cannot be elected as president, vice-president, general secretary, or treasurer, according to Article 23, para. 10.[23]

A particularity of Greek law is the establishment of a strong state presence in cooperative matters. Although cooperatives are private organizations and function under private economic criteria, the state recognizes their important socioeconomic role and provides them with increased privileges. The question is How much and what kind of support can the state give to the cooperatives without creating undesirable effects upon them and upon the private sector? Generally, we could say that direct economic support for financing cooperatives' losses deriving from bad investments and sloppy situation analysis is not acceptable.

According to Article 32 of Law 1541/85, "The agricultural cooperatives are under the supervision of the State." Such a supervision is exercised by "a body of cooperative organizations' controllers." This body is established by presidential decree, issued after proposal by the Ministry of Agriculture and the Panhellenic Confederation of Agricultural Cooperatives (PASEGES), and is supervised by the Ministry of Agriculture, which assigns a seven-member board of directors. This supervision aims at

1. the legal operation of agricultural cooperatives and especially control over the application of the law, the articles of the corporation charter, and the regulations;
2. managerial and accounting control over agricultural cooperatives and, more generally, the supervision of their economic situation;
3. support of the agricultural cooperatives for rational operation, the development of appropriate entrepreneurial activity, and, more generally, their effectiveness and efficient functioning; and
4. support of the supervisory councils in the discharge of their duties.

The cooperative movement in Greece is based on the prototypes of other European countries and on the same basic internationally accepted principles that marked its birth--the free and voluntary participation of members; democratic management based on one vote per member, regardless of the lot he or she possesses; legal protection of the funds invested; distribution of surplus whenever possible according to the participation of the members or its disposal for broader social goals; training of the members; and intercooperative collaboration at the national and international level.

The pyramid of the cooperative organization in Greece includes first-degree cooperative organizations in every village, which elect their representatives and have farmers as members; second-degree cooperative organizations at the level of associations (unions), usually within the prefectures, having cooperatives as members; third-degree cooperative organizations, which cover the whole country and refer to specific products or groups of products (KYDEP, SEKE, ELAIOURGIKI, etc.). On the very top is PASEGES (Panhellenic Confederation of Agricultural Cooperatives).

The most interesting characteristic of the cooperatives is that they constitute independent local democratic economic organizations, and in many ways they have the characteristics of the community. If they are properly activated, they can play a leading role in the development of the Greek countryside.

For analytical purposes, we distinguish cooperatives into three basic categories: agricultural cooperatives, urban cooperatives, and new innovative types of semi-cooperatives.

Agricultural Cooperatives

Agricultural cooperatives in Greece are still under-developed; the Greek cooperative movement is one of the least developed in Europe. According to data of the Agricultural Bank of Greece (ATE), in 1984 there were about 7,500 first-degree agricultural cooperatives operating at the local level (village) and having farmers as members, but only 40 percent showed satisfactory activities. The general picture given by the Agricultural Bank of Greece is as follows: 60 percent of the total number of first-degree agricultural cooperatives represent small cooperatives with few members, that is, 7 to 100 members (28 percent have from 7 to 50 members, 17 percent have from 51 to 75 members, and 15 percent have 76 to 100 members); about 20 percent of first-degree agricultural cooperatives are production cooperatives involved in the collection and processing of agricultural products, while the rest are credit cooperatives and multiple-purpose cooperatives. Sixteen percent of the communities and municipalities of the country do not have any cooperatives; in 25 percent of the communities and municipalities there are more than one cooperative. Only 12 percent of the agricultural cooperatives have clerical staff; while only 11 percent have machinery and buildings—and those are mainly unions and federations, 72 percent of Greek farmers are registered in cooperatives.

Depending on the way they are formed, agricultural cooperatives are distinguished into two main categories: free cooperatives, which represent the majority (94 percent) and are divided into subcategories according to their objectives (like credit, trade, production, fishing), and compulsory cooperatives, which are established by law and refer to specific activities of certain regions.[24]

Urban Cooperatives

This category of cooperatives is limited in Greece. We distinguish them as 1) consumer cooperatives (which provide products and services both to members and non-members); 2) professional and manufacturing cooperatives (which either provide their members with raw materials and products substituting for private trade or establish cooperatives with the collective work of their members); 3) construction cooperatives (which buy, arrange, and distribute land for building houses for their members, who

deposit their savings at the cooperative); and 4) workers'
cooperatives (in which the employers are at the same time
employees who offer their labor and tools to form a new
productive organization that allows them to collaborate
under equal terms). Participation of workers in decision
making constitutes a basic characteristic that differentiates
the workers' cooperative from a capitalist enterprise.

The presence of workers' cooperatives within the
Greek cooperative movement is very limited. There is no
specific law for workers' cooperatives as such, but they
are covered by the law regarding urban cooperatives.
Owing to the limitations of this legal framework, however,
several workers' cooperatives operate under a different
legal status, i.e., as limited liability companies. In
several cases, companies established by carpenters, engineers, cargo drivers, and craftsmen operate as workers'
cooperatives. With the entry of Greece into the EEC, a
number of workers' cooperatives have been founded, but
they did not appear as very successful up to now. The
EOMMEH has expressed its interest in the development of
workers' cooperatives and since 1983 it has provided them
technical and economic support.

Workers' cooperatives had (and still have) to face
serious problems that restrict their development. The lack
of cooperative ideals in the broader sense as well as the
lack of a specific legal framework that would provide for
the future of workers' cooperatives explain the absence of
a substantial workers' cooperative movement in Greece.
Other main problems that restrict the operation and promotion of workers' cooperatives in Greece are an absence of
capital and of a cooperative bank, the paucity of economic
incentives, a lack of education on cooperative issues, and
the difficulties involved in keeping discipline and interest
in participation.[25]

Innovative Types of Semicooperatives

In this category we consider two types of cooperatives that could be recognized as innovative, although their
roots can be traced to the past: school cooperatives and
the women's cooperatives. They both have potential in
revitalizing community life. These are special producer
and marketing cooperatives and are initiated by groups
such as pupils and women farmers.

School cooperatives are small, self-managed self-
regulated, democratically organized communities. It is

held that school cooperatives are tools for providing democratic education to today's pupils and tomorrow's citizens.
Pupils by themselves manage the cooperative with the assistance of a teacher. They produce and sell the products
of their labor. The money collected is used for, among
activities of mutual aid inside and outside the school, improving school and work conditions. With the initiative of
some teachers, school cooperatives first appeared in Greece
in 1925. In the period 1981–82, 703 school cooperatives
operated with 36,800 members. The majority of school cooperatives function at the elementary school level in the
provinces and have developed several remarkable activities
(like, for example, raising rabbits, selling books, writing
materials, and creating handicrafts). The Confederation
of Agricultural Cooperatives promotes and assists school
cooperatives and offers annual awards to successful
cases.[26]

Women's cooperatives constitute a recent development
in the cooperative movement and are not widely known as
yet. We can see the first women's cooperative, in Samarina
of Grevena Prefecture, in 1957, but up to 1974 there were
still only nine women's cooperatives. In the period 1982–85,
26 more were created. It is recognized that women farmers
are among the least–advantaged women in Greece. Today
there is an effort made to activate women in the country's
agricultural cooperative movement, so they can have economic self–sufficiency and develop their personal potential.
Women are encouraged to get into production by establishing agrotourist women's cooperatives. Although there are
some major problems, because most women farmers had
never participated in an organized collective effort and
their resulting economic position is weak, the program is
considered successful.[27]

Public Representation at the Prefectural and
the Local Level: Democratic Planning

The participation of people in exercising authority at
the local level is provided for by Law 1270/82, which sets
the legal framework for municipal decentralization, the
promotion of public participation, and the autonomy of
Local Government Authorities in local matters.[28]

In every municipality, neighborhood assemblies and
neighborhood councils are being created with the purposes

of increasing public participation in local matters and of mobilizing and organizing the inhabitants within the context of local government. Members of the neighborhood assembly are all those who have the right to vote. Tasks of the neighborhood assembly are research, definition, inventory, specification of priorities, and working out and pushing forward solutions for local and more-general problems.

The neighborhood councils exercise control over the committees, which are created for neighborhood matters. These are organs for the implementation of decisions made by the neighborhood assembly and for the support of local government. They consist of eight members, who must also be members of the neighborhood assembly. The councils have an advisory function and make proposals to the prefectural council on matters related to the neighborhood. The mayor and elected members of the town council participate in the meetings of the neighborhood council, as well as one representative of the "pupils' community," of the schools in the area, who has the right to express his or her opinion.

In the above new model of development, which is based on democratic planning and involves the participation of people and the local government in discussions formulating plans for economic and social development in each prefecture all over the country, the prefectural council is the responsible organ for coordinating planning at the prefectural level.[29] At the local level, the organ responsible for planning is the council of the first-degree local government, with the participation of worker representatives and the other sectors of production. The inhabitants' assembly, established by Law 1270/81, has also an important role in defining social needs, collecting proposals, and defining priorities.

The responsibilities of Local Government Authorities and prefectures for democratic planning are defined by Law 1622/86 (Articles 15 and 22). According to this law, Local Government Authorities submit their proposals for development projects and policy measures that concern their communities to the prefectural council and formulate their local plan of development. At the prefectural level, proposals are made for projects of development and policy measures of regional or national concern for which the prefecture has a special interest. Prefectural councils are also responsible for formulating a development plan for the prefecture and for distributing the public-investment program allocation to local projects.

The above collective organs constitute primary forms of citizen participation under the Plan. They represent a new mentality, a collective expression of the will of the provinces for local development. But the members participating in such organs lack experience. This and the inadequacy of services for providing technical support prevent them at the moment from carrying out their purpose as satisfactorily as they could and from showing any remarkable initiatives. As a consequence, such collective organs cannot function as efficiently, for the time being at least, as expected.

Decentralization and Regional Division

The Local Self-Government Charter (Presidential Decree 76/1985) and Law 1622/86 provide for the decentralization of administrative authorities envisaged in Plan 1983-87 as well as their mobilization for the development of communities and regions.

Prefectural self-government is defined as second-degree local government, responsible for the economic, social, and cultural development of their regions with the active participation of citizens in the administration of local matters. In particular, the second-degree local government is responsible for democratic planning, social welfare, health, cultural affairs, environment, education, athletics, the agricultural sector, industry, tourism, labor, transportation, and programs for raising the educational level of the people in the area. The responsibilities of the second-degree local government do not interfere with those of the first-degree local government. First-degree and second-degree local government are independent levels of local administration and there is no hierarchical relation between them.

The organs of the prefectural self-government are the prefectural council and the prefectural committees. The prefectural council consists of elected members; elected representatives of trade, professional, cultural, and syndicalist organizations and chambers that have their seat in the prefecture; and representatives of the central administration. The prefectural council makes the decisions on all matters for which prefectural self-governance is responsible.

Third-degree local government takes the form of regional committees. The regions into which the country is divided for the planning and coordination of regional development are to be defined by presidential decrees. In the regional committees participate the prefects of the area and the presidents of the prefectural self-government, as well as one representative of the Local Union of Municipalities and Communities (TEDK). The regional council is responsible for submitting to the central state services proposals for projects and policy measures of national concern that are of interest to the region and are provided for in the national development plan as well as proposals for projects and policy measures for the regions that are financed by the public-investment program, formulating the regional development plan on the basis of the proposals of the prefectural councils, and distributing the allocations of public-investment programs for projects of prefectural and local concern.

Decentralization is to be implemented with the transfer by presidential decree (Law 1416/84, Article 8) of those responsibilities of ministers, prefects, and divisions of central government (at the ministerial, regional, and prefectural level) that concern local affairs to Local Government Authorities (OTA). This law also provides for the transfer of required funds for those responsibilities to the LGUs. Provisions are also made for the decentralization of public-investment program.

The mobilization of the OTA for the development of communities is being enhanced by enabling legislation such as Law 1416/84, which permits them to get involved in tasks of a broader nature that promote the social, economic, and cultural interests of the citizens. To that end, they are allowed to set up small enterprises, municipal enterprises, popular companies, and sociétés anonymes together with cooperatives in the region. Special incentives are also provided to encourage entrepreneurial activity among OTA.

CONCLUDING REMARKS

In the 1980s in Greece there is a sincere concern about the decline of communities. Existing and new structural arrangements are mobilizing for regional development and the strengthening of the role of communities. These changes aim to upgrade community life and develop activities in the regions and local communities that are accountable to land, labor, and capital in order to control distorting influences coming from the imperfect competitive market. Actually, a reconstruction of the local community is planned to take charge of the market forces that have played havoc with social control. Altering the social structure of the private sector as well as creating a social sector to allow people to become more important than generally occurs in a highly competitive market are both envisaged. The whole endeavor involves processes of bottom-up development and top-down policy making.

Emphasis is given to the social sector by the present government in order to encourage investment by forces outside the conventional public and private sectors. The social sector, a third sector of the economy, depends mainly on local government investment activities taking the form of municipal enterprises and companies of popular base. This new role assigned to local government is undoubtedly a step toward the somewhat comprehensive socialization of investment. Moreover, it can stimulate and guarantee social participation in planning and social control over the corporate sector. Investment activities undertaken by local authorities in the form of municipal enterprises and companies of popular base are intended to play a steadily increasing role in the Greek economy.

We observe also in Greece a potential new framework for enabling legal provisions to develop the institution of local self-government on the basis of participative structures and decentralization of decision making. Autonomy, viability, and democratic polity seem to be the main principles upon which the government attempts to establish a social foundation for local self-governance in Greece. Decentralization of decision making and participative policies reflect many of the principles in our conceptual framework of community self-governance as analyzed in Chapter 5. However, a major difference rests on the accent given to a top-down process involving legislative mandates, presidential decrees, and extensive government involvement at the local level as opposed to an accent on the socialization of the enterprise system itself.

A thorough evaluation of the implementation of the above plans of the government is not possible. It is a process that demands time, and the implementation of the 1983-87 Plan had not yet developed up to the time of submission of the manuscript to a degree necessary to reach objective conclusions; most new developments are at the moment in an experimental state. Nevertheless, it must be mentioned that, owing to economic difficulties, the objectives of the Plan seem ambitious.

It must be noted also that the massive changes envisaged for a local government that has been for so long characterized by a climate of inertia and perpetuation of the status quo as well as by structural weaknesses and organizational problems will be difficult to implement. The extent of the innovative nature of the new structural changes (institutions) that are under formulation for the Greek scene are often entangled with ideological and political perceptions. Such entanglements have created some ambiguities about the specific direction they will be taking and have blurred the clarity of models observed in other countries.

The rather rapid rate with which some of the above changes have been promoted do not secure the required necessary conditions, especially professional knowledge, expertise, and research (which are scarce resources in Greece) as well as the required funds, and the results may not be satisfactory.

Finally, the nonrealization of the rate of growth foreseen by the National Plan for Economic and Social Development 1983-87 and the continuous economic problems faced by Greece seem to limit severely the financial resources available for the implementation of the projects required to upgrade community life.

NOTES

1. Irwin T. Sanders, Rainbow in the Rock: The People of Rural Greece (Cambridge, Mass.: Harvard University Press, 1962), especially chaps. 10, "Mutual Aid and Cooperatives in Rural Greece," pp. 191-204; 12, "Local Government," pp. 218-40; and 15, "The Village Community," pp. 275-88. See also Ioannis Tsouderos, Greek Agricultural Cooperatives within the Framework of the Greek Social Fabric (Chicago: Fund for International Cooperative Development, 1961); Dimitrios Tsaoussis, Aspects of Greek Society in 19th Century (Athens: Estia, 1984), in Greek; C. Caravidas, Rural Issues. A Comparative Study (Athens: Papazissis, 1978, reprint of edition 1931), in Greek; and

idem., The Problem of Autonomy, Socialism, and Communality (Athens: Papazissis, 1981, reprint of editions 1930, 1936), in Greek; G. Contogeorgis, Community Dynamics and Political Self-Government. The Greek Communities during the Ottoman Rule (Athens: Nea Synora, 1982), in Greek; C. Coukidis, The Spirit of Association of Modern Greeks and Ambelakia. The First Cooperative in the World (Athens: n.p., 1948), in Greek; Evan Vlahos, Modern Greek Society: Continuity and Change (Fort Collins: Department of Sociology, Colorado State University, 1969), mimeographed.

2. The term community is used here to refer to a locality where people have a common identity and share a common life through the administration of basic institutions, such as the government, the church, and business. This term also includes an administrative unit of local government. Communities in Greece are those relatively autonomous neighborhoods, villages, or settlements that have 1) at least 500 inhabitants; 2) a school of elementary education; and 3) economic means to sustain the secretary of the community, to accomplish works of public utility, and to cover other current expenses. Communities constitute the first-degree local government. For an analysis of community decline and urbanization trends in post-World War II Greece, see, B. Kayser, P. Y. Pechoux, and M. Sivignon, Exode rurale et attraction urbaine en Grèce (Athènes: Centre National de Recherches Sociales, 1971); Guy Burpel, Athens: The Development of a Mediterranean Capital (Athens: Exantas, 1976), in Greek; Calliope Moustaka, The Internal Migrant (Athens: Social Science Center, 1964); Eva E. Sandis, Refugees and Economic Migrants in Greater Athens: A Social Survey (Athens: National Center of Social Research, 1973); S. Damianakis, "Aspects du changement social dans la campagne grecque," Review of Social Research, Special Issue (Athens: National Center of Social Research, 1981), pp. 3-10; Damianakis, Etudes rurales et monographies locales en Grèce (Paris: CNRS, Université de Paris X. Nanterre, Groupe de Recherches Sociologiques, 1978); Helen T. Covani, Empirical Studies in Rural Greece (Athens: National Center of Social Research, 1986); Manesis-Verpopoulos-Rozakis-Veremis-Mouzelis-Tsoukalas-Jannitsis-Carageorgas-Pakos-Kravaritou Manitaki-Veltsos-Zouraris, Greece in the Process of Development (Athens: Exantas, 1986), in Greek.

3. Center of Planning and Economic Research: Plan for Economic and Social Development, 1983-87: Preliminary (Athens: Center of Planning and Economic Research [KEPE], 1983), in Greek; also, ibid., Local Self-Government. Report No. 3 published in the context of the Five-Year Economic and Social Development Plan, 1976-80 (Athens: KEPE, 1976), in Greek; and ibid., Regional Development. Report No. 10 published in the context of the Five-Year Economic and Social Development Plan, 1976-80 (Athens: KEPE, 1976), in Greek.

4. The GDP per capita in the region of Athens is estimated at 40 percent to 100 percent more than the other regions (except for Thessaloníki). In the underdeveloped regions, the utilization of human and natural resources is limited, whereas the cost of production in many secondary and tertiary sectors is relatively higher. This imbalance is owing to the small size and the inefficient organization of the productive units, the inadequate infrastructure, and the great distances and difficulties of transportation. Many regions have an unbalanced intersectoral structure: they depend excessively on one sector, e.g., Epirus and Thrace depend on seasonal, one-crop agriculture, while Dodecanese, Cyclades, and Corfu depend on tourism. See George Cottis, Industrial Decentralization and Regional Development (Athens: Institute of Economic and Industrial Research [IOBE], 1980), in Greek; Center of Planning and Economic Research, The Incentives System of Regional and Economic Development: Description, Evaluation, New Proposals, Report in the context of the Five-Year Plan of Regional Development (Athens: KEPE, 1980), in Greek; and idem., The Framework of Regional Development, Series of Lectures No. 23 at the Polytechnic School of Athens (Athens: KEPE, 1970), in Greek.

5. Center of Planning and Economic Research, Preliminary.

6. Hellenic Organization of Small and Medium Sized Industries and Handicraft, EOMMEH and Its Activities (Athens: EOMMEH, n.d.), in Greek.

7. See Bank of Greece, Annual Report of the Governor of the Bank of Greece for the Year 1985 (Athens: Bank of Greece, 1986), in Greek.

8. N. Zagouras, "The Introduction in Greece of the Institution of 'Worker Participation' in Management," Review of Labor Law 43 (1984):686-87, in Greek.

9. According to D. Stergiou, the role of the OAE
is questionable. This organization is neither a credit institution nor a development organization, but a bureaucratic section of the Ministry of National Economy. (Parallel to the establishment of the OAE was the establishment
of the Consortium of Banks that also participates in the
rehabilitation procedures of problematic enterprises, and
of which the OAE is a member.) One solution for these
enterprises would be the abolition of the OAE and the
transformation of the Consortium of Banks into a substantial credit institution. This solution was proposed also by
economist Aggelos Aggelopoulos, former governor of the
National Bank of Greece, in 1978 (see D. Stergiou, "Problematic Enterprises: Suitable Solution, Unsuitable Methods,"
Economic Herald 43 (1642), October 24, 1985, pp. 11-12, 68,
in Greek.

10. Ibid.

11. See statement made by Deputy-Minister Vaso
Papandreou, "Only Enterprises of Strategic Importance Will
Remain with the Industrial Reconstruction Organization,"
Express Daily, December 5, 1986, p. 3, in Greek.

12. Theodoros Papalexopoulos, Speech of the President, Association of Greek Industries (SEB), Annual General
Assembly, May 16, 1955; see Industrial Review, no. 607/608,
1985, pp. 23(155)-26(158), in Greek. S. Mantzavinos, Speech
of the Treasurer, Association of Greek Industries, Annual
General Assembly, May 16, 1985; see Industrial Review, op.
cit. L. Melas, Speech of the General Secretary, Association of Greek Industries, Annual General Assembly, May
16, 1955; see Industrial Review, op. cit. Theodoros Papalexopoulos, Speech of the President, Association of Greek
Industries, Annual General Assembly, May 14, 1986; see Industrial Review, no. 617, 1986, pp. 17(145)-22(150), in Greek.

13. European Economic Community, Council Regulations No. 2088/85, July 23, 1985. Official Journal of the
European Communities No. L 197, 27.7.1985.

14. An ECU amounts approximately to US$ 1.

15. See P. Maistros, "The New Institutions for Decentralization, Local Self-Government, Democratic Planning and
Local Development," Paper presented at the Training
Seminar for Planning Specialists (Athens: Center of Planning and Economic Research, February 1985), in Greek
(mimeographed); also A. Kalliatzides, "The Investment Activity of Local Self-Government," Economic Annals, no. 19,
February 1986, in Greek.

16. See Chapter 5 of this volume, "The Concept of Community Self-Governance."

17. Maistros, The New Institutions; also Ioannis Vavouras, "Local Government and the Social Sector: An Evaluation of the Recent Institutional Arrangements in Greece," Annals of Public and Cooperative Economy, vol. 56, no. 4, pp. 497–512, 1985.

18. In the period 1982–84, according to Law 1069/80, 20 municipal enterprises of water supply and drainage were established. Until January 1986, the consulting firm EOEM conducted feasibility studies for 40 municipal enterprises and started research for 14 more ("New Feasibility Studies for Municipal Enterprises," Profit, January 5, 1985, in Greek). Between February 1984 and May 1985, 27 new municipal enterprises were created. Since the publication of Law 350, proposals have been submitted to the Ministry of the Interior for approval (see Table: "Establishment of Local Municipal-Communal Enterprises according to L. 1416/84," Ministry of Interior, Section of Legal Entities, Institutions and Enterprises, n.d., in Greek) (mimeographed).

19. Ministry of Interior, Planning Contracts, A New Institution in Local Self-Government (Athens: MOI, August 1986), in Greek.

20. See Ioannis Vavouras and Constantinos Archontakis, Popular Shipping Companies (Athens: Papazissis, 1982), in Greek; Stavros Theophanidis, "The Consumer Firm: The Popular Shipping Companies in Greece: A Case Study of Consumer Participation in the Creation of Firms," Economic analysis 15 (1981):231–49; Kyriakos S. Sahanidis, Representative of the Association for the Establishment of an Economic Chamber of Greece (SDOEE), "Companies of Popular Base," Paper presented at the Conference on the Development of Greece, Technical Chamber of Greece, Athens, May 25–30, 1981, vol. 1, pp. 199–203, in Greek.

21. See P. Efstathiou, "Workers' Cooperatives," Athens, General Confederation of Workers of Greece (n.d., in Greek); also Sanders, Rainbow in the Rock, pp. 197–201.

22. Constantinos Papageorgiou, Agricultural Cooperatives (Athens: Evgenidio Idrima, 1985), p. 60ff, in Greek.

23. The corporation charter of each agricultural cooperative can provide for the operation of local assemblies of its members when special geographical, social, and economic conditions impose it. If there is a disagreement between the local assembly and the board of directors, then the only body responsible to give a solution is the

general assembly. Supervision and control over the administration and management of the cooperative are exercised by the supervisory council. The supervisory council consists of three members at least. Among its jurisdictions are reporting for each fiscal period to the general assembly and checking the application of the law, the corporation charter, and the decisions of the general assembly.

24. For a detailed presentation of the development of agricultural cooperative experience in Greece, see Ioannis Tsouderos, Agricultural Cooperatives (Athens: Estia, 1960), in Greek; G. Grammatopoulos, Contemporary Cooperative Movement in Other Countries and in Greece (Athens: 1960), in Greek; T. Tzortzakis, Cooperatives in Greece (Patra: D. Fragoulis, 1932), in Greek; P. Avdelidis, Agricultural Economy and Prospects for Its Development (Athens: Gutenberg, 1976), in Greek; idem, The Agricultural Cooperative Movement in Greece (Athens: Papazissis, 1976), in Greek; idem, Cooperative Problems (Athens: Nea Synora, 1981), in Greek; idem, Issues in Agricultural Economy (Athens: Nea Synora, 1981), in Greek; Papageorgiou, Agricultural Cooperatives; D. Mavrogiannis, Regards sur le developpement des cooperatives en Grèce, 1915-1966 (Athens: PASEGES, 1977).

25. Alkis Raftis and Dimitrios Stavroulakis, "Workers' Cooperatives as Self-managed Enterprises: The Case of Greece" (Paper presented at the XI International Congress of Sociology, International Sociological Association, New Delhi, August 1986).

26. See I. Syggelakis, "School Cooperatives Are a Nursery for the Development of the Cooperative Spirit," Agriculture (March 1983), in Greek; Fotini T. Tzortzaki, School Cooperatives (Athens: Panhellenic Confederation of Agricultural Cooperatives, PASEGES, 1978), in Greek; Constantinos Papageorgiou, Agricultural Cooperatives, Ch. 7, "Cooperatives and Education," pp. 192-212.

27. See Eleni Papagaroufalis, "Self-Management and Women's Cooperatives in Greece: The Case of Petra," in E. Papagaroufalis, Greek Women Farmers and Women's Cooperatives (Athens: Mediterranean Women's Studies Institute [KEGME], 1987), pp. 17-47; Sotirios I. Agapytidis, "Agrotourist Cooperatives," The Cooperative Way, No. 10 (April-June 1988):92-94, in Greek; "Petra, Mytilene—The Successful Experiment of Agrotourism," Agricultural Cooperativism 42 (November 1987):56-59, in Greek; C. Laiou-Antoniou,

"Women's Cooperatives: A Hellenic Experience" (Paper presented at the International Conference on the U.N. Decade for Women, Nairobi, 1985).

28. Maistros, "The New Institutions"; also, Government Gazette, A, No. 80, August 10, 1982, in Greek.

29. Center of Planning and Economic Research: Plan for Economic and Social Development, 1983–1987, Preliminary.

PART III

CONCLUSIONS

8. Evaluation of Developments in the United States and Greece

We have discussed selected aspects of labor and community self-governance in the United States and Greece as part of a system of social governance developing in the economy. We have described social governance as a pattern of organization and management developing autonomously within the private sector of the economy, outside the immediate control of the state, but intricately interdependent with it. Within the context of a nation under a socialist-oriented government, social governance, as it is exemplified by the case of Greece, could be described in part by the "de-statification" and socialization of the economy promoted by action of a responsible government. In such cases, usually we encounter a more advanced conceptualization of social governance. When the change is promoted and/or imposed primarily from the top, however, it does not necessarily secure a steady advance toward a reduction in government controls. Within the context of a capitalist nation, it is at best a process by which the private sector itself must assume initiatives to become more accountable to the people it affects without requiring government regulation. When the government and the private sector both take initiatives in this direction, it is a process of social development within the economy.

Social development involves the upgrading of human resources such as individual skills, leadership abilities, imagination, and personal authority among workers in the economy as part of augmenting the self-governing powers of the economy. This upgrading occurs with structural changes in corporate life and the creation of educational programs in schools and the organization of training insti-

259

tutes to make the changes possible and effective. The purpose of social development is to increase the level of competence of people for treating all sorts of problems hindering the enhancement of social and economic life. We have chosen to discuss only selective aspects of this development process: the way in which workers and communities are increasing their levels of self-governance in the life of the nation as a whole.

The differences between the social economies of the United States and Greece in the fields of labor and community organization are extraordinary. This should be expected in two nations so opposite in size, history, tradition, stage of development, and political orientation of their governments in the 1980s. Since there are lessons to be learned from these two national experiences, we now review our findings in the light of what we think are possible prospects for social development and make evaluations of the actual developments taking place in each nation. Then, we draw appropriate comparisons that have implications for future policy research. We conclude with some suggestions on what all this means for the broader international issues in social economy.

EVALUATION OF DEVELOPMENTS IN EACH NATION

We have focused our analysis on creative social policies in the fields of labor and community development in each nation, but we have not analyzed problems within the political economy as a whole. The focus of the chapters on Greece necessarily takes into account the larger political scene, because the government is actively promoting a change in policy that affects the whole country. It behooves us here to offer a brief review of actual developments in the larger political economy of both nations to provide a more-comparable setting within which to make comparisons between developmental processes in each country.

We noted that the governments of these nations have promoted policies that seem to take them in opposite directions. In the United States, the Reagan administration has moved decisively to the conservative right, while in Greece the Papandreou administration, in the early 1980s at least, moved to the moderate left. In each country there are still more extreme positions on the right and the

left, but each move represents a strong political direction
not fully experienced before in the recent history of each
nation. We said both economies have a market system but
with different kinds of government intervention. Also, as
relatively open economies, they are both subject to the
international economic fluctuations associated with Western
capitalism.

Both countries, as we saw in Chapter 1, have experienced continuous growth in government activity during
the postwar period. In the United States, the policy to
reduce government intervention in the economy has been
intensified; at the same time in Greece the policy has been
to increase the power of the central government to lead
the way toward a new society. The U.S. policy under
Reagan has covertly encouraged the market forces in the
economy to expand and to allow business sectors to become
more conglomerate, while the Greek policy under Papandreou
has overtly encouraged decentrist forces and followed policies in favor of small business units and the social sector, especially at the local level. The two government
policies could hardly be more opposite, as U.S. policy
openly favors capitalist development and Greek policy
openly favors a special decentralized pattern of socialist
development.

Both governments have tended to expand. While the
Reagan administration sought to reduce government activity
in many sectors, including social services, research, and
small-business support systems, government expenditures
mostly went up. Defense expenditures that had started to
expand under Carter continued to expand under the Reagan
administration, increasing government debt to the highest
level ever experienced in U.S. history. The Papandreou
administration expanded the broad spectrum of central
government activities, in particular social services, and
created a most-favorable climate for the expansion of
local-government activities and cooperatives while at the
same time also incurred one of the largest debt problems
in Greek history. Both governments are in economic trouble
because of their high debt-service payments.

On the basis of these two national developments and
the general context of the economies and institutions in
the two nations, we want to draw conclusions about what
we can learn for future policies leading toward social development. We explore the positive and the negative sides
of these policies from our perspective.

THE UNITED STATES

While we have been describing innovative experiments leading toward selective decentralization, the U.S. economy has experienced trends toward greater centralization. Critics have noted that the policies of the Reagan administration to deregulate and be more permissive of private actions also resulted in the formation of corporate conglomerates. These national developments stand in contrast with the small experimental changes we have been describing and they should now be noted to clarify the direction of economic forces in the larger political setting.

First, current policies of deregulation have led toward corporate mergers in an unprecedented fashion. The $140 billion business in mergers, acquisitions, and leveraged buyouts in 1984 exceeded its previous mark in 1983 by $54 billion, and the pace continues. This trend is permitted by the present administration without any recognition of its negative impact on the corporate system or on labor and the life of the community.

In 1982, investment bankers participated in takeover transactions of more than $20 billion that brought them over $100 million. Many analysts have decried the unproductiveness of this activity. Robert Reich, an industrial analyst at Harvard University, has pointed to the economic losses that take place with this type of activity and labeled it "paper entrepreneurialism." Most important for our purposes, the big mergers have shifted centers of business decision making away from cities such as Buffalo, Syracuse, Utica, Scranton, Toledo, Dayton, San Jose, Phoenix, and Youngstown toward larger metropolitan centers such as Dallas and Boston. These communities have now lost much of their regenerative capacity, since their economic life has come under the dominion of distant corporate policies. We have discussed the negative impact of absentee-owned companies on localities and the economic alternatives that offer greater prospects for genuine development in community life.

The irony of these policies lies in the fact that the reasons for instituting government regulations have been forgotten and that new regulations can be predicted to correct future abuses of workers, consumers, and the environment. During the next five years, when problems from market forces again become manifest to a concerned public, another political administration will simply reintroduce government regulations. At present, there is no plan to establish economic alternatives based on principles of business accountability, no social vision of how to alter the business system to take away the necessity for the government to control corporate conduct. The lack of any alternative planning means that history is destined to repeat itself in the form of new government regulations.

Second, the growth in corporate, household, and government debt has never been greater in U.S. history. The cost in the expansion of the defense industry and the refusal to introduce taxes to compensate for the added government costs under the Reagan administration has led to a major debt crisis. The total debt in the U.S. economy (government, corporate, farm, and consumer) has risen from $1.6 trillion in 1970 to $4.6 trillion in 1980, and reached $7 trillion at the end of 1986. The rate of growth of debt did not slow down when inflation collapsed and actually rose from 11 percent in the 1970s to 12 percent in the 1980s. Debt has grown much faster than the GNP. The rate of growth of debt has doubled since Ronald Reagan came into office, while consumer and corporate debt have also grown enormously. Many economists predict disaster, that the house of cards will fall before the 1990s.[1]

Innovative experiments in self-governance are important in part because many economists have argued that these tendencies in the economy are leading the country toward financial collapse. We would argue that the decentrist alternatives we have been discussing not only help create stability but are also socially and economically rewarding. They answer the question of how an economy based on free enterprise can lead toward systems of social justice.

Our question has been: How can accountability systems be introduced into the national economy as a pattern of social self-regulation? The answers are found within our discussion of development toward labor and community self-governance. We want now to evaluate how these systems bear on future government policies and social research.

First, a prefatory note. The actions taken by the U.S. Congress to encourage changes in private enterprise toward greater social accountability have been based on "enabling legislation" and tax incentives. In this pattern of development, business has taken advantage of economic incentives to become socially accountable rather than being forced by legislative mandate to change their way of doing business. The voluntary nature of the changes encouraged by these types of legislation alters the climate for change. There is less resistance and more interest in experimentation.

One example of "enabling legislation" is the new state charter for worker self-governed firms, or producer cooperatives. It encourages firms to organize with "internal accounts" for their employees and to provide a basis for them to vote per person rather than per share. Five states have enacted new statutes for this purpose. Without this legislation, these special types of cooperatives could not avoid the problems of ordinary business as well as avoid the problems of other types of cooperatives (e.g., the Plywoods in Oregon) in which stock is sold publicly and the price expands on the market beyond the reach of ordinary workers.

One example of tax-incentive legislation is the ESOP law, which makes it attractive for firms to become employee owned. This law reduced the cost of borrowing capital for conventional firms through the authority of ERISA, a pension law, while encouraging business leaders to share ownership with their employees.

These lessons are important because we have seen in Greece how political pressures, socialist rhetoric, economic policy and in particular the income policy up to the end of 1985 by the Papandreou government, and legislative mandates have intensified the already unfavorable climate for investment and created a fear among industrialists leading to curtailed production schedules, capital flight, and other reactions that helped cause a slowdown in the economy as a whole. Our argument is that there are more-effective ways to achieve objectives of socializing the economy.

In sum, the U.S. experience with free enterprise and legislative incentives has yielded unique experiments in socializing land, labor, and capital without government controls over the enterprise system. These models of social development represent perhaps the most innovative contribution of the U.S. economy to international policies of development. Indeed, we would argue that this pattern of social development is worthy of careful study by Third World nations.

Let us now review the policies we have been discussing for our evaluation of their contribution to social development. We will add facts that lead more clearly toward an understanding of their international significance.

Worker Self-governance

In the United States we have said that the future of worker self-governance is forecast by the relative growth of two subtrends: worker ownership and worker participation in higher levels of management. We conclude that neither of these two developments shows signs of making massive leaps forward but both show signs of continuing in the same positive direction they have been heading for the last decade. The question is whether these two trends will converge as one major trend toward worker self-governance in the next decade. The issue is whether there is sufficient political interest in providing additional incentives to advance these developments in selective industries so that they provide models of development in the U.S. economy.

Worker ownership has been implemented by the passage of the Employee Stock Ownership Plans. About 400 new companies each year become worker owned in some measure. Even though it is likely that the tax-credit legislation supporting ESOPs will be dropped, the remaining portions of the federal program will remain in operation. The future on this development front looks promising.

Political leaders in both political parties have endorsed worker ownership. The Democratic party has shown a special interest in worker participation and worker ownership and made the idea of worker ownership a part of its political platform in 1984. The White House and the House of Representatives both took stands in favor of increased voting rights for ESOP programs in 1985. The ESOP association--a membership organization composed of ESOP businesses lobbying on behalf of its members, usually conservative on legislating voting rights for employees-- has claimed now to be in favor of these voting rights while still favoring the idea that the action should remain optional rather than required by federal law. The association has also indicated that it would not oppose a full voting rights requirement for firms in which a majority of stock is employee owned. This is important because an advance in voting rights with ESOPs links the ownership movement with the movement in worker participation.

We have discussed the limitations of ESOPs in their pattern of voting per share rather than per person and the restricted proportions of labor involvement in the program, but we have also stressed the symbolic importance of this trend in providing legitimacy for worker ownership and also for providing a basis for a cooperative pattern of ownership to develop based on one vote per person in firms choosing to do so.

Labor participation in management in the United States also continues to advance significantly through quality-of-work-life programs, autonomous work groups, labor-management committees, Scanlon plans, and selected cases of employee representation on corporate boards. We have discussed the issues of whether these labor-management programs have introduced management skills among workers at the middle and lower levels of administration and whether they are simply new steps for management manipulation and control.

Irving Bluestone, retired vice-president of the United Auto Workers, describes worker participation in management in two fundamental ways: "managing the job" and "managing the enterprise." Managing the job has received increasing attention so that workers have become newly engaged in making decisions on "work processes, the methods and means of production, plant layout, quality of product control, job design and many other areas of management." Bluestone claims that there is a progressive history of increasing worker participation in all such areas of corporate management. The task of managing the whole enterprise is simply another major step that is "down the road" and only beginning to be seriously considered on the agenda of unions.[2]

We mentioned that the first widely publicized breakthrough for managing the enterprise was through the cooperative agreement between the UAW and Chrysler Motors in which the president of the UAW, Douglas Fraser, was elected to the board of directors. Fraser made his presence felt as a representative of the workers in a period of weeks. It was on his initiative that the board formally adopted a resolution dealing with the pressing problem of plant closings and consolidations. The board agreed to establish a plant utilization and human resources committee to ensure that alternative employment was found for laid-off employees during necessary shutdowns. Though Fraser did not choose to continue on the board after his retirement, this major step was recognized as having opened the door for other advances toward worker control.[3]

Since the Chrysler experience there have been numerous worker takeovers. These takeovers range from relatively large firms such as Weirton Steel (7,000 workers) in West Virginia to medium-small firms like Seymour Specialty (300 workers) in Connecticut. There are now estimated to be about 1,000 self-governed firms in the United States (producer cooperatives). These producer cooperatives now serve as a prototype for self-management consultants. They are models of development for consulting institutes such as the Industrial Cooperative Association in Massachusetts and PACE in Pennsylvania. These institutes respond to requests for information about cooperatives and occasionally from managers in the 8,000 ESOPs. The ESOPs that have been transformed into worker cooperatives are still only a half dozen in the United States, but self-management consultants believe this number will increase in the coming decade.

A number of new steps have been taken by labor unions to cooperate with management at the national level over critical issues in corporate policy. For example, the Communication Workers of America (CWA) negotiated with AT&T to establish a national committee to generate initiatives for cooperative labor-management activity among Bell system affiliates. Its purposes include encouraging greater employee participation. Similar national committees are already in place in the automobile industry.

At the heart of the many innovative new labor pacts is the belief on the part of management that the new steps will make their firm more competitive. The idea is that labor helps management raise productivity in return for lifetime jobs and institutional security for the union.

In many cases, labor leaders have argued that these participatory programs have helped orient workers toward dealing with management problems and are thus preparatory for the responsibilities of ownership. For example, in such simple matters as joint preretirement programs, workers have learned how to instruct and provide pertinent information on pension funds that are administered jointly by management and union representatives. The advantages of this type of participation are subtle in their learning dimensions. These programs have increased the awareness of labor leaders about how pension funds work. Today, the overall goal of the AFL-CIO is to develop a pattern of tripartite control over the allocation of capital from these funds at the national level through the joint oversight of labor, management, and government working together. It is argued that the experiences of working with these programs are cumulative and provide a foundation for managing the enterprise as a whole as well as becoming acquainted with the operations of the larger economic system.

Another example: joint apprenticeship training programs are of long standing with union and management making certain that apprentices are properly selected and their training appropriate to their trade. The union is now engaging in still higher levels of management policy based on this experience. Still another example: joint administration of worker benefit plans, such as health care and pensions, have become traditional. Together the parties determine the facts in any disputed situation, apply the provisions of the program, and correct errors in payment or coverage. This has led to greater union control over the process. Still another example: there are joint health and safety committees in which thousands of corrective actions are taken each year. Unions have increased their level of control as a result of joint studies by these committees. The joint health and safety committees normally arise from collective bargaining, but once the provisions are written as part of the labor contract, their implementation becomes a matter of mutual concern and cooperation.[4]

We have noted that labor-management cooperation can cut two ways. First, it can become another method of management to control workers and subdue union activism. Second, it can be a subtle stage in the long-range movement to integrate the two subtrends of worker participation in higher management and worker ownership. The difference between these two interpretations on the role of labor participation is fiercely debated today by leaders in the United Auto Workers. The subject of the debate was their new contract with General Motors.

A recent significant step in the direction of labor-management cooperation has been that of the UAW and General Motors in the new Saturn Project. In this case, the UAW helped G.M. design work practices to be used with new technology in producing a car to compete with low-priced imports. In return, G.M. pledged to hire UAW members from other plants in starting up its Saturn plant in Tennessee, thus ensuring the UAW as the bargaining agent for the new employees. The new agreement thus involved the union in the most advanced level of codetermination of plant policies in the United States to date.

The National Right to Work Committee charged that the special provision on hiring through union leadership violated the federal labor law, but after six months of study, the National Labor Relations Board decided to dismiss the charges without a trial. This means that the Saturn Project plan for high-level joint policy making will probably have a number of new models developing in the United States.

The UAW and G.M. technicians jointly designed the new work system and the agreement gives employees a strong voice in all operations. It says that a majority of the initial complement of Saturn workers will come from other G.M. plants and therefore that the UAW is recognized as the bargaining agent for these new workers. This new step toward top-level cooperation is of course undergoing debate from the right and the left. Critics on the right believe that it gives the union too much power while critics from within the UAW have claimed that it will pit team against team in the workplace and represents only another example of the collusion of the union with the competitive purposes of corporation.

The public issue is whether management or labor is winning in each new step toward collaboration in higher levels of corporate administration. We have said that both sides can win at the same time but that each case must be evaluated on its own terms. The criteria for evaluating these cases include knowing the degree to which labor unions are strengthened, the degree to which responsible labor leaders understand what they are doing in terms of long-range strategy, the degree to which a vision of worker self-governance is retained and management skills are learned, as well as the degree to which advances are made in efficiency and productivity within the corporation.

Community Self-governance

The number of new innovative firms and the strength of subtrends leading toward community self-governance in the United States show no signs of a revolutionary progress and also no signs of stopping in their slow advance. New policies continue to be formulated at state and city levels to advance local controls over land, labor, and capital. For example, combinations of grants, technical assistance,

and financing are provided for community development corporations in Florida, Illinois, Massachusetts, Minnesota,
New Hampshire, and Wisconsin. Massachusetts and Florida
supply grants to CDCs to hire core staff. The city of
Boston designates CDCs as priority when properties are
taken by the city for nonpayment of taxes; the property is
rehabilitated into low-income housing by a CDC through
the Boston Housing Partnership. There are now over 1,000
CDCs organized in the United States.[5]

Massachusetts has organized its support for CDCs
into three distinct programs. The Community Development
Finance Corporation (CDFC) provides debt and equity
financing and loan guarantees to business ventures and
real estate development projects sponsored by CDCs. The
Community Economic Development Assistance Corporation
(CEDAC) offers technical-assistance services to CDCs. The
Community Enterprise Economic Development Program (CEED)
helps communities organize new CDCs. Together, these
programs give CDCs access to the full range of resources
that are necessary to undertake successful local development.[6]

The National Congress for Community Economic Development studied carefully the activities of 18 CDCs in the
United States. The researchers found them productive in
aiding business development, housing, employment and
training, and many other developmental activities in local
economies. They also found them to be of mixed ethnicity,
including white, black, Hispanic, and Native American as
well as mixed genders of men and women.[7]

Citizen networks for socially innovative development
in localities include the Association of Community Organizations for Reform Now (ACORN), which has 25,000 member
families in 19 states working a range of issues surrounding
local self-governance. There is also a string of public
interest groups in half the states, supported by a check-
off on student tuition fees and door-to-door canvassing for
contributions. The New York Public Interest Research
Group (PIRG) is one example with a gross budget of $2
million. The Ohio Public Interest Campaign and the Illinois Public Action Council each contain dozens of local
action groups in coalitions that have prominently fought
successfully against a number of local issues such as
plant closings.[8]

Apart from statewide groups, there are thousands of
local action groups in every major city in the nation. The

National Commission on Neighborhoods report in 1979 listed 8,000 community organizations in the country. These are nonstatist (voluntary organizations) organized in the social sector.[9]

From the standpoint of the vision of some proponents of labor and community self-governance today, very little can be said about major progress in these two fields. The United States remains a strongly capitalistic nation charac- terized by command systems in the corporate economy. It is also characterized by its big cities and centers of con- trol in metropolitan areas. At the same time, from the standpoint of what is happening steadily to change these patterns of corporate command and metropolitan dominance, progress can be clearly seen. While there is no reason to believe that these changes could alter the dominant trends fundamentally before the turn of the next century without more government incentives, there is every reason to be- lieve that these trends will continue by themselves well into the future. The question remains whether this slow advance will accumulate in their patterned significance and draw enough national attention to stimulate government policies to quicken this process of social development.

GREECE

Worker Self-Governance

The issue of participation and self-governance at the corporate and community levels in the 1980s in Greece can- not be viewed outside the political and economic context of the country. It has been associated with the political decisions of a socialist-oriented government and economic difficulties in the private and public sectors.

The socialist-oriented government in 1981 declared that it would follow "a third way" toward socialism, name- ly, a socialist system that would be different than that of communist countries and Western social-democratic countries. Despite this declaration, after 1985--under the pressure of economic problems--government policies have been more con- servative; the leftist rhetoric has declined, especially in economic policy. The Greek government seems more recently to be adapting its political ideology to that of Western social-democratic parties as concerns economic policies, whereas, as concerns social policies, the orientation toward

the welfare state remains steady.   This development is
mostly due to the fact that Greece remained a member of
the European Economic Community and had to face the
realities of an open economy, and government policy had
to take into consideration the laws of the market.   To that
trend also contributed the need to attune the policy of
some sectors gradually with EEC policy.[10]

Summarizing, the transition. from the third-way-toward-
socialism policy to Western social-democratic policies was a
necessity coming from the economic conditions that prevailed, and the participation of Greece in the EEC.

The socialist-oriented government proposed the creation of new institutions and brought forth new legal measures and a great deal of discussion on the concepts of
democratization, modernization, and self-governance at
various levels of the political, economic, and social life
of the country.   The government, as part of its underlying
ethos and political rhetoric, gave an emphasis to the cooperative idea and to the promotion of decision making at
the local level, with the participation of inhabitants in
local affairs.   Yet the outcomes of these intentions are
highly disputed.   It remains for future evaluations to determine the extent to which decentralized democracy has
actually occurred versus to what extent the creation of a
powerful party apparatus, controlled from the top, comes
to pervade all aspects of local life.

We have said that the problems faced by the political administration in Greece show some similarities to
policies in the United States in the growth of government
activity and the public debt in spite of the apparently
different ideology.   At the same time, there were also important differences.

New institutions and legislation seem to have been
hastily made in Greece by the present government.   Defects
of planning; the lack of the appropriate infrastructure,
training, and sufficient information about corresponding
empirical models from the international experience; the introduction of new concepts and the vagueness and obscurity
of their content; as well as the ideological differences even
among the theorists of PASOK have created confusion,
strengthened the reaction against the proposed institutions,
and provided reasons for severe criticism of the institutions
of participation and self-management at the level of the
enterprise.   These unfavorable developments have been intensified by the serious economic problems that Greece is

facing at present (deficit in the balance of payments, low rate of development, inflation, lack of interest for investments among Greek and foreign entrepreneurs, loss of competitiveness of native products, overindebtedness of large enterprises, increasing unemployment, etc.), which seem to force the government to draw back in order to secure stabilization of the economy in 1985–87, the necessary foreign loans, and the needed investments. It could be maintained that these developments have inhibited the government from proceeding to active implementation of new institutions and experimentation to avoid any further criticisms and discouragement of the entrepreneurs.

The model set by the public sector (where the already-existing serious problems seem to have been intensified by measures concerning remuneration, the rights of workers, etc.) creates serious reservations for the private sector. In other words, the possibility of reproduction within the private sector of a model with serious problems seems to discourage such developments in the private sector. Everyone in Greece hopes and searches for a job in the public sector, and clamors for the expansion of the state bureaucracy. But productivity of public employees is low, since the public sector does not operate efficiently and lacks management skills.[11]

Beyond the above factors, which seem to affect the rate of development of trends, the connection of the new institutions exclusively with political ideologies creates some concern as to the smooth development of the trends that started being traced out at the beginning of the decade 1980.

Community Self-governance

The effort to develop community self-governance has been instituted so quickly that there is some doubt about the desired results, owing to the difficulty in overcoming technical and organizational deficiencies and mobilizing initiative and resources for local and regional development at a level adequate enough to secure restructuring of the Greek countryside. The required funds, on the other hand, for such an endeavor seem to be missing, as the government is obliged to check the growth of deficits and of foreign loans, while the prospects for growth in Greece seem to be rather limited in the coming decade. The objective of a balanced regional development, of revitalized country-side, despite its wide acceptance, does not seem a possible reality in the near future.

The obstacles to effective decentralization are formidable. Greece has a large nationalized sector—the state runs about 60 percent of the economy—characterized by a pervasive patronage system resistant to popular control. The country is politically highly centralized (demographically and industrially) and many trade unions are controlled by the state. Added to these are barriers imposed by the international economy. Pressures for increased productivity in the name of competitiveness are great and are expected to be intensified in the near future, especially in the early 1990s. Furthermore, the existing pressure to cover the extended needs of the Greek economy for managerial and technical expertise may slow down the trend toward increased popular control. The government's decision not to embark on a more-extensive program of worker self-management that would aim at democratizing the workplace as well as the economywide decision-making process is already a concession to that pressure.[12]

The degree of possible mobilization of the social sector in which this effort is mostly based and the efficiency and ingenuity with which the resources will be utilized has to be proved. The implementation of a well-integrated setup, owing to the experimental stage of the efforts made, is not possible to evaluate as yet.

On the other hand, the new institutions, the measures, the continual reference to the concepts of democratization, modernization, and self-governance at the various levels of the economic and social life have advanced social consciousness versus individualism, and have influenced attitudes that may contribute to new participative schemes and promote social justice. But the intense projection of the political factor has limited the broader acceptance of the institution of participation and self-management as forms of social development generally desired and approved and will possibly delay the realization of the desired social developments.

In order that the above developments in the critical sector of production lead to higher forms of social development and responsibility of the interested parties, workers, and employers, it is necessary to proceed to a re-examination of the present positions and attitudes on the basis of social and labor criteria beyond conflicting political ideologies and with the purpose of selecting models able to achieve managerial effectiveness and enlargement of worker self-governance and autonomy.

Under these conditions, such policies of socialist governance may become the most significant contributions to the field of political development. In a world that is now half-populated with socialist-oriented governments, it carries special significance. It may also provide a model for overcoming the problems of state socialist command systems. The antihuman tendencies in state bureaucracies may thus be treated through a similar development. The new policy simply requires time and research to determine its capacity to be efficient as well as responsive to labor and community needs.

The objectives for integrated plans of regional and community development, for participation in the formulation and implementation of the plan, and the agent selected-- the social sector--for the development of local communities may point to a rational process of decentralization and democratic planning worthy of study.

We will now define developments that have prospects for the social development of the country and possible usefulness for small nations that seek their own path, or a "third way."

THE SELF-GOVERNING DEVELOPMENTS IN REVIEW: FUTURE PROSPECTS

With the coming to power of a socialist-oriented government in Greece in 1981, certain policies are being formulated for securing worker participation in the public sector and for obtaining a broader representation of social constituencies in critical sectors of the economy and in the development at the regional and community levels with new structural and institutional arrangements and policy measures. The institutional changes pursued at the socioeconomic level and the questioning over the social, economic, and political structures have pushed forward some important changes in labor relations.

Of special importance may be the participation of the workers in the control of public enterprises together with the community and several social constituencies in order to function in favor of the public interest. Equally remarkable may be the development toward participation of social

groups at the regional and local levels in the choice of
the developmental model of the country through the procedures of democratic planning.

The new institution of worker participation (one-third
board representation) in control over public enterprises
does not by itself seem to have contributed for the time
being to adequate levels of economic efficiency and productivity, as officially stated, and contrary to some studies
of what has happened with worker participation in the
United States. The abrupt change, the novelty of the
approach for the Greek scene, have deprived this interesting social experiment of an adequate supply of competent
people to treat the problems, for there has not been the
required preparation to upgrade skills, to disseminate information, and secure documentation. Doubts are expressed
about up-to-date information on the development of worker
participation abroad of the PASOK planners, which may be
responsible for mistakes made in the planning and implementation of the new institution in the public enterprises.

Some of the criticisms are not unrealistic because of
the way worker participation has been implemented by the
government. The government has not developed fully adequate programs for training and implementation of the new
idea. Therefore, worker participation does not appear to
have wide appreciation as the most efficient way to manage
an enterprise. There is criticism of the new institution
as being more of a political and ideological character.
Those doubts were reinforced with state involvement in the
cooperative system in its attempt to promote worker participation and "protect" the system. The cooperative movement
was considered with some justification, of course, an attempt to limit the private sector of the economy and to
develop the social sector.

It should be noted however that the extended participation of labor representatives in the organized system
through consultative and planning committees at sectoral,
national, and regional levels seems to be accepted by all
social groups. It is through this form of participation
that the role of the working class in the organized system
has been extended. This trend is expected to continue
and labor will play a greater role in shaping policies of
wider interest for society as well as an active role in the
enactment of labor and social legislation. Some dissent
appears to be related today to new legislation and the
political appointments by the government for enforcement
of the participatory process.

In Chapter 1 we discussed the unplanned overurbani-
zation process in Greece during the 1960s and 1970s and
its social consequences. Restructuring of the Greek countryside—community self-governance—is a major priority of
government policy. A consistent effort is being made to
reverse past trends of abandonment of local communities by
their populations and of lack of interest of private enterprise for investment and development in those regions. The
government's document for economic and social strategy,
the 1983-87 Five-Year Plan, a synthesis of local and national priorities, although almost forgotten today because
of the stabilization policy in effect since late 1985, provides a desired framework of action, projects of development, and policy measures for community and regional
development. In particular, the 1983-87 Plan entails
structural arrangements, financial and technical support,
and promotion of the social sector of the economy (the enterprises of local government, the companies of popular
base, and the cooperatives) as the main agents for community development. Restructuring of the Greek countryside
clearly will take much more time and effort than envisaged
in the Plan.

Furthermore, this model of decentralized development
seems to depend also on the political power of local PASOK
branches. If they lose any control in the decision-making
processes, things will be reversed; the decentralization
and more generally the socialization will become just one
form of state power.[13]

The Greek model differs from the U.S. model in the
pattern of development envisaged. In Greece the process
of change is initiated by legislative mandate and party
involvement; in the United States autonomous developments
are encouraged by economic incentives for a more socially
accountable entrepreneurship. The Greek model differs
from the U.S. model insofar as it emphasizes local government participation, even though recent policies of the
Reagan administration have accented cost sharing at state
and local levels in a parallel fashion. Decentralization
and strengthening of local government authorities (OTA).
are decisive factors for the local and regional economy.
A development model is envisaged based on decentralization
of planning and decision-making processes as well as participation by social partners in the determination of priorities in an effort to reach national consensus of the action
undertaken. The Greek Plan does not emphasize social

controls in the same manner as CLTs and CDCs in the United States.

Such measures of vital importance as deconcentration of public administration; increased funds under the control of local authorities; increased responsibility and independence of local authorities; the widening and strengthening of the cooperative movement and the municipal enterprise; encouragement of joint ventures among private firms, cooperatives, and local and central government, and more have begun to be cultivated. Entrepreneurial activity at the local level is mostly entrusted to the social sector of the economy. It remains to be seen if the succession of a different government will strengthen these developments or will let them die.

This model of regional and community development is expected to set free creative forces and initiative for development at the local and regional level. It is also expected to contribute in the short run to the solution of critical problems and in the long run in a more-balanced development of the country, that is, in controlling the potential imperfect competitive market forces in the interest of the community. With the development of the social sector, certain indirect social controls of the private sector's productive activity and of market forces seem possible. This development implies an extension of the planned sector of the economy that does not have all the disadvantages of the state so long as it is not politically controlled. A gradual socialization of the means of production is attempted in this way in the hope that workers will have greater interest and will take better care of their collective property. But socialization includes also government controls and government participation in ways that differ significantly from the U.S. experience.

Nevertheless, an interesting attempt has been made in Greece to set up a favorable institutional base that aims to upgrade community life and develop activities in the regions and local communities that are accountable to land, labor, and capital. The purpose in part is to control the deteriorating influences of the potential imperfect competition market forces on the countryside. This development entails a new social orientation in the productive sectors and also public administration. The whole endeavor involves accenting processes of bottom-up development in contrast to the current top-down process of policy. The top-down accent gives a nationwide sense of urgency and a basis for widespread structural change, but policies today need more balance with local incentives and grass-root efforts.

Attempts at community self-governance in Greece show promise of a more-extended and more-integrated process as well as of a more consistent effort than in the United States. Set against the spontaneous, sporadic development in the United States, largely outside of state control, in Greece there is commitment of the government for action in restructuring the countryside and an institutional setup that harmonizes with its ideology and attempts to implement its objectives. It remains to be seen which approach will prove to have greater potential.

FUTURE POLICY RESEARCH: COMPARATIVE ADVANTAGES

Important lessons can be learned from the experience in both these nations for policy research. In particular, some scholars are interested in how studies on these experiences may show degrees of convergence and divergence in patterns of development.

We noted at the outset that some scholars question whether Greece is experiencing a divergence from Western patterns of development and establishing its own unique form of development or experiencing a convergence with Western patterns. Our belief is that there are dimensions of development in Greece that show signs of both convergence and divergence, but that each dimension is of comparative advantage to each country.[14] Put another way, certain patterns of development in the two nations show comparative advantages.

Much has been said in economics about how comparative advantages may provide different nations with greater wealth and security in their separate economies; when a nation can compete better by specializing in a product that other nations have not developed, it serves to their advantage on the world market. This specialization increases their competitive edge in sales. But we are not talking here about economics. We are talking about a comparative advantage in social and economic organization from which each nation can learn. These are developmental advantages gained by each nation that can be shared to the benefit of both nations.

A special advantage in the United States is evident in the innovative firms contributing to greater measures of self-governance and social accountability in the economy. Americans have conducted significant corporate experiments on a small scale that suggest important new policies to be made on a national scale. We want to evaluate the experimental areas that require further study for Greek researchers.

A special advantage in Greece is in the recognition of the need for a national policy to implement change. Greece has attempted some major steps on a national scale, the outcomes of which need to be carefully studied. Government leaders have been seeking to create a fundamentally different system of governance in the life of the economy, which must be studied in depth and evaluated by American researchers.

If comparative advantages exist in each nation, what can we suggest for future studies in light of our conceptual framework?

The United States: Recommendations for
Research on Comparative Advantages

The lack of U.S. government policies to counteract tendencies toward corporate centralization and metropolitan dominance may be the most-serious problem to be addressed in the next decade. The United States thus contrasts with Greece by its failure to implement national policies to counteract these trends. It now behooves us to point toward principles of government policy and social research that could lead successfully in the direction of decentralizing corporate and metropolitan life without the loss of effective industrial organization and productivity.

The distinctive contribution of the American experience lies in the fact that new types of businesses can be designed to socialize land, labor, and capital without requiring government controls. These new socially oriented businesses offer special promise for their accountability to constituencies. They are unique social experiments within a capitalist setting that could be studied further for their adaptability to a socialist setting.

It is important to note the capitalist context under which they have developed in the United States. First, worker self-managed firms, CDCs, CLTs, and CDFCs have not been implemented by government mandate. They have been spurred into existence by enabling legislation and tax-incentive programs and have all emerged on a voluntary basis. Part of their value and effectiveness may rest in this voluntary process under which they are emerging. Second, they remain relatively unstudied in their internal life. It is not clear to what extent such attributes as self-interest, profiteering, winning market dominance, and so forth remain a part of this innovative management's orientation. There is reason to believe that these conventional interests remain in some cases.[15]

The degree to which these corporate structures lead workers toward higher values, such as a social concern for the impact of their product on the community, would be of interest to socialist leaders. The question is whether these types of corporations, derived in a capitalist setting, can be transferred in principle to a socialist setting. There is a second question that should be raised here: Can government incentives encourage a more-rapid development of these innovative firms?

We think there can be affirmative answers to these questions but they are not easily found. We would say that subtle changes toward broader social values may be one of the most difficult dimensions to develop in a market system. We can only suggest that these key corporate structures show promise in laying the foundation for a new system of values.

Third, these innovative firms (CDCs, CDCUs, CLTs, etc.) have not been observed for their effectiveness to operate in greater numbers on a national scale and the introduction of incentives for them to develop together have yet to be studied. The legal, social, and economic dimensions of these social innovations in land, labor, and capital have yet to be examined more extensively for their collective impact on the larger society.

We are talking about new types of democratic corporations whose counterparts are not the same in other nations and which have not developed in large numbers. We are suggesting that a new combination of these corporations related to land, labor, and capital can be put together effectively but that this special combination has never been put into practice fully at the national level. In light of this possibility, let us now review them and add facts about them for clarification.

The New Democratic Corporations in Review

The type of self-managed enterprise (worker cooperative) we recommend has been designed by the Industrial
Cooperative Association (ICA). This model was adapted
from the system of Mondragón cooperatives in northern
Spain and adjusted to the American scene. This type of
worker cooperative was devised in part because the stock
of U.S. worker-owned firms often become purchased by outside financiers. When this happens, the value of local
worker control is lost. The ICA prototype keeps this from
happening by keeping co-op stock within the domain of the
firm. Also, this corporate model has an internal account
for workers' savings, which are drawn from a portion of
the profits. Workers cannot withdraw their savings until
they separate from the firm and the firm itself has achieved
sufficient success as an economic entity.

This profit-sharing account has three advantages to
be studied in further detail. First, the plan rewards
workers for their productivity and thus offers an incentive
system for work. Second, the internal accounts for each
worker accent the value of the individual in the firm, as
opposed to the collective, where individual savings are not
accumulated. Third, the capital savings of employees can
be utilized by the firm for corporate investment in new
technology and expansion. Thus, it provides an internal
motive for corporate development. The lack of motive for
corporate development was first observed in Yugoslav firms
where internal capital was not accumulated and the firm
had little incentive and capacity to develop itself. The
features of this prototype, therefore, usually require special statutes to operate in a capitalist or socialist setting.
Comparative studies are needed to show their advantages
and disadvantages in different cultural settings.

Similarly, a special model for socializing landed
property is provided in the U.S. experience with the community land trust (CLT). This model was developed by
the Institute for Community Economics in Greenfield, Massachusetts, and also requires study for its intercultural advantages and disadvantages. The United States has many
types of land trusts, but they are different from this important community model. Ordinary land trusts can fall
prey to the destructive forces of the market or become
elitist even in their purpose to conserve land in the public interest. So, it is important to see the distinction of
the CLT. It is also different from land trusts in other
nations such as Israel, Mexico, and Tanzania.

For example, the CLT is designed with a board of trustees represented by one-third lessees (workers), one-third community (not the municipality), and one-third public (not necessarily the government). The local community representatives are not drawn from the municipal government but rather from an electoral process legally instituted by the CLT itself as part of the private sector. The CLT is a form of self-government within the local economy operating outside the control of the state or the municipality. The public representatives in some cases are selected by the board itself. The board makes the selection from community-based organizations, which can be the municipal government, a community council, a church council, or others. This representative may also be a professional person who is known for an expertise associated with the problems of the trust. A rural land trust may choose a soil expert where the problem of soil erosion is high so that the farmers renting the plots can be kept informed about the need for preserving the productivity of the land. The CLT is a democratic institution responsible to the community as a whole and operating outside the government. It is part of what we have described as the social sector.

Other U.S. prototypes that we find significant for international study also have special features that are not duplicated in other nations. They require special study for their implementation as models of social development.

The community development corporation, for example, is a democratic corporation operating in the private sector with similar functions to the local government but separate from it. It is an independent entity designed to coordinate the development of the local economy outside the mandate of the state or the local municipality. It can be organized as a profit or a nonprofit entity, but its own mandate is to make money in the interest of the whole community.

The community development credit union is a customer-owned bank that is designed not only to invest capital in the best interest of its owners, but to be accountable to its customers' values. It is thus different from a conventional bank that invests anywhere to make a profit. It is also different in being designed to educate its local owners about its social purposes and the nature of its business. Many of these community-oriented banks have developed in poor neighborhoods where citizens lack an education in home accounting and banking practices. It is therefore

organized to train its local customer-owners about the
discipline of capital savings, which in some cases may
involve training them in literacy. It also teaches about
the tendencies of big corporations to squeeze local capital
from local use and how to increase the capacity of local
people to develop their own system of capital accounting.

These corporations are unique in that they provide a
basis for constructing an economy with a social foundation.
They offer a basis for social development that otherwise
could become entrenched with local elitism. Elitism develops easily through the private sector in the capitalist
tradition, but it also develops easily through a political
party in the state socialist tradition. Either form of
elitism can cause a slowdown in the growth of a social
economy. These corporations offer an alternative. Combined together they lessen the likelihood that local elitism
will develop.

These firms have shown great merit individually in
separate locations but they have not been tested together
as part of a coordinated plan in large geographical
areas.[16] If they are to become a system of community
corporations operating nationwide and independent of the
municipality and the state, they need their own arbitration boards and social federations. Each democratic corporation is still experimenting in their separate environments in special ways: For example, CLTs are adjusting
to city zoning codes even though they have shown suc-
cesses by "legislating" in this area; worker cooperatives
are still developing charter principles that protect workers
against ethnic dominance and can affirm the principles of
equality between men and women within their own firm,
even though most of them practice gender equality on an
informal basis. The point is that without testing their
own accountability systems to establish social standards
of operation, they—like traditional business firms—may
invoke government controls. Our argument is that they
should require much fewer outside controls than conventional business enterprises because their self-accountable
structures give them this advantage. They reduce the
necessity for government controls while maintaining efficiency and productivity.

In sum, all these models have yet to be tested as
part of a regional or national experiment. Creative national legislation has yet to be formulated that offers
them incentives to develop together on a large scale. But

their success on a small scale in overcoming select problems of both corporate and state dominance suggests that they be given primary consideration in new policy initiatives. They represent important models for nations to examine in efforts to advance social development within the local economy.

Greece: Recommendations for Research on Comparative Advantages

The Greek experience complements the lack of U.S. experience with national legislation. Here we have a government policy to encourage democratization and self-governance at the national level. A national policy now exists for some forms of worker and citizen participation in economic affairs. Political mistakes and corporate failures point to a need for study, evaluation, and experimentation.

First, it is important to recognize certain aspects of the large-scale picture that require sociological analysis. Such aspects include the practicality of a social vision that encourages desired change at the national level related to a human-oriented government policy for labor, the adequacy of attempts to modernize economic sectors with new structures of social accountability, the ability of a program to bring up the less-advantaged segments of society within a policy of redistribution of income, the capacity to revitalize communities and regions through the development of a social sector, the degree to which citizens are inspired to public involvement, the extent of voluntarism, the character of participatory democracy, and so forth. The emphasis in this sociological analysis is on development on a large scale having an impact on all aspects of social, economic, and cultural life.

Second, it is important to study the weaknesses and mistakes in government policy, including the absolute or unrestricted emphasis given to the political factor, the accent on legislative mandates as opposed to incentives, the unrealistic goals promoted by a grandiose plan, the lack of long-term planning and consideration of the need for implementing middle-range objectives, lack of serious study and consideration of other existing models and experiences, the expansionary macroeconomic policy and its consequences on the economy and the objective pursued,

reaction of the private sector, confusion around terms and
concepts used, increased government regulation, costly
programs, fast announcements and their impact on people,
and lack of experience and knowledge among government
officials, consideration of present realities, indifference
for sound management principles, and finally the strengthening of corporatism and the creation of the PASOK <u>nomen-
klatura</u>, its development and social characteristics.

Third, dimensions of this national vision that seem
potentially effective are important to study. These include the socialization of the government sector; the various participative structures in the social sector, in particular the companies of popular base; locally owned
shipping companies; women's cooperatives; the efforts to
promote agricultural cooperatives and other cooperatives as
agents of local and regional development; the formulation
of a social vision in the Five-Year Plan for Economic and
Social Development 1983-87; and the structures for providing citizen involvement in national planning, participative
structures in higher education, and a national health plan.
Although ill implemented and disfunctioning or utopian in
some respects, these dimensions need serious study and
consideration for their positive impact on social and economic development. They are interesting in that they en-
visage a social foundation for the Greek economy and may
offer an alternative course for social development.

It should be emphasized that in the Greek case corporate elitism developed in certain instances through the
private sector in the capitalist tradition, while more recently cases also are observed of political party elitism
more or less in the state socialist tradition. Both these
tendencies could be detrimental to the future development
of a socially oriented economy in Greece. Such tendencies
should be detected and evaluated. Furthermore, it should
be of interest to study in particular the relation of the
government to the party, party influence and involvement
in policy making, and evaluate populist policies.

A national vision for independent policy in a small
and dependent economy that introduces new modes of development and serious changes of the institutional setup requires careful studies that critically examine mistakes. It
is important for such national policy to consider various
models of development and be eclectic while at the same
time building gradually its own realistic model, fitting
best into its national and cultural setting.

Fourth, the role of socialist ideology in motivating and in demotivating people (causing resistance) is an important factor to study, as it impacts on the performance of the economy. We have noted the negative results of fears among corporate leaders. The rhetoric of political parties too often entangled in dogmatism that is surpassed by present realities can make a major difference in the outcome of policies. Also, the symbolism surrounding political acts has a major impact on economic life.

Fifth, it is important to study in Greece how the appropriate infrastructure and work toward the goals of efficiency and effectiveness can be built up beyond the traditional ideologies. The ideologies can be unrealistic, ill adapted, or inappropriate for providing solutions to Greece's specific problems. Greece must develop its own managerial support system apart from the political slogans that may separate or bind it to the rest of the world.

This may be one of the most-important lessons to be drawn from the examination of these cases: capitalist and socialist economies or economies of the mixed type in big and small nations that may show convergent, divergent, or even segmented courses of development should rather be seen under the perspective of social management. All economies need to manage socially complex systems. They need a managerial support system to enhance their development along desired goals. The need to work toward important goals of efficiency and effectiveness beyond the competing ideologies that separate the world is a key factor common to all societies. Managing complexity is the challenge of the future. The accent on ideology without a parallel promotion of a realistic managerial support system can prove to be disastrous for efficient national development as well as for international cooperation, understanding, and peace.

INTERNATIONAL ISSUES IN SOCIAL ECONOMY

Keeping in mind our conceptual framework, certain aspects of these two cases have implications of international research.

One interesting political concept developed within the Greek case is the social sector. In the American context, the idea of a social sector is implicit in the enactment of legislation (CDCs, CLTs, CDFCs, ESOP) to encourage the socialization of the private sector. The study of the applicability of this concept on an international basis could lead toward a new direction for the politics of nations occupying some point in the continuum of regulated markets.

There is a difference in emphasis between the concept of the social sector as conceived within our theoretical orientation and the political formulation of the concept in the Greek context. The formulation of this term to guide new directions for social policy is critical for all modern nations and therefore worthy of further examination.

Early statements about the meaning of the social sector in Greek government policy refers primarily to local development. This sector includes cooperatives, municipal enterprises, and enterprises with a popular base, like the shipping companies. According to Vavouras, the local government is considered the most significant agent of the social sector.[17] He notes that in Greece, local authorities were considered until recently merely instruments for the implementation of the centrally determined general public policy and that the new PASOK policy seeks to change this tendency so that local authorities have more power to implement social development. Also, joint ventures by private firms, agricultural cooperatives, and local and central government are particularly encouraged to develop under this new policy.[18]

The meaning of the social sector is still being defined in the political context of Greece and is part of the effort to implement the vision developed by PASOK; it is important, therefore, to add some clarification to the meaning of the term within our conceptual framework.

The term as we see it refers to the whole range of democratic enterprises developing within the private sector. Development of a social sector cannot be simply legislated, although this does not mean that legislation cannot be enacted to encourage its development. It emerges by definition as part of the social development of the business sector and the socialization of government sectors. Government enterprises (including centrally and locally controlled) are not included conceptually in this category. If they become socialized in the manner that Greek policy intends, with employee and community representation in policy making, they begin to move significantly toward what we have described as the social sector. But the meaning of the social sector in its ideal typical form as we conceive it, refers to the development of a nonstatist (or nongovernmental) sector that becomes socially responsible to its constituencies and local communities while remaining effective and productive. This includes large-scale corporations that become decentralized by employee representation through their subsidiaries and develop social audits to monitor their own activities in the public interest. It includes social federations that help govern the competitive activities between corporations in the interest of the larger society. In many countries, employee associations have begun to monitor the ethical practices of firms in the marketplace. They become part of the self-governing formation of a social sector.

The social sector, a working concept in our theoretical framework of social economy, is clearly one of the most important areas to develop in the economic life of modern nations, and the typical traits of this sector have yet to be fully identified. The social concept leads toward studies of not only local life but interpersonal life as an important part of a self-governing social sector. But it also has broader implications that include the development of social charters, social constitutions, and by-laws and social audits for corporations. It includes the nonstatist development of judicial systems, interindustry councils, and social audits for whole industries. It includes social federations of employee-owned firms with self-initiated ethical codes and standards of conduct in the public interest. It means the development of consumer councils in some countries as a replacement for government participation in utilities. It means the development of buyers clubs to counteract the tendency for producer firms to become dominant in the economy. The social sector is evolving both with government support and on its own through voluntary action. In sum, the concept of the social sector refers to a nonstatist economy that has become structurally accountable to the people it affects and is therefore relatively self-governing.

The policy dimension in our conceptual framework is thus in tension with the prevailing practices in both the United States and Greece. It points in the direction of policies that elicit greater support for the development of a social sector. In other words, the social sector in the United States could develop more fruitfully through stronger government incentives for private corporations to promote accountability systems such as we have described and through more encouragement of the developing social move-

ments that we have described. The social sector in Greece,
described in the early 1980s as a political vision for the
reorganization of production and municipal life, could develop still more fruitfully as a social policy grounded in
wide popular support with a greater accent on methods of
social self-regulation in the private sector. In both nations, special attention needs to be given to the way the
private sector can develop its own systems of participation
and accountability around the people it affects.*

The general direction needed by government policy
in both nations can be easily discerned from this analysis,
but creating the actual basis for the social development
of enterprises is a complex process requiring both government incentives and grass root support. Such a policy
requires support not only from national leaders but from
the public, where its implementation is related to the time-
liness and readiness of people to understand its value.
For this reason, our key recommendation for both countries
involves the development of research programs that have

---

*Both nations will also be facing many problems that
we have not discussed. For example, we have said nothing
about the new class of professionals emerging in capitalist
nations undergoing a social transition and the impact of
this new class on labor and community life. See: Charles
Derber, Professionals as Workers (Boston: G. K. Hall,
1982). We have not discussed the possibilities of trade
federations and consumer federations serving as a social
foundation for price determination and the establishment of
ethical codes within the marketplace. A step in this direction has been taken by Wolfgang Streeck and Philippe C.
Schmitter, eds., Private Interest Government: Beyond Market
and State (London: Sage, 1985); Gene Laczniak and Patrick
Murphy, Marketing Ethics (Lexington, Mass.: D. C. Heath,
1985); Richard Farmer and W. Dickerson Hogue, Corporate
Social Responsibility (Lexington, Mass.: D. C. Heath,
1985); Severyn T. Bruyn, The Social Market (forthcoming).
We have not analyzed the political basis for multinational
corporations to operate between nations with the purpose
of optimizing both social and economic returns in home and
host nations. See: Bart Fisher and Jeff Turner, Regulat-
ing Multinational Enterprise (New York: Praeger, 1983).
The study of such questions remains ahead as international
issues developing in the social economy of modern nations.

guided this analysis. This means the formation of research institutes and the promotion of university programs in each country to study precisely the development of a social sector.

These institutes and university programs can then begin to examine particular cases for the manner in which social transformations that reduce the necessity for government intervention and controls take place. Their purpose would be to study the power of people to develop a social foundation to the economy--a power that emanates from the synergy between higher levels of productivity with social accountability and greater proportions of profitability with grass roots participation.

If a large nation like the United States and a small nation like Greece can take the lead in moving in this direction, we should see a future more promising for other nations. We may see the first significant signs of socially self-governed economies developing in post-modern society.

NOTES

1. Michael Moffitt, "Reaganomics and the Decline of U.S. Hegemony," World Policy Journal (Fall 1987):561-62.

2. Irving Bluestone, "The Workers' Role in Decision-Making," in Eurosocialism and America, ed. Nancy Lieber (Philadelphia, Pa.: Temple University Press, 1982).

3. Ibid., p. 190.

4. A detailed study on these issues can be found in David Montgomery, Workers' Control in America: Studies in the History of Work, Technology, and Labor Struggles (New York: Cambridge University Press, 1979).

5. Severyn T. Bruyn and James Meehan, eds., Beyond the Market and the State (Philadelphia, Pa.: Temple University Press, 1987).

6. "Resource Centerpiece," Changing Work, Spring 1986 (Newton, Mass.: P.O. Box 261), p. C 3.

7. Robin J. Erdman, et al., Community Development Profile (Washington, D.C.: National Congress for Community Economic Development, 1985).

8. For a detailed picture of these organizations, see Mark Green, Winning Back America (New York: Bantam Books, 1982).

9. For case studies of what is happening in communities across the United States in nonmunicipal action organization, see Harry C. Boyte, Community Is Possible (New York: Harper & Row, 1984).

10. See John Loulis, "The Greek Malaise," Encounter 67 (July–August 1986):68–70, 72–73.

11. Ibid., pp. 72–73.

12. Nicholas Xenos, "Economic Democracy in Greece," New York Times, May 6, 1982.

13. Ibid.

14. Litsa N. Nicolaou, The Growth and Development of Sociology in Greece (Boston: Department of Sociology, Boston College, pp. 78–79, mimeographed).

15. It is not clear to what extent changes in corporate structure in these new firms have altered typical business attitudes and what we described earlier as social character. We mentioned studies by writers in the 1950s claiming existence of the "organizational man" and the "other–directed" self. There is reason to believe that not much change in character has occurred among employees within worker self–managed firms, in part because of the larger impact of business culture on them. Clearly, there are also not the society–oriented motives involved in the work culture of some of these innovative firms. See Edward S. Greenberg, "Producer Cooperatives and Democratic Theory," in Robert Jackall and Henry Levin, Worker Cooperatives in America (Berkeley: University of California Press, 1984). Finally, limited studies of these firms suggest that there is no vision among workers of how to overcome the problems of aggressive self–interest engendered by the competitive market system. A few studies approach the answers to these questions, but they are not sufficiently focused on these questions or broadly based in their statistical coverage of these firms to draw firm conclusions on the internal subculture and the impact of their structure on the life of workers. For CDCs, see A Review of Abt Associates, Inc., Evaluation of the Special Impact Program, Center for Community Economic Development, 639 Massachusetts Avenue, Cambridge, Mass., 1977.

16. Since each model has been implemented independently on a voluntary basis and furthermore not operated frequently in geographic proximity with each other, there is reason to expect that new problems in the relationship to rights of control over property could be a problem. They need to be tested in practice together on an experi-

mental basis. Also, these firms would require a new legal foundation for them to operate effectively together in most national contexts.

17. Ioannis Vavouras, "Local Government and the Social Sector: An Evaluation of the Recent Institutional Arrangements in Greece," Annals of Public and Cooperative Economy, Vol. 56, No. 4 (1985):497-512.

18. P. Maistros, "The New Institutions for Decentralization, Local Government, Democratic Planning and Local Development," paper presented at the Training Seminar for Planning Specialists (Athens: Center of Planning and Economic Research, February 1985) (in Greek) (mimeographed).

Appendix/Social Federations: The Foundation of Democratic Enterprises

The development of democratic enterprises such as worker-owned corporations, consumer cooperatives, community development corporations, community development credit unions, and community land trusts is becoming notable in many nations, but their survival is made difficult by the competitive environment of big business and sometimes the restrictive practices of government. These new enterprises, in which local members have equal votes for their boards of directors, are not typical of either capitalist or state socialist systems and so their appearance as seedling enterprises is interesting and important to empirical research. They point toward the possibility of an entirely new pattern of social economy developing selectively in nations today.[1]

Modern textbooks assume that the market system and state socialism are the prototypical economic systems of contemporary nations and that the choices for societies developing beyond them are impossible. Some theorists point toward a third prototype called market socialism, but few would acknowledge the possibility of nations breaking through the key traits of the market and the state and developing an entirely new system.[2] A new economic system would mean going beyond the hegemony of the competitive market and the regulatory state or any strong combination of these two systems. It would mean establishing a social foundation for the economy that would reduce the need for state regulations and the competitive marketplace. The prospect that an economy could develop organizations based on principles of mutual aid and social controls beyond the competitive market and state controls is remote indeed. And yet these democratic enterprises show quiet signs of evolving toward this possibility. They are therefore worthy of our attention as they emerge successfully and significantly as a system in certain nations. If we can understand the social foundation that gives these fledgling firms comparative power in selective nations today, we may learn how they avoid being destroyed by the unfavorable climates of market and state economies.

The failure rate of small-business enterprises is high; it is also high for innovative business and community-oriented ventures. The reason is partly because big business competes aggressively to stop their growth or buys them out and makes them part of their command system when they are successful and also because innovative enterprises do not have the financial support and federal assistance they need to survive in a hostile environment.[3] If these socially innovative enterprises are seen to be important to the development of a new pattern of social economy, that is, an economy more accountable to the people it affects and therefore more self-regulating, it behooves us to find the environment in which they can survive. This means studying strategies taken in those countries where these enterprises have become successful and have flourished.[4]

Our purpose is to examine how democratic enterprises have survived in Israel, Yugoslavia, and Spain with the aid of social federations at regional and national levels. Our principal case will be the Israeli kibbutzim, whose federations have successfully supported their development to the point where they are one of the most-advanced examples of a democratically oriented economy in the world today. We will then look briefly at enterprises in Yugoslavia and in Mondragón, Spain, where comparably innovative self-managed systems have developed. Each system shows signs of self-regulation and a capacity to reduce competitive forces in their internal market systems by means of social federations. At the same time, they each show evidence of introducing new types of stratified power at different levels. We speculate on how some of the new problems of stratification may be treated by community self-studies. We are interested in the possibilities of a decentralized system of federal development in the social (nonstatist) economy of each nation.

THE SOCIAL FEDERATION

We noted that the concept of the federation first began with the ancient Greeks, but it became largely an invention of the modern period when Johannes Althusius described the principles of federation on the basis of their
application to a wide range of authority.[5] The federal
concept has developed in succeeding centuries to become
one of the most important ideas of modern times, making
possible the democratic development of government in contemporary societies. Virtually every nation in the world
is now organized by means of a political federation. This
includes such diverse countries as the United States, the
Soviet Union, Canada, China, Australia, Malaysia, Nigeria,
and Switzerland. The concept of the political federation
has been applied to both capitalist and socialist nations
alike as it has become a part of contemporary democratic
culture. Federal structures have proven to be a successful
response to popular demands for autonomy in different regions, provinces, and states of modern nations.

Our interest is focused on social (not government)
federations. These are nonstatist organizations whose
membership is composed of relatively autonomous corporate
units joined together democratically to advance their common cause in the private sector of the economy. Social
federations have allowed enterprises to innovate structures
and cooperate successfully in many nations. At the same
time, they show a potential to decentralize the command
bureaucracies of corporate and state enterprises in the
economy. They do not eliminate bureaucracy, as we shall
see, but they significantly alter the character of bureaucratic oppression generated in the command systems of
governance. Finally, they become a substitute for key
mechanisms of control exercised through the competitive
market and the state.

The most successful experiment in which social federations have aided the development of democratic, community-oriented enterprises has been in Israel. The Israeli
kibbutzim are well known throughout the world for their
egalitarian practices, but the support for their growth in
a capitalist environment has remained relatively unpubli-
cized and hidden from view. Our purpose is to examine
how the kibbutzim have been supported through the operation of social federations that extend their powers among

regions and Israeli society. These brief notations then lead us to discuss how democratic companies within Yugoslavia and Spain have likewise gained a firm foothold in the economy through the establishment of social federations that go beyond the destructive forces of the market or the state. The Israeli kibbutzim are the most publicized example of community self-governance, the Yugoslav system is most renowned for worker self-governance, and the Mondragón system is the most recognized for having unique economic measures of self-governance in the context of the community.

THE KIBBUTZIM IN ISRAEL

Kibbutzim are organized autonomously through a system of regional and national associations that has developed with them over the decades. These associations are relatively independent of one another and yet together they compose a web of critical support for the kibbutzim in Israeli society.

The associations linking kibbutzim together and providing them with support are many, but four types of federal organizations appear noteworthy for our purposes. First, the kibbutzim have established movement federations, which bring them together on religious, ideological, and political grounds within Israeli society. Second, kibbutzim have brought their separate movement federations together into a superfederation, which provides the necessary support and guidance for the whole kibbutz system. Third, kibbutzim have established regional councils, which are based on federal principles and located on the uninhabited land between them. Fourth, kibbutzim are members of a national labor economy organized federally through the Histadrut, a labor organization that provides a still wider base of support for kibbutzim in Israel. Let us look briefly at how these support systems work.

The Kibbutz Federations

There are four major kibbutz movements in Israel with other kibbutzim also developing outside them. There is the Kibbutz Artzi movement, with 77 kibbutzim and 21,300 members; the Ichud Kibbutzim, with 90 kibbutzim and 20,700 members; and the Kibbutz Meuchad, with 62 kibbutzim and

16,400 members. The Ichud and Meuchad movements have
recently joined their federations into one large federation
called Brit Hakibbutzim. In addition, there is a religious-
ly based federation composed of 14 kibbutzim with 2,800
members as well as two more religious kibbutzim and one
communist kibbutz.[6]

These major movements are all democratically constituted in federations. Each federation has a national congress that convenes every four years and also holds conventions twice a year on special issues. Each kibbutz
sends delegates to the congress and the conventions to
represent them in general policy making. Each kibbutz
also sends a quota of individuals to staff the departments
of the federation and is obligated to send 4.5 percent to 5
percent of its members for activities in the federation and
in the affiliated organizations.

For example, the Kibbutz Artzi has about 900 individuals from kibbutzim working in their federation and
affiliated organizations. For a single year, it has recorded the percentages of its 900 members in the following
activities: 4 percent in general administrative operations,
12 percent in departments dealing with the social organization of the kibbutzim, 30 percent in economics, 3 percent
in education, 5 percent in cultural activities, 13 percent
abroad in the youth movement (e.g., in the United States
and Latin America), 10 percent supporting the political
party associated with the federation, 9 percent represented
in activities of the labor sector such as the Histadrut,
and about 15 percent working for the federation of all
kibbutzim. It is clear by these figures that over 50 percent of these members are working outside the administration of the federation itself in affiliated activities.[7]

To support their federations, a tax is levied against
each kibbutz based on the numbers of its members in addition to a separate tax based on the percent of profits
made by each kibbutz.

Each federation has established a department composed of people with skills appropriate to each area.
These areas include (1) education, (2) social and personal
problems, (3) cultural activities, (4) kibbutz youth movement, (5) second generation, (6) economics and management,
(7) industry, and (8) mutual funds.

Each federation also has a mutual fund that serves
as a bank for its kibbutzim. The fund's capital increases
each year through the annual tax payments from the kib-

butzim. The staff administering the fund seeks to help
economically weak kibbutzim to overcome their financial
difficulties. The bank actually aids all communities in
times of emergency through common grants and loans. It
also has established programs of joint funds with public
and private banks in Israel that have a good standing in
the financial market of the country.

Since departments of federation are staffed by members of the kibbutzim, each kibbutz is asked periodically
to release its members who have skills in key areas.
These people spend two to four years on special tasks and
then rotate back into kibbutz residence. Such a practice
has two advantages. On the one hand, it can open up a
path for personal growth for members. Horizons of individual members have been known to widen as their movement work provides them with new experiences and an opportunity to view old problems with fresh insights. On
the other hand, it helps to keep the federation from dominating member-kibbutzim through a professional staff and
a bureaucracy outside the traditions of the movement. The
control of the federation thus remains within the hands of
the kibbutzim themselves.

In other words, the kibbutzim supply the leadership
core of their federation, while leaders maintain key ties to
their original communities. The kibbutzim staff are usually
assigned to tasks and posts that include key decision
making. Travel expenses are provided, but it is customary
that all members of kibbutzim receive no salary. Staff
members who work at a considerable distance from their
kibbutz generally return to their communities on weekends
to be with their families. The federations in this way
are operated very much within the tradition and purpose
of the kibbutzim they represent.

The General Association of Kibbutz Federations

A federation of kibbutz federations was established
in 1963 as an umbrella organization to support the activities of all 250 kibbutzim. It grew out of a desire to
have a wider influence within the society and to promote
cooperation among the kibbutz federations.

This superfederation is headed by an executive committee. The executive committee is the policy-making body
and consists of the general secretary of each kibbutz fed-

eration and an elected chair who serves as general secretary of the federation. The chair is rotated every few years among all the secretaries. Policy decisions are made by consensus and not by majority rule.

The general federation supports a number of important interfederation committees. One of the most important is the economic committee, consisting of delegates from all kibbutz federations and some kibbutz individuals who are nominated as ex-officio members. The committee, concerned with improving the economic conditions of all kibbutzim, represent their interests to the Israeli government on issues of agricultural and industrial development and seek to secure loans for construction of houses, schools, and public buildings in the kibbutzim.

Interfederation committees have been established in such fields as education, culture, social problems, health, clothing, and others. Some committees have themselves created joint ventures. For example, the clothing committee has established a large clothing shop in Tel Aviv. It seeks kibbutz collaboration on establishing quality standards and agreements on prices in the production and sale of kibbutz clothing.

The federation has established major projects in a number of fields of interest to all kibbutzim. For example, it has created the Kibbutz Industries Association, which negotiates with the government in the search for new investment sources for factory development, the cultivation of export opportunities, and so forth. It maintains a staff of engineers for counseling and for planning new projects in the kibbutzim.

Another major project is the Inter-kibbutz Economic Research and Advisory Agency. It accumulates data from comparative economic research for all kibbutzim on costing techniques, the computerization of accounting, financing and budgeting techniques, and the application of modern analysis techniques to kibbutz economics. Overall, it conducts research on major economic problems of the kibbutzim.

In addition, the federation supports several higher education institutions such as the School of Education for the Kibbutz, The Kibbutz Management Center at the Ruppin Institute, and the Institute for the Study of the Kibbutz at Haifa University.

Other educational and cultural organizations are affiliated with the federation, such as the Kibbutz Clinic

for Rehabilitation and Retraining, the Kibbutz theater, the
Kibbutz orchestra, and film production. In effect the
federation has become a significant force in supporting
the development of kibbutzim in the context of Israeli
society.

Regional Councils and Joint Enterprises

Abraham Daniel describes six stages of regional development for Israeli settlements. The first was the municipal stage, which appeared during the prestate days
when bloc committees were established for communications,
municipal services, and common guard duty. After the
state was established, these organizations served as the
basis for the creation of a legally recognized network of
regional councils. The second consumer stage began as
farmers sought to free themselves from their dependence on
commercial firms and middlemen and established purchasing
organizations. The third production stage was marked by
the need to use modern equipment such as heavy agricultural machinery and techniques of processing-sorting, packing, cold storage, and so forth. The fourth social and
cultural stage involved the establishment of joint activities
in education, health, and culture among settlements. The
fifth marketing stage saw regional centers beginning to
serve as intermediate links between the individual settlement and national marketing organizations. In the final
stage, a financial administration came to characterize the
regional organization.[8]
The trend toward regional associations for separate
kibbutzim became significant in the early 1930s when purchasing organizations were established with the aim of
achieving better credit conditions and lower purchasing
prices. In recent decades, rural development enterprises
have gained momentum as joint ventures. Regional councils have also developed to encourage interkibbutz industry.
The councils are given the responsibility for developing
land existing between kibbutzim.
In the Beit Shean Valley, for example, a regional
council consists of representatives from 19 communities, of
which 14 are kibbutzim and 5 are moshavim (small family
farm communities). The overall population of the region
is around 6,000. A regional center was established on a
site with a large complex of processing plants, service

enterprises, municipal offices, an adult education center, and an amphitheater. Today farm products are processed in the plants for sale by the regional enterprises.

The enterprises in such regions can be quite profitable. A survey showing the depth of integration of a specific kibbutz in the Beit Shean Valley revealed that the additive value (in Israeli pounds) of the regional processing of its farm products consisted of 8 percent in 1962, 10 percent in 1964, 20 percent in 1966, and 33 percent in 1970. The income from such enterprises is generally reinvested in the regional centers, giving the center more economic power each year.

This type of regional activity has increased the strength of individual kibbutzim, but it also has led to greater dependence upon the common enterprises. More and more members of kibbutzim are beginning to work outside their own kibbutz in such economic enterprises. In 1970 the regional centers were taking about 3 percent of the work force of its kibbutzim. Like the federations, the regional centers require staff from member communities in order to keep them from dominating the creators, the kibbutzim. In 1968 a special conference was held by the kibbutz federations on the issue of regional development and power. A special survey followed to determine the extent to which regional associations had developed among kibbutzim. The survey revealed 23 regional associations with 100 regional co-op enterprises. The following types of co-op enterprises had developed within the regions: "mixture factories" to supply food for cattle and poultry, alfalfa dry flour producers, poultry meat processors, cattle slaughter houses, fruit processing plants, cotton gins, packing sheds, cooling houses for fruits and potatoes, heavy farm machinery, garages, and other miscellaneous enterprises.

The development of regional centers is defined by their leaders as an extension of the economy of each kibbutz. The regional enterprise is designed to function according to kibbutz principles and to contribute economically to the movement in ways that the single kibbutz could not do by itself.

Kibbutz members have tended to resist the development of large production units and also see their own autonomy threatened to some extent by the regional enterprises. For this reason it was decided recently that the overall federation of kibbutzim be given supreme authority

over the direction of regional projects. A special department in the federation has been created to aid regional
centers in confronting their common concerns on economic
development.

One active goal given to the federation has been to
reduce the percent of paid labor in the regional centers
from 75 percent to 40 percent in the coming years. The
number of nonkibbutz labor involved in regional centers
can present a threat to kibbutz control of regional activity.

Daniel notes that the advantages to regional integration for agricultural settlements have been that it (1)
makes it possible for farmers to control the process of
supplying produce to outside markets and frees them from
the need to depend on outside commercial interests, (2) allows for the utilization of agricultural surpluses that cannot be marketed (such as fresh fruit) by processing them
in regional enterprises, (3) permits the accumulation of
technological know-how in organization and finance, and
(4) adds employment opportunities for people made redundant in agriculture by mechanization.[9]

The regional centers and interkibbutzim co-ops represent an important strength to the kibbutzim. They have
helped kibbutz communities economically and have resolved
problems that small size and distance have presented.
The centers have offered another method of mutual aid,
enabling kibbutzim to survive as innovative systems within
a capitalist society.[10]

Finally, the kibbutzim own nationwide cooperatives
for marketing their agricultural products and for purchasing such supplies as trucks and tractors. The marketing
cooperative (TNOVA) and the purchasing cooperative
(HAMASHBIR) enable them to buy and sell in large quantities, with a greater effectiveness and strength in the marketplace of Israel's capitalist economy. They help create
the larger environment of economic support for the kibbutzim.

The National Labor Economy: The Histadrut
and Nationwide Enterprises

All kibbutz members are members of the Histadrut, a
general federation that embraces workers from every sector of the Israeli economy. It contains representation
from such independent communities as the kibbutzim,

moshavim, and cooperatives involved in branches of agriculture, transportation, and trade, while it also owns its
own enterprises directly. The Histadrut is a holding company with the right to control its own enterprises. It is
also a trade union that has organized 90 percent of the
working population.

For the kibbutzim, it provides comprehensive medical
care, social security, and educational and cultural benefits. Kibbutz members automatically belong to a health
fund. The Histadrut's financial and cultural institutions
have offered extensive support in meeting the needs of the
agricultural sector of Israel of which the kibbutzim represent a major part. The funds of federations are closely
associated with the Histadrut Bank, with commitments to do
business together. The labor-managed economy is also
supported through loans drawn from the Histadrut's pension funds.

All agricultural workers are organized in an association called the Agricultural Center, which is affiliated with
the Histadrut. The kibbutzim play an important role in
this Center. Yet the Center has its own autonomy and is
also connected to the overall policy decisions of the Histadrut and other labor institutions in Israel.

In these ways, kibbutzim federations have been central to the support and development of these socially based
enterprises and at the same time have reduced the need for
government functions in such areas as banking, marketing,
medical care, social security, and educational and cultural
benefits.

YUGOSLAVIA

Democratic worker self-management developed in Yugoslavia in 1950 as part of a socialist and nationalist re-
bellion against the Soviet Union. Yugoslavia was largely
an agricultural country at the time with over 76 percent
of its workforce in farming. Its economy was in a depression after World War II when the government sought to
collectivize agriculture following the model of the Soviet
Union. But the government faced powerful peasant resistance. Some scholars argue that the attempt to nationalize
the farm system failed because the government did not
have the power of an urban working class to control the
peasantry in the same fashion as its Soviet counterpart.

Partly because of these political realities and partly out of socialist belief, the government broke from the Soviet sphere of influence and began to mobilize the entire society around the political principle of labor self-management.[11]

This was made possible through a political federation of regions otherwise riddled with strife and opposition to one another. Each region had its own history, culture, and economic organization, which played a major role in causing strife in national politics. But the political federation permitted the necessary autonomy for each region to maintain its own identity. Still today, the major differences in the political economies of each region slow down the realization of socialist goals. The economic differences among regions have created major problems. The per capita income in Slovenia is today six times greater than in Kosovo, the poorest region. The government has sought to equalize the income differences but without success. Nevertheless, national unity has been maintained through a common belief in socialist ideas and in part because political leaders have found that they have greater strength standing together against threats from neighboring nations.

The success of the political federation in helping to resolve regional conflicts and develop an innovative system of labor-managed firms is critically important, but it is still only part of the story. Yugoslavia had previously developed a significant (social) cooperative base in agricultural federations before the government sought unsuccessfully to nationalize them. In 1938, 37 federations existed, including consumer, producer, and credit cooperatives. These federations represented over 10,000 cooperative societies and over a million members. These cooperative federations provided an important foundation for the advancement of self-management in the economy.[12]

There are three levels of political organization in Yugoslavia: the commune, the state (or region), and the federation. Like residents in Switzerland, residents in Yugoslavia have three citizenships: the local community, the (ethnic) state, and the national federation. In principle, decisions are made at the lowest level and elevated to the next higher level only if they affect a wider set of communities. The political federation is therefore concerned with internal coordination primarily at the highest levels as well as with matters of defense and foreign relations. Its general assembly passes "framework laws" and decides on overall policy measures. There is therefore the potential in Yugoslavia to develop a decentralized pattern of communities similar to the kibbutzim. The internal organization of the local market then could become altered from being characteristically based on competition to one based on cooperation in the same manner as Israel.

In 1959, the Law on Association in the Economy abolished trade associations in their traditional sense and introduced a new form of "business associations." These associations were given the status of juristic persons and permitted to act legally as commissioned agents in behalf of their corporate members. Members conduct affairs through a management board in which each enterprise has the same number of votes. In succeeding years, the Law on Association and Business Cooperation in the Economy expanded the organizational powers of associations by introducing a new type of cooperation involving the possibilities of entering into business-cooperation and technical-cooperation contracts. This law simplified contracting among firms for long-term cooperation.[13]

In 1964, enterprises were encouraged to join economic chambers—associations organized locally and regionally by industry branch. The legal status of the chambers was defined in the Basic Law on Unified Chambers of Economy and Business Cooperation in the Economy and included the provision for "joint activities for the advancement of production, trade in commodities and the provision of different services." Economic chambers have some formal power in price administration and they seek to influence overall enterprise policy.[14] They serve as a key structure for reducing the dominance of competition in the market as the determining cause for economic development in Yugoslavia. The market could become increasingly characterized by fair cooperation rather than primarily by fair competition.

The concept of federalism usually refers to the government in Yugoslavia, because the political federation has been such a distinctive force in the development of the nation, but the social federations of cooperatives and labor-managed firms have also played a significant role in the development of the economy. These federations include not only cooperative chains but also business associations of self-managed firms in industry. These business associations have enabled labor-managed corporations to integrate their activities and strengthen themselves hori-

zontally in regions. The government has thus played a
key role in stimulating the development of democratic enterprises and these social federations, which are providing
the nonstatist foundation for their socialist development.
They become part of a social outlook for reducing the
power of the state in the life of the Yugoslavian society.

MONDRAGÓN IN SPAIN

Another innovative system of democratic enterprises
exists in the Basque region of Spain. The Basques have
maintained their own culture and history, which distinguishes them from the rest of Spain. Their special identity and autonomy may explain partly why they have
generated a unique system of social enterprises without
being influenced or destroyed by the surrounding environment. Like Israel and Yugoslavia, the Basques in their
own way have stood in political opposition to outside influences and have thus acquired an independent spirit and
an internal cohesion that provides part of the motif underlying their social economy.

This Basque system of cooperative enterprises began
in the city of Mondragón during an economic depression in
the mid-1950s. Five men, inspired by a priest, Jose Maria
Arizmendi, founded the first industrial co-op in 1956.
Other co-ops were encouraged to develop through the establishment of a labor-oriented bank in 1958. The bank
became a social federation composed of the firms it created.
It was the primary instrument for promoting rapid growth
among the industrial cooperatives in the region. Today
Mondragón has 81 industrial firms, 6 construction firms, 5
agroindustrial firms and employs over 17,000. This regional system of innovative enterprises has also developed
a cooperative for research and development and a nonstatist system of health care, food distribution, and schools
that is based on principles of social federation. It is one
of the most unique regional systems of self-management in
the world today.

The most unusual federation is perhaps the cooperative bank (Caja Laboral Popular) designed for the social
development of labor in the regional economy. It supports
the self-managed firms through loans, feasibility studies,
and extended technical assistance, but part of its unique-
ness rests in the fact that all the new firms it creates

eventually become its owners. Each cooperative firm has workers represented in the general assembly of the bank. The bank has developed as a social federation of the enterprises that it has spawned in the region.

The system is community oriented as well as labor oriented. At the end of each fiscal year, the surplus (profit) of the companies is divided into three parts. A total of 30 percent is set aside for two purposes: 10 to 15 percent goes for the benefit of the community (e.g., co-op schools) and the remaining 15 to 20 percent goes to a reserve fund maintained by the company itself. The other 70 percent is distributed to the workers in proportion to hours worked during the year and the rate of pay received. This bonus, however, is not paid in cash to members but is deposited to the account of each member within the firm. This internal account is then treated by the firm as debt to members on which interest is paid. Each co-op, therefore, maintains its own internal banking system. If a member is discharged for disciplinary reasons, the firm retains up to 30 percent of his or her account, but when the member reaches retirement, he or she may withdraw the whole amount. The Caja Laboral Popular maintains the accounts and oversees the system.[15]

These cooperatives have not only federated successfully and thus gained power to develop a diverse democratic economy in the region, but they have also developed a social ecology that has enabled the development to take place effectively. The grade schools train students in co-op values; the vocational college trains workers in the technical skills needed in the industrial firms; the industrial firms contribute a portion of their profits to support other co-operatives in the community; and a research and development cooperative provides the technical assistance needed for the industrial and agricultural firms in the system. It is indeed a phenomenal system of regional self-development.

THE PROBLEM WITH FEDERATIONS: STRATIFICATION AND BUREAUCRACY

The advantage of organizing federations rests clearly in the strength they provide for fledgling enterprises that would otherwise be demolished by themselves in a hostile environment. Federations are democratic organizations in which all member-corporations have an equal vote and thus they serve as an alternative to the command systems of capitalist and state enterprises. They advance the cause of democratic development in the economic system. At the same time, however, these federations can generate their own systems of stratified power and bureaucracy that threaten and compromise the egalitarian values of their members.

In the case of the kibbutzim, Paula Rayman argues that stratification and bureaucracy began developing with the advent of regional organizations that carry some characteristics of the federation. She concludes that the kibbutzim have had to confront four major consequences of regional organization: (1) an increase in specialization and stratification; (2) the movement from manual labor norms to professionalism; (3) a concentration on standardization and routinization; and (4) the isolated nature of building a kibbutz regional infrastructure.[16] In her regional study of western Galilee, she found that kibbutz values were threatened by the emerging bureaucracy of the municipal council, the introduction of a new division of labor in regional factories, the development of specialized courses in the curriculum of the regional high school, and the exclusion of hired (nonmember) labor from the privileges given to kibbutznicks in the region. For example, hired workers did not have access to regional libraries or share in the profits of their enterprises in the manner of kibbutz members. The regional organization thus began to compromise the universal egalitarian beliefs of the kibbutzim as it competed in the region for its share of the nation's resources.[17]

In the case of Yugoslavia, democratic self-management was introduced effectively within the whole nation through the government federation, but this is also a story filled with paradoxes and unintended consequences. The party took an important lead in advancing self-management in basic institutions, but at the same time it has become a political monopoly with negative as well as positive outcomes. While it has pressed positively for worker self-management, to the point that the national system is one of the most-advanced in the world today, it has also become a defender of the status quo and has often resisted innovative ideas and retarded social development within the economy. The advantage of a state federation providing rapid development toward worker self-management is compromised by the political bureaucracy it created in the process. The government has been the focus of student riots and the source of political repression as well as the subject of national uprisings. In the face of a single-party system and the singular command structure of a state as the primary agent of social change in the economy, the system fosters resistance and resentment. The power of police enforcement of government laws and the dominance of party dogma has resulted in creating conditions opposed to the values of the nation's ideology of self-management.

In the case of Mondragón, problems of stratification and bureaucracy began with the growth of a large-scale organization. The first problem began initially within its largest cooperative, Ulgor. In 1974, Ulgor had developed a command bureaucracy that caused the only labor strike in the history of the system. A brief 48-hour strike of some 400 workers (out of 3,400) was an embarrassment to corporate leaders. They quickly sought to assess the problem and to redesign the corporate structure. The new design involved decentralizing authority in the work system.

The Mondragón banking system has also experienced bureaucratic problems in its central administration. The bank has operated allegedly like a patron and the bank staff member assigned to supervise new enterprises is frequently referred to with mixed affection as the Godfather, because of his command authority. It has perpetuated the tradition of male dominance in management hierarchy. The extent to which the size and bureaucratic organization of the bank has caused an unnecessary division of labor and stratified power has not been studied carefully, but the problem has been claimed by both insiders and outsiders. Many professional consultants in the field of self-management have held the Mondragón system as an ideal model for developing nations, but clearly it too has been subject to bureaucratic problems and stratification as it has grown into a large-scale system of enterprises.

TOWARD SOLUTIONS

Clear solutions have not yet developed for treating the stratified power and bureaucracy produced by large-scale (albeit democratic) federations, but certain concepts are worth exploring to orient social research. We propose that some answers to bureaucracy may rest partly in the creation of new inventions--technological and social--that place authority closer to lower units in the hierarchy of organization. This means decentralizing large corporations and federations through a series of systematic studies and educational programs.

Technological inventions that decentralize organizational authority are important to keep in mind even though they are not the focus of our attention. Corporate computer systems with word processors requiring a new specialized division of labor can centralize print-outs and thus clog the system with requests from the lower echelons of the organization and require rule-making priorities at the top to obtain print-outs on time. This type of new technology centralizes and adds to bureaucracy. But the invention of a low-cost word-processing system for the whole corporation that allows departments and individuals to control the entire process from input to output eliminates the rules and decentralizes the bureaucratic authority. In a similar vein, the invention of electric cars energized by solar cells rather than by gasoline is an example of how a whole industry dominated by bureaucratic trade associations, big oil companies, and world cartels could be significantly altered and decentralized. The elimination of oligarchy and unnecessary bureaucracy can be effectively introduced by new technology.

Technological change is intricately interrelated with social inventions that allow large-scale bureaucracies to change and decentralize authority. The social invention critical to our purposes is the federation, which plays a major role in decentralizing power to local communities. This is an important part of their flexibility in the democratic development of the economy.

The process of overcoming stratification in federations can best be illustrated on a continuum where different types of organizations are represented with different degrees of decentralized authority. The organizations classified below in Figure A.1 as Command, Federation, Confederation, and Alliance are prototypical forms of organizational governance evident today in both capitalist and socialist systems. We have alluded to this theory in Chapter 5, but we can now discuss it further in this international context.

Figure A.1

Patterns of Organizational Governance
(Degrees of Decentralized Authority)

Command ----- Federation ----- Confederation ----- Alliance

These four prototypes represent stages in the development of authority at lower levels of stratified organization. In a command system, power is located at the top
of the organization and is administered through a hierarchy of offices. In a federation, the power and final
authority is also located at the top in the formal structure
but it is mediated through a democratic system of elected
representatives who together determine overall policy for
the organization. In a confederation, the final authority
is located at the bottom of the organization in its separate
corporate-members, but it is guided from the top by member-
representatives. In an alliance, the final authority is
also at the bottom, but there is no chartered corporation
with designated powers for the top board. Our theory of
the process of overcoming stratified bureaucracy involves
moving from the left to the right of the continuum. But
it is a very complex political process.[18]
    We are saying theoretically that the next step in
overcoming bureaucracy in the organizations we have been
discussing involves decentralizing authority and in some
cases cultivating the attributes of the confederation and
the alliance. A confederation comes in many forms, but
its prototype is evident in most nations today. Max Weber
described its origins in medieval Italian cities among
civic and religious organizations seeking to maintain their
individual authority while establishing a broader base of
influence within cities and regions.[19] Today in the United
States, a confederation can be illustrated in the community
council composed of the Girl Scouts, the Boys Club, the
YMCA, or the council of churches containing separate
protestant denominations. It is also observed in the
structure of trade (employer-capital) associations organized by businesses in capitalist countries.
    Taking steps to reduce stratified power and bureau-
cracy requires studies of how a federation can decentralize
authority appropriately within a political environment. The
danger in creating a confederation rests in the possibility

of losing the unity and the power maintained in a centralized federation. The possibility is that the confederation may not be able to sustain itself in the face of opposing interests among its members or be able to protect
itself against outside enemies.

The United States fought a civil war partly around
the issue of establishing a confederation and abolishing
the centralized power of the federal government. The
question was whether the center could hold among states
with vastly different beliefs and economic systems. The
central government and the northern states were not ready
for the confederation demanded by southern states. Also,
a confederation of states would not have served well in a
jungle of competing nation-states. Centralized power
seemed essential at least until a greater degree of political security, racial integration, and economic equity
could be developed.

On the other hand, the advantage of a confederation
is in the fact that it may reduce the central bureaucracy
of a federal system and offer member-organizations a
greater degree of autonomy and power. Trade associations, for example, give their member-firms full authority
to operate independently, while the firms gain power collectively by acting together rather than alone.

The task in each case of federations in Israel,
Yugoslavia, and Mondragón is to study how stratification
can be overcome through a decentralizing process in the
political context of the nation. Our argument is that each
case requires study by its members to determine how the
attributes of a nonbureaucratic confederation can be developed safely and effectively.[20]

In the case of the kibbutzim, for example, there are
many political issues that would need to be addressed before taking these new steps. The Sulam Tsor Regional
Council in western Galilee may be a case in point. It
administers the functional activities of its district and is
sustained by the eight cooperative settlements: six kibbutzim and two moshavim. When the Council was first
proposed, some kibbutzim viewed the idea of federating as
a threat but then later saw that they could thereby
strengthen their position in the region. Their security
would be increased and they could lower their cost
through the collective administration of district legal services, construction, industry, education, health, and
tourism.

At the same time, no Arab villages were included in the Council. This exclusion accentuated the problem of class structure and stratified power in the region. Other regional councils reportedly include Arab villages together with the kibbutzim, but in this case the question is how to introduce greater economic equity and religious-ethnic integration in the Council. It would clearly involve a local community study of how the kibbutzim relate to Arab villages and to Arab labor. It would involve a joint study with local Arab leaders on how security problems could be resolved and bureaucratic costs reduced in a new and broader Council relationship. It could include the question of how hired labor could be given incrementally the privileges now excluded from them and whether Arab villages could contribute resources to the Council.

The same joint study would apply to the social development of the regional high school. Secondary education in the region is limited in membership to the kibbutzim and does not include residents of nearby towns or villages. In the predominately North African population of Shlomi, residents of Nahariya and the region's Arab population are not included in the federation. Like the different provinces of Yugoslavia, these ethnic groupings within the region of western Galilee are marked with major cultural and economic differences. The process of overcoming the differential in income alone is enormously complex because it alters the balance of power in the region. The task of kibbutzim to overcome the problems of education in a capitalist society required the creation of separate schools over 50 years ago. Now, to add the complexity of compromising education with Arab culture may be an impossible task. But it clearly becomes a part of the resolution of the problem of privileged versus poor strata accentuated by the power of regional organization of kibbutzim. The study question is How can a new relationship with the Arab population increase economic resources for everyone and increase political security through a redesigned regional organization?

Similar types of studies-in-transition would need to be made in the case of federations in Yugoslavia, but the political context is different. Studies in Yugoslavia are best directed toward the role of social federations (trade associations of labor-managed firms) in the development of the interregional economy. The key point here is that trade associations would become key agents helping to

facilitate socialist development as opposed to the singular
direction of the political party and the Yugoslavian government. The government has begun to see the importance
of trade federations in stimulating interregional trade.
By shifting attention to the trading powers and mutual-aid
interests of social (nonstatist) federations, the government
keeps its original goals to reduce state bureaucracy. It
offers a basis for fulfilling Marx's hope to lay a social
foundation for the economy that would allow the state to
"wither away" in favor of an administrative organization
within the society.

The problem is that the government still views trade
associations largely as agents supporting the competitive
market rather than as agents of socialist development.
Recognizing a greater social role for trade associations
would allow the state to provide incentives for them to aid
in the democratic development of the economy. The government would no longer need to mandate that development
by itself. This policy would transfer the power of a
political federation to a social confederation. At the same
time, it could increase the probability that the change
toward greater equity would be voluntary and enforced
from within the organization of the change agents themselves.

The Yugoslavian government has not always served
effectively as the (primary) change agent in the society.
For example, it introduced a well-intended law for the
basic organization of associated labor designed to create a
federation of the economic units within each labor-managed
corporation. Advocates of the law hoped to decentralize
authority in corporations by making each department-unit
autonomous and free to trade its products or services on
the market. The outcome of the law in certain respects
was almost disastrous. It tended to create chaos in some
firms while other firms tended to lose their "center hold"
as their units began to compete in the market place. In
some cases, it increased the power of the government as
an agent of local control. It is an example of how legislating social change can result in producing the opposite
of what is intended.

The government, however, can provide attractive incentives for corporations to experiment with socially oriented
(not market-oriented) decentralization and furthermore can
encourage trade federations to observe the process. Trade
federations could conduct studies of these new experiments

in a manner that would retain the integrity and social-
economic well-being of its corporate members. This could
be a social function of the trade federation--as opposed to
the state federation taking the action by itself. It suggests what we mean by transferring a greater social responsibility to the nonstatist sector of the federated
economy for future socialist development.

The Mondragón system would likewise benefit from
studies of how to reduce bureaucracy and the patron powers of the bank without destroying its effectiveness. The
bank has reportedly developed a system of bureaucratic
command that suggests excessive stratified power and bureaucracy. Mondragón leaders know that when any corporation becomes too large, it is usually time for it to
divide again into units that provide controls closer to its
membership. Mondragón managers themselves have practiced this principle.

The problem of bureaucracy had been anticipated and
actually treated with success in the case of Ulgor, the
largest co-op in the system. The founders expected that a
company could reach a point where it was too big to manage even with labor representation on the board of directors. A bureaucratic system of command develops within
the management hierarchy. Thus, management in the firm
of Ulgor, anticipating the problem of bureaucracy, divided
itself corporately into separate firms as the original company expanded. Ulgor has given birth to six other firms
as new lines of production provided the basis for them.
The six firms growing out of Ulgor now have their own
boards and have combined with the original firm to establish a business federation called Ularco. Ularco jointly
manages finance, legal services, market research, and
certain personnel functions of each member firm, while the
line management of each firm remains independent of the
confederated body. This decentralized federation of firms
has given an advantage to corporate members in the sense
that it has increased their financial and marketing power
while at the same time contributing to the larger welfare
of the workers. The confederation makes it possible to
shift workers made redundant in one firm to employment in
another firm of the federation, thus avoiding unnecessary
layoffs. When one firm lays off workers and another firm
is expanding, the central administration arranges the
transfer. This eliminates government bureaucracy in welfare and unemployment compensation. New patterns of

social decentralization thus provide a basis for eliminating
unnecessary bureaucracy and stratified power among federations of self-managed firms in the private sector.

There are three problems to resolve in the practice
of organizational decentralization. The first problem is
to decentralize the organization in such a manner that the
whole enterprise does not fall apart into political factions
or so that separate units do not begin competing unfairly
with one another. This process can involve planning
studied steps, whereby new degrees of authority are experienced and practiced in lower units of a corporate
heirarchy. Each new step toward higher levels of self-
governance among lower-level units is decided upon gradually and by agreement in these cases.

Second, a decentralized federation should be observed
for the way it affects organizations outside itself. For
example, in the United States, the National Association of
Manufacturers is a confederation of thousands of corporations and is decentralized and powerless relative to what
it would be if it existed as one conglomerate command system. At the same time, it gains power by its size relative
to other trade associations and by the loyalty given to it
by its many members. Loyalty is obtained in part because of the freedom for members to act independently
while a new collective power is gained through the federation. The NAM has established a powerful computer network by which it supplies information to its members on
new legislation and on outside competitive threats to itself.
The NAM can rally its members quickly over national issues
in its own self-interest. Other trade associations live in
its shadow. The decentralization of power in any real
sense must take account of the interorganizational context
in which the action may take place.

Third, the interorganizational context is important to
examine not only for the way in which a confederation may
become another bigger monopoly but for whether it may become structured in the public interest. The big confederation can become another dominating force in the market or
it may serve the purposes of social development while
meeting its own economic objectives. The big organization
can maximize social development through the formulation
of ethical codes, product standards, training programs for
quality-of-work-life projects, and worker self-management.
Many trade federations have already developed ethical
codes and tribunals to settle conflicts arising from code

violations. Thus, socially constructive developments can become applicable on a wider geographical area through a big decentralized organization. Interorganizational committees can develop social charters that can judge corporate conduct by public standards.

Examples of how federations can cultivate the power of employee authority among their private business members is found in some European associations that have members already organized with a measure of employee authority. The most-significant political action of a European federation to develop employee authority took place with the enactment of the Fifth Directive by the European Economic Community. The EEC is the most influential federal association active in issues of worker self-management. Its Fifth Directive urges country-members to require firms to develop practices of codetermination among their enterprises. Choices are provided among a number of different models (e.g., the German model or the Dutch model) as a type of employee participation that firms may develop to remain a member of the EEC. Put another way, this Directive requires private enterprises to become at least partially democratic in order to participate in the European market system. Thus, private enterprises in nations like Ireland and Greece must cultivate a new social authority for workers within their businesses in order to trade within the European Economic Community. Indeed, the EEC may be more powerful than the socialist Greek government for persuading firms to become worker self-managed.

IN CONCLUSION

The three self-managed systems we have reviewed are similar in that they have emerged uniquely in a polity that stands in opposition to neighboring governments, each with a set of social beliefs that provide an important motive for their development. They are each expressions of a political community, which explains part of the reason for their success.

This suggests that these systems are not easily duplicated in other capitalist and socialist environments, but it does not mean that we cannot learn from the more-successful features of each of them. It is notable, for example, that the Mondragón bank was able to initiate such a rapid development of labor-managed firms without legislation and without a government to enforce and actively support the process. We need to learn more about how this was done so successfully. We also could learn more about how the schools in the kibbutzim and in Mondragón teach cooperative values supporting their systems and thus prepare young men and women to enter the system effectively. Additionally, it is noteworthy that these systems have encouraged systematic research on their self-managed enterprises to provide a self-critical basis for their development. This effort serves as an example for other nations experimenting with democratic enterprises. Finally, we need to learn more about how Yugoslavia's social federations have participated in the effort to introduce cooperative relationships among competing labor-managed firms and thus have contributed to socialist development in the economy as well as facilitated access to markets in the manner of capitalist trade associations. This action could tell us more about how statism is reduced in socialist nations today.

The democratic enterprises in Israel, Yugoslavia, and Mondragón have survived and developed through the support of federations operating at regional and national levels. Our argument is that the development of these federations is essential for such innovative firms to acquire power in an alien or competitive environment. At the same time, these federations can develop stratified power and bureaucracy themselves that contradict and compromise the values of their egalitarian members. An irony develops here. The democratic firms were organized initially to overcome stratification in the command bureaucracies of capitalist and state enterprises, but then they confront the problem again in their own federations.

The solution can be conceptualized as a process of decentralizing authority. The federation can be seen as one point on a continuum of organizations expressing relative degrees of decentralized power. It is more advanced than the command system in its capacity to decentralize power, but it is also more centralized than a confederation or an alliance. We argued theoretically that the problems of a federal bureaucracy are best treated through a process of self-study and decentralization of authority. This process alters the character of the federation gradually to the point where it acquires the attributes of a new organization approximating the prototype of a confederation.

We noted that the bureaucracy and stratified power evident in the federations of Israel, Yugoslavia, and Mondragón may be studied for their prospects for cultivating power and responsible authority from the bottom of the hierarchy. The process of decentralizing power of course requires careful study and training for members who normally experience major changes in moving from one type of organization to another. The studies and educational programs attending such changes must take serious account of the interests of corporate members of a federation and the political context within which the changes are implemented.

The process by which these steps are taken are more complex than we can summarily represent here. The varieties and subvarieties of federations and confederations have yet to be studied and typologized. This is an important area of research in the future.[21] Our theoretical premise is that while the steps toward decentralization are quite variable--centralizing firms under a limited command structure in certain cases and in other cases perhaps starting with an alliance and staying with it, depending upon the political context--the long-range process of social development in the economy involves cultivating responsibility and authority at the base of the organizational hierarchy. It is this distinctive process that has been leading toward a new social economy.

The careful observer may see how these self-managed systems show signs of creating a social economy that goes beyond market capitalism and state socialism. None of the three systems have transcended the market outside their own internal economies, but the interesting point is that the competitive market does not exist characteristically within the local life of the kibbutzim communities or the Mondragón cooperatives. Their internal economies are based on cooperative (not competitive) exchange. The firms within these two systems do not compete against each other. The kibbutzim are designed to aid one another through their regional federations. The Mondragón corporations likewise do not compete but instead help one another through their federations. The Yugoslav system is different in that it is designed so that firms compete within its own political community, but if trade federations assume a greater social role and purpose in the economy, we may even see the basis for their members transcending the competitive market. All three systems of course engage in

external markets in Europe, Africa, and other continents
while they continue to engage in a unique social transformation of their home economies.[22]

In sum, social federations have supported the development of these new democratic enterprises attempting to
develop themselves in three nations. They offered these
innovative enterprises the support they needed to survive
and flourish. The primary characteristics of their development were mutual aid and cooperation rather than self-
interest and competition. New problems of stratification
arose in each case that compromised some of their original
values, but each case shows a potential for decentralized
economic development retaining the advantages of self-
governance. They have demonstrated a unique capacity to
remain accountable to constituencies and the people they
affect in communities while also maintaining productivity
and profitability. These are key measures in the development of a social economy.

We have suggested that the next step in these cases
involves studying and implementing a process of decentralization through self-directed action, allowing member-
corporations the opportunity to assess their future together
and to establish the necessary consensus to transform the
organization. This methodology of change appears to be
one of the pathways toward overcoming the bureaucracy
and stratified power that develops typically in large-scale
systems today and points selectively toward the possibility
of developing decentralized, self-managed economies in the
context of capitalist and socialist nations.

NOTES

1. As noted in Chapter 5, Karl Polanyi argues that
capitalism emerged from feudalism by means of small legal
innovations freeing land, labor, and capital from bondage
in the estate system. The implication of his study is that
today's legal innovations leading to democratic enterprises
may also lead toward a new economic system. The literature on these diverse types of democratic enterprises is
quite extensive, but the following books may provide some
orientation: Severyn T. Bruyn and James Meehan, eds.,
Beyond the Market and the State (Philadelphia, Pa.:
Temple University Press, 1987); Carole Pateman, Participation and Democratic Theory (London: Cambridge University

Press, 1970); David Jenkins, Job Power (New York: Penguin Books, 1973); and Derek Jones and Jan Svejnar, Participatory and Self-Managed Firms (Lexington, Mass.: D. C. Heath, 1982). Also cf. Karl Polanyi, The Great Transformation (Boston: Beacon Press, 1965).

2. For example, Charles Lindbloom discusses these two major prototypes and a third type called market socialism but never discusses the possibility of a new system whose characteristics are not determined primarily by the state or the competitive market. Charles Lindbloom, Politics and Markets (New York: Basic Books, 1977).

3. One study shows the failure rate of small businesses in the United States is 80 percent in the last five years. J. Zupnick and S. Kats, Case Studies Profiles (Worthington, Ohio: Enterprises Institute, 1980), p. 3. The failure rate of producer co-ops is reviewed by Derek Jones in "U.S. Producer Cooperatives: The Record to Date," Industrial Relations 8 (1979):342-56. On the failure rate of innovative communities, see Rosabeth Kanter, Commitment and Community (Cambridge, Mass.: Harvard University Press, 1972). For a study of the high failure rate of self-managed firms in an unfavorable climate, see J. G. Espinosa and A. S. Zimbalist, Economic Democracy: Workers Participation in Chilean Industry, 1970-1973 (New York: Academic Press, 1978). An interesting case study of a worker-owned firm developing in a hostile environment is found in Claire Bishop, All Things Common (New York: Harper and Bros., 1950). Boimondeau lasted three decades. Newcomers to the business had been socialized to capitalist values and tended to work "for wages" without any sense of responsibility to the corporate community. Like Owenite, Fourierist, and other communal experiments, it lost the struggle to survive against an alien and competitive environment. It was finally sold in 1971.

4. The question of why these democratic firms have failed to become widespread in capitalist and state-socialist environments is too complex to pursue here, but our argument is that one reason is the lack of support from mutual-aid organizations. Many studies show strong economic performance of self-managed firms in Yugoslavia, e.g., B. Balassa and T. J. Bertarand, "Growth Performance of Eastern European Countries," American Economic Review 60 (1970); in Mondragón, Spain, e.g., R. Oakeshott, The Case for Worker Co-ops (London: Routledge & Kegan Paul, 1978); and in Israeli kibbutzim, e.g., S. Melman, "Industrial

Efficiency under Managerial versus Cooperative Decision
Makings: A Comparative Study of Manufacturing Enterprises in Israel," in Self-Governing Socialism, ed. B.
Horvat et al. (White Plains, N.Y.: International Arts and
Sciences Press, 1975). The evidence suggests that the
political environment is a factor explaining the success in
these countries. One other common factor in this environment is the social federation.

5. The first modern reference to a federal concept
was reportedly made by Jean Bodin, who advocated the
idea of a sovereign state in 1577 and included the concept
of cooperative relations between states. In 1603, Althusius
explained the concept in more detail by discussing roughly
the difference between a federation and a confederation.
Sobei Mogi, The Problem of Federalism (London: George
Allen & Unwin, 1931), p. 21ff.

6. Some of the information that follows on kibbutzim
was drawn from interviews with Dr. Menachem Rosner,
director of the Institute for the Study of the Kibbutz and
the Cooperative Idea, and other information from visits to
Israel.

7. Naphtali Golimb, "Kibbutz Reinforcement Organizations" (Unpublished paper, Kibbutz Management Center,
Ruppin Institute, Israel, n.d.).

8. Abraham Daniel, Regional Cooperation in Israel
(Cambridge, Mass.: Harvard University Center for Jewish
Studies, 1988), p. 4.

9. Ibid., pp. 3-5.

10. The kibbutzim are more independent of government
controls than other types of Israeli towns and suburbs and
have virtually eliminated the competitive market within
their own internal systems of exchange. The government
is of course still a strong factor determining their policies.
Kibbutzim have several sources of investment financing,
including development loans provided by the government
for regional plants. The government sets conditions via
the ministries according to the 1950 Capital Investments
Promotion Act, the object of which was to encourage the
flow of both foreign and domestic capital.

Certain financing conditions are granted by the Ministry of Commerce and Industry to approved enterprises
that are contributing to the improvement of the balance of
payments. For example, an approved enterprise undertakes
to export a certain percent of its output according to its
classified region. If the equipment used is domestically

produced, certain benefits are given, such as grants for
buildings, land, and equipment and are made equal to 15
percent of the purchasing price. But the main source of
capital for the development of kibbutzim is the self-managed
system of enterprises that do not require government controls. Their social federations have substituted self-
accountable systems for what would otherwise have been
relegated to government agencies.

11. Branko Horvat, The Political Economy of Socialism (New York: M. E. Sharpe, 1982).

12. Jozo Tomascvich, Peasants, Politics, and Eco-
nomic Change in Yugoslavia (Stanford, Calif.: Stanford
University Press, 1955), quoted in Joseph Blasi, Perry
Mehrling, and William F. Whyte, "Environmental Influences
on the Growth of Worker Ownership and Control," in Inter-
national Perspectives on Organizational Democracy, ed.
Bernhard Wilpert and Arndt Sorge (New York: John Wiley
& Sons, 1984)2:297.

13. Josip Obradovic and William Dunn, Workers'
Self-Management and Organizational Power in Yugoslavia
(Pittsburgh, Pa.: University of Pittsburgh, 1978), pp.
124-25.

14. Howard Wachtel, Workers' Management and
Workers' Wages in Yugoslavia (Ithaca, N.Y.: Cornell
University Press, 1973), p. 85.

15. Ana Gutierrez Johnson and William Foote Whyte,
"The Mondragon System of Worker Production Co-operatives,"
in Workplace Democracy and Social Change, ed. Frank
Lindenfeld and Joyce Rothschild-Whitt (Boston: Porter
Sargent, 1982).

16. Paula Rayman, "Co-operative Movement Confronts
Centralization: Israeli Kibbutz Regional Organizations,"
Economic and Industrial Democracy 2 (London: Sage,
1981):483-520. Membership of kibbutzim in the regional
organization is limited to specific activities. You can be
a co-owner of one regional factory and not of another,
depending upon your economic interest. In contrast, membership in the kibbutz federation is comprehensive. The
kibbutz federation has at last some authority on all areas
of kibbutz life and activity.

17. Other kibbutz scholars find Rayman's interpretation to be too extreme. For example, Menachem Rosner
finds the municipal council dealing with very limited issues without relevance to kibbutz values. He sees nothing
wrong with specialist courses in regional high schools.

The only real issue, he says, is "that of hired labour in the regional enterprises belonging to the Kibbutzim. . . . The Kibbutz federations try to counter these developments that are opposed to Kibbutz values." In certain cases, for example, there are proposals to sell a part of the enterprises to the Histadrut. Menachem Rosner, personal correspondence with Severyn Bruyn, November 27, 1985.

18. There is no reason to hypothesize that a confederation will always be less bureaucratic than a federation. In Israel, for example, the ideologically based nationwide federation appears to be less bureaucratic and less hierarchical than the regional organizations that approximate the confederation type. The difference in this case may be based on the purpose of the organization and the nature of its activity. The nationwide federation is not engaged in economic activities as is the case of the regional organization. Studies are needed to reveal the variables that may contradict our theory that generally the confederation is less bureaucratic and permits greater social authority in the membership base.

19. D. Martindale and G. Neuwirth, The City (New York: Free Press, 1958).

20. The variables involved in decentralizing power from the federation to the confederation need to be carefully explored. There should be cases in which this hypothesis would not hold. For example, the kibbutz nationwide federation maintains a continuous rotation of office holders and a large participation of the kibbutzim in the decision-making process. Such unique factors can reduce the more-centralized bureaucratic character of the federation. The federation in this case may be less centralized than the regional councils that approximate the confederation type.

21. We have used the concepts of federation and confederation in gross terms here, because their specific attributes have not yet been adequately characterized for scientific study. For example, Yugoslavia is a political federation but relative to the centralized structures of other governments like the United States and the Soviet Union, it clearly leans more toward some attributes of a political confederation. A precise study of federations as ideal types has yet to be made.

22. These systems are all designed to be self-managing so that they reduce the necessity for state regulations and statism. They show the potential for creating

the sort of economic order that Marx once dreamed would evolve with communal systems. At the same time, history tells us that it takes many centuries for entirely new economic systems to evolve in whole societies. Furthermore, a glimpse of the stage of evolution in the international market leads us to conclude that the realization of Marx's world vision of socialism is still too complex to conceive in the practical future. Nevertheless, the fact that these three systems are linked to international markets does not detract from our interest in the way social federations have begun to support an internal domestic system of cooperative exchange and have begun to point the way toward a system of self-governance in the modern economy.

Selected Bibliography

Adizes, Ichak. Industrial Democracy: Yugoslav Style.
    New York: Free Press, 1971.

Adizes, Ichak, and Elisabeth Borgese, eds. Self-Manage-
    ment: New Dimensions to Democracy. Oxford, England:
    Clio Press, 1975.

Aivaliotis, Apostolos. Community Development. Athens:
    Thomas Rammos, 1980. In Greek.

Androulakis, M. Socialist Self-Government--Self-Management.
    Athens: Synchroni Epochi, 1983.

Avdelidis, P. The Agricultural Cooperative Movement in
    Greece. Athens: Papazissis, 1976. In Greek.

_____. Cooperative Problems. Athens: Nea Synora,
    1981a. In Greek.

_____. Issues in Agricultural Economy. Athens: Nea
    Synora, 1981b. In Greek.

Bank of Greece. Annual Report of the Governor of the
    Bank of Greece, 1985. Athens: Bank of Greece,
    1986. In Greek.

_____. Summary of Annual Report of Governor D.
    Chalikias, 1985. Athens: Bank of Greece, 1986. In
    Greek.

_____. The Greek Economy. Vol. 2. Athens: Bank of
    Greece, 1982. In Greek.

_____. Annual Report of the Governor of the Bank of
    Greece, 1981. Athens: Bank of Greece, 1982. In
    Greek.

Bender, Thomas. Community and Social Change in America. New Brunswick, N.J.: Rutgers University Press, 1978.

Berle, Adolph. Power without Property. New York: Harcourt, Brace, Jovanovich, 1959.

Bernstein, Paul. Workplace Democratization. Kent, Ohio: Kent State University Press, 1976.

Blumberg, Paul. Industrial Democracy. London: Constable, 1968.

Blumer, Herbert. "What Is Wrong with Social Theory." American Sociological Review 19 (1954).

Boyte, Harry C. Community Is Possible. New York: Harper & Row, 1984.

Bradley, Keith, and Alan Gelb. Worker Capitalism. Cambridge, Mass.: MIT Press, 1983.

Braveman, Harry. Labor and Monopoly Capital: The Degradation of Work in the Twentieth Century. New York: Monthly Review Press, 1974.

Brenner, M. H. Mental Health and the Economy. Cambridge, Mass.: Harvard University Press, 1973.

Bruyn, Severyn T. The Social Economy: People Transforming Business. New York: John Wiley & Sons, 1977.

_____. The Field of Social Investment. Cambridge, England: Cambridge University Press, 1987.

Bruyn, Severyn T., and James Meehan, eds. Beyond the Market and the State. Philadelphia, Pa.: Temple University Press, 1987.

Caravidas, C. D. Geoeconomy and Community: A Collection of Texts. Athens: Agricultural Bank of Athens, 1980. In Greek.

Catsanevas, Theodoros. Trade Unions in Greece. Athens: National Center of Social Research, 1984a. In Greek.

_____. Labor Relations in Small and Middle Enterprises in Greece, in collaboration with Maria Dotsika-Papavasiliou. Athens: Ministry of Labor, Manpower Employment Organization, 1984b. In Greek.

Center of Planning and Economic Research (KEPE). Local Self-Government, Report No. 3 published in the context of the Five-Year Economic and Social Development Plan 1976-1980. Athens: KEPE, 1976. In Greek.

_____. The Greek Economy Today. Athens: KEPE, 1984.

_____. Regional Development Report No. 10 published in the context of the Five-Year Economic and Social Development Plan 1976-1980. Athens: KEPE, 1976. In Greek.

_____. Plan for Economic and Social Development, 1983-1987. Athens: KEPE, 1985. In Greek.

Chandler, Alfred. The Visible Hand: The Managerial Revolution in American Business. Cambridge, Mass.: Harvard University Press, 1977.

Chiotis, George. The Framework of Regional Development: A Series of Lectures in the National Metsovion Polytechnic School. Athens: Dardanos-Karatsanis, 1970. In Greek.

Climis, Aristidis. Cooperatives in Greece. Athens: Pistelon, 1985. In Greek.

Clogg, Richard, ed. Greece in the 1980's. New York: St. Martin's Press, 1983.

Cobb, Sidney, and Stanislau Kasl. Termination: The Consequences of Job Loss. Research Report no. 77-224, National Institute of Occupational Safety and Health, June 1977.

Committee of European Communities. Social Policy in Greece: Trends, Problems, Prospects. Athens: CEC, 1983. In Greek.

Conte, Michael, and Arnold S. Tannenbaum. "Employee-Owned Companies: Is the Difference Measurable?" Monthly Labor Review (July 1978).

Couloumbis, Theodore, and John Iatrides. Greek-American Relations. New York: Pella, 1980.

Coutsoumaris, George. The Morphology of Greek Industry. Athens: Center of Economic Research, 1963.

_____. Economic Development and Developmental Policy. Athens: Sbilias, 1979. In Greek.

Derber, Charles. Professionals as Workers. Boston: G. K. Hall, 1982.

Drucker, Peter. The Unseen Revolution: How Pension Fund Socialism Came to America. New York: Harper & Row, 1976.

Economic Report of the President, 1984. Washington, D.C.: Government Printing Office, 1984.

Economic Report of the President, 1986. Washington, D.C.: Government Printing Office, 1986.

Edwards, Richard. Contested Terrain: The Transformation of the Workplace in the Twentieth Century. New York: Basic Books, 1979.

Erdman, Robin J., et al. Community Development Profile. Washington, D.C.: National Congress for Community Economic Development, 1985.

Evangelinides, Maria. "Core-Periphery Relations in the Greek Case." In Underdeveloped Europe: Studies in Core-Periphery Relations, edited by D. Seers, B. Schaffer, and M. R. Kiljunen. Atlantic Highlands, N.J.: Humanities Press, 1979.

Featherstone, Kevin, and Dimitrios K. Katsoudas, eds. Political Change in Greece. Before and After the Colonels. London and Sydney: Croom Helm, 1987.

Filias, Vasilis. Society and Authority in Greece. Athens: Synchrona Kimena, 1974. In Greek.

Freris, A. F. The Greek Economy in the 20th Century. New York: St. Martin's Press, 1986.

Frieden, Karl. Workplace Democracy and Productivity. Washington, D.C.: National Center for Economic Alternatives, 1980.

Galbraith, John Kenneth. The Industrial State. Boston: Houghton Mifflin, 1967.

The Boston Globe. June 24, 1987.

Gouldner, Alvin. Patterns of Industrial Bureaucracy. New York: Free Press, 1954.

Grammatopoulos, G. Contemporary Cooperative Movement in Other Countries and in Greece. Athens: 1960. In Greek.

Green, Mark. Winning Back America. New York: Bantam Books, 1982.

Heenan, David A. The Re-United States of America. Reading, Mass.: Addison-Wesley, 1983.

Hitiris, Theodore. Trade Effects of Economic Association with Common Market: The Case of Greece. New York: Praeger, 1972.

Honigsberg, Peter J., Bernard Kamoroff, and Jim Beatty. We Own It. Laytonville, Calif.: Bell Springs, 1982.

Horvat, Branko. The Political Economy of Socialism. New York: M. E. Sharpe, 1982.

Horvat, Branko, et al., eds. Self-Governing Socialism. White Plains, N.Y.: International Arts and Sciences Press, 1975.

Hudson, J., et al., eds. Uneven Development in Southern Europe. London: Methuen, 1985.

Institute for Community Economics. The Community Land Handbook. Emmaus, Pa.: Rodale Press, 1982.

International Research Group. Industrial Democracy in Europe. Oxford, England: Clarendon Press, 1981.

Jackall, Robert, and Henry Levin. Worker Cooperatives in America. Berkeley: University of California Press, 1984.

Jecchinis, Chris. Trade Unionism in Greece: A Study in Political Paternalism. Chicago: Roosevelt University, 1967.

_____. Preconditions for the Success of Workers' Participation in Management. Athens: Manpower Employment Organization, 1986. In Greek.

Jecchinis, Chris, and Theodoros Catsanevas. The Trade Unions Movement in Greece. Athens: Manpower Employment Organization, 1985.

Jenkins, David. Job Power. New York: Penguin Books, 1973.

Jones, Derek, and Jan Svejnar. Participatory and Self-Managed Firms. Lexington, Mass.: D. C. Heath, 1982.

Kanter, Rosabeth. Commitment and Community. Cambridge, Mass.: Harvard University Press, 1972.

Kasimati, Koula. Labor Mobility Trends in Greek Industry. Athens: National Center of Social Research, 1980. In Greek.

Kerr, Clark. The Future of Industrial Societies: Convergence or Continuing Diversity? Cambridge, Mass.: Harvard University Press, 1983.

Kourvetaris, G., and W. Dobratz. A Profile of Modern Greece. Oxford, England: Clarendon (Bound), 1987.

Lalonde, Robert, and Nick Papandreou. The Manpower Report of KEPE: The Characteristics of the Greek Labour Market. Athens: Center of Planning and Economic Research, 1986.

Lambiri, Ioanna. Social Change in a Greek Country Town. Athens: Center of Planning and Economic Research, 1965.

_____. Social Stratification in Greece 1962–82. Athens: Sakkoulas, 1983. In Greek.

Lansdale, Bruce M. Metamorphosis. Teaching Peasants Management. Boulder, Colo.: Westview Press, 1986.

Lemonias, Hermes. Developmental Incentives in Greece and the EEC. Athens: Center of Planning and Economic Research, 1985. In Greek.

Lieber, Nancy, ed. Eurosocialism and America. Philadelphia, Pa.: Temple University Press, 1982.

Lindbloom, Charles. Politics and Markets. New York: Basic Books, 1977.

Lindenfeld, Frank, and Joyce Rothschild-Whitt, eds. Workplace Democracy and Social Change. Boston: Porter Sargent, 1982.

Local Self-Government: A Modern European Expression—Studies and Findings of Specialists in Greece and Abroad. Athens: Tamesos, 1983. In Greek.

Loulis, John. "The Greek Malaise." Encounter 67;2 (1986): 68–70, 72–73.

McGregor, Douglas. The Human Side of Enterprise. New York: McGraw-Hill, 1960.

MacIver, Robert M. Society. Philadelphia, Pa.: Century Bookbindery, 1937.

Manesis, Aristovoulos, et al. Greece in the Process of Development. Athens: Exantas, 1986. In Greek.

Marglin, Stephen. "What Do Bosses Do? The Origins and Functions of Hierarchy in Capitalist Production." Journal of Radical Political Economy.

Mason, Ronald. Participatory and Workplace Democracy. Carbondale, Ill.: Southern Illinois University Press, 1982.

McNeil, William E. The Metamorphosis of Greece since World War II. Chicago: University of Chicago Press, 1987.

Meek, Christopher. "Employee Ownership and Union Activism: The Rath Packing Company Case." Social Report 3 (1983).

Ministry of Interior. Local Self-Government, Regional Development, Democratic Planning. Athens: MoI, 1986. In Greek.

Mitropoulos, Alexis. Labor Institutions in Greece. Athens: Sakkoulas, 1985. In Greek.

Mogi, Sobei. The Problems of Federalism. London: George Allen & Unwin, 1931.

Montgomery, David. Workers' Control in America: Studies in the History of Work, Technology, and Labor Struggles. New York: Cambridge University Press, 1979.

Morris, David. The New City States. Washington, D.C.: Institute for Local Self Reliance, 1982.

Moschonas, Andreas. Traditional Lower Urban Strata. The Case of Greece. Athens: Institute of Mediterannean Studies, 1986. In Greek.

Mouzelis, Nicos P. Modern Greece: Facets of Underdevelopment. London: Macmillan, 1978.

Mumford, Lewis. The Culture of Cities. New York: Harcourt, Brace, 1938.

Nicolaou, Litsa N. The Growth and Development of Sociology in Greece. Boston: 1974 (mimeographed).

Nicolaou-Smokoviti, Litsa. "The Psychosocial Contract: Its Nature and Effects for Greek Industry." In The Greek Review of Social Research, no. 26–27. Athens: National Center of Social Research, 1976:110–28.

_____. "Industrial Organization of Greece: Some Major Dimensions Related to Success of Industrial Firms." In Work and Technology, edited by Marie R. Haug and Jacques Dofny. London: Sage, 1977.

_____. New Institutions of Labor Relations. Participation and Self-Management. Athens: Papazissis, 1988. In Greek.

Nicolaou-Smokoviti, Litsa, and Severyn T. Bruyn. "A Theoretical Framework for Studying Worker Participation: The Psychosocial Contract." In The Greek Review of Social Research, no. 32. Athens: National Center of Social Research, 1978:60-73.

_____. "The Social Structure of Self-managed Firms in Greece: Guidelines to Policy Studies." Studies, no. 1. Piraeus: Piraeus Graduate School of Business Studies, 1984, pp. 73-108.

Nicolinakos, Marios. "Transnationalization of Production, Location of Industry, and the Deformation of Regional Development." In Peripheral Countries: The Case of Greece in the Uneven Development of Southern Europe, edited by R. Hudson and S. Lewis. London and New York: Methuen, 1985.

_____. Self-Management and Workers' Participation. A Review of International and Greek Bibliography. Athens: Greek Productivity Center, 1986. In Greek.

Nisbet, Robert. The Quest for Community. New York: Oxford University Press, 1953.

Oakeshott, R. The Case for Worker Co-ops. London: Routledge & Kegan Paul, 1978.

Obradovic, Josip, and William Dunn. Workers' Self-Management and Organizational Power in Yugoslavia. Pittsburgh, Pa.: University of Pittsburgh, 1978.

Organization for Economic Cooperation and Development. Community Business Ventures and Job Creation: Local Initiatives for Employment Creation. Paris: OECD, 1984.

_____. Economic Surveys 1985/86: U.S.A. Paris:OECD, 1985.

_____. Economic surveys 1985/86: GREECE. Paris:OECD, 1986.

_____. Economic surveys 1986/87: U.S.A. Paris: OECD, 1986.

Papageorgiou, Constantinos. Agricultural Cooperatives.
Athens: Evgenidio Idrima, 1985. In Greek.

_____. "Thoughts for the Development of Agricultural
Cooperatives." The Cooperative Way 7 (1987):121-31.
In Greek.

Pateman, Carole. Participation and Democratic Theory.
London: Cambridge University Press, 1970.

Petmezidou-Tsoulouvi, Maria. "Approaches to the Issue of
Underdevelopment of Greek Social Transformation: A
Critical Perspective." Current Issues 22 (1984):13-29.
In Greek.

_____. Social Classes and Mechanisms of Social Repro-
duction. Athens: Exantas, 1987. In Greek.

Photopoulos, Takis. Dependent Development: The Greek
Case. Athens: Exantas, 1985. In Greek.

Piore, Michael, and Charles Sabel. The Second Industrial
Divide. New York: Basic Books, 1984.

Polanyi, Karl. The Great Transformation. Boston:
Beacon Press, 1965.

Raftis, Alkis, and Dimitrios Stavroulakis. "Workers' Cooperatives as Self-managed Enterprises: The Case of
Greece." Paper presented at the XI International
Congress of Sociology, International Sociological Association, New Delhi, August 1986.

Rosen, Corey, et al. Employee Ownership in America.
Lexington, Mass.: D. C. Heath, 1986.

Rosner, Menachem. "Theories of Cooperative Degeneration
and the Experience of the Kibbutz." No. 63, University
of Haifa, Institute for Research and Study of the
Kibbutz and the Cooperative Idea, July 1985.

Rowe, Jonathan. "Buying Out the Bosses." Washington Monthly 15, no. 10, 1984.

Sacks, Stephen. Self-Management and Efficiency: Large Corporations in Yugoslavia. London: George Allen & Unwin, 1983.

Sahanidis, Kyriakos S., Representative of the Association for the Establishment of an Economic Chamber of Greece (SDOEE). "Companies of Popular Base." Technical Chamber of Greece, Conference on the Development of Greece. Athens, May 25-30, 1981, Vol. 1, pp. 199-203. In Greek.

Sanders, Irwin T. Rainbow in the Rock: The People of Rural Greece. Cambridge, Mass.: Harvard University Press, 1962.

Skountzos, Theodoros. Structural Changes in Greek Economy: A Diachronic Analysis. Athens: Center of Planning and Economic Research, 1980. In Greek.

_____. Tables of Social Accounting of Greek Economy: Year 1975. Athens: Center of Planning and Economic Research, 1985. In Greek.

_____. Economic Development: Theory-Practice-Planning. Athens: Caramberopoulos, 1986. In Greek.

Smelser, Neil. Sociology. Englewood Cliffs, N.J.: Prentice-Hall, 1984.

Smith, James. "The Labor Movement and Worker Ownership." Social Report: Vol. 11, no. 2. Boston: Boston College, Program in Social Economy and Social Policy, 1981.

Stavrianos, Leften. The Promise of the Coming Dark Age. San Francisco: W. H. Freeman, 1976.

Stern, Robert, and Sharon McCarthy, eds. The Organizational Practice of Democracy. New York: John Wiley & Sons, 1986.

Streeck, Wolfgang, and Philippe C. Schmitter, eds. Private Interest Government: Beyond Market and State. London: Sage, 1985.

Sturmthal, Adolfo. Workers' Councils. Cambridge, Mass.: Harvard University Press, 1964.

Tatsos, Nicos. "Local Self-Government and Economic Development: Possibilities and Constraints." Study no. 1, The Piraeus Graduate School of Business Studies, 1982. In Greek.

Theodori-Markojiannaki, E., P. Cavvadia, and D. Catochianou. Basic Data per Prefecture and Region. Athens: Center of Planning and Economic Research, 1986. In Greek.

Theodorou, T. Issues of Local Self-Government. Articles and Studies of Mayors. Athens: Tolidis, 1982. In Greek.

Toby, Jackson. Contemporary Society. New York: John Wiley & Sons, 1971.

Tomascvich, Jozo. Peasants, Politics, and Economic Change in Yugoslavia. Stanford, Calif.: Stanford University Press, 1955.

Toqueville De, Alexis. Democracy in America. New York: Harper & Row, 1966.

Tsaousis, Dimitrios. Morphology of Modern Greek Society. Athens: Gutenberg, 1971. In Greek.

Tsenes, Elias. Local Self-Government: Theory and Practice. Athens: Foivos, 1986. In Greek.

Tsouderos, Ioannis. Agricultural Cooperatives. Athens: Estia, 1960. In Greek.

————. Greek Agricultural Cooperatives within the Framework of the Greek Social Fabric. Chicago: Fund for International Cooperative Development, 1961.

Tsoukalas, Constantinos. State, Society, and Work in Post-War Greece. Athens: Themelio, 1986. In Greek.

Tzortzakis, Theodoros. Cooperatives in Greece. Patra: D. Fragoulis, 1932. In Greek.

_____. Cooperativism: From Its Application in Greece. Athens: Cooperation, 1980. In Greek.

_____. Cooperative Economy: History-Theory-Applications of Cooperativism. Athens: n.p., 1981. In Greek.

U.S., Joint Economic Committee. Estimating Costs of National Economic Policy.

Vavouras, Ioannis. "Local Government and the Social Sector: An Evaluation of the Recent Institutional Arrangements in Greece." Annals of Public and Cooperative Economy 56 (1985):497–512.

_____. "Local Government Investment Planning: A Proposed Approach Applied to Greece." Comparative Economic Studies 28 (1986):1–11.

Vavouras, Ioannis, and Constantinos Archontakis. Popular Shipping Companies. Athens: Papazissis, 1982. In Greek.

Vergopoulos, Costas. The Agricultural Issue in Greece. Athens: Exantas, 1975. In Greek.

Wachtel, Howard. Workers' Management and Workers' Wages in Yugoslavia. Ithaca, N.Y.: Cornell University Press, 1973.

Warren, Roland. The Community in America. Chicago: Rand McNally, 1963.

Watts-Glen, E. "New Challenges in Collective Bargaining." Social Report 2 (1981).

Weber, Max. Economy and Society. New York: Bedminister Press, 1968.

Whyte, William Foote. Worker Participation and Ownership. Ithaca, N.Y.: ILR Press, Cornell University, 1983.

Wilpert, Bernhard, and Arndt Sorge, eds. International Perspectives on Organizational Democracy. Vol. 2. New York: John Wiley & Sons, 1984.

Wirth, L. "Urbanism as a Way of Life." American Journal of Sociology 44 (1983):3-24.

Wolin, Seldon. Politics and Vision. Boston: Little, Brown, 1960.

Xenos, Nicholas. "Economic Democracy in Greece." New York Times, May 6, 1982.

Zagouras, Nicholas G. "The Introduction in Greece of the Institution of 'Worker Participation' in Management." Review of Labor Law 43 (1984):681-97. In Greek.

Zagouras, Nicholas G., and Chrisostomos G. Ioannidis. "Autonomous Work Groups at the Emery Mines of Naxos." Paper presented at the Conference on "Self-Management: Experiences and Perspectives," Center of Planning and Economic Research. Athens, May 28-30, 1986. In Greek.

Zupnick, J., and S. Kats. Case Studies Profiles. Worthington, Ohio: Enterprises Institute, 1980.

Zwerdling, Daniel. Democracy at Work. Washington, D.C.: Association for Workplace Democracy, 1982.

Index

name of specific corpora-
tion or topic
corporatism, 114, 286
cottage industry, 226, 231-
32
Coulistandis-Coutsakis & Co.,
S.A., 125
creative destruction, 151
credit unions, 184-85, 205-6,
227, 283-84
Crete, 237, 239, 240
critical perspective of worker self-governance, 57,
58-64, 69, 70-75

debt, 25-26, 31, 33, 261,
263, 272, 273
decentralization: and capital, 225-26; and commu-
nism, 134; and community
self-governance, 9, 157,
195-200, 208, 210, 219,
220, 223-24, 225-26, 228-
29, 237, 249, 274, 277;
and contraction/expansion,
200; and corporations,
74, 173-74, 210; definition/
function of, 171; federal,
197-98, 200; and the Five
Year Plan, 228-29; in
Greece, 171, 219, 220,
223-24, 225-26, 228-29,
237, 249, 261, 272, 274,
277; and municipal enter-
prises, 237; and public
participation, 228-29,
245-47; social, 171-74;
socialism/socialization,
261, 277; and the social
market, 171; and the so-
cial sector, 171, 289; in
the U.S., 195-200, 210,
262, 263, 280; worker
participation/self-gover-
nance, 197, 272. See also

autonomy; polity; viabil-
ity; name of specific
company
deconcentration, 171, 277-78
democracy, 30, 72, 74, 158,
172-74. See also name of
specific topic
democratic corporations,
174, 179. See also name
of specific type of cor-
poration
democratic federations, 30,
181, 200
Democratic party, 20, 100,
103-4, 265
democratic planning, 31,
220, 224, 245-47, 275-76
Democratic Renovation party
[DA], 134-35
dependency, 1-2, 15, 17,
32-33. See also autonomy;
viability
deregulation, 25, 31-32, 262
Detroit, Michigan, 189-90,
192, 194-95
development: definition of,
7; process of, 11
dominance, 55-58, 69, 70,
72-73, 280, 285
Douglass Aircraft, 197
Drucker, Peter, 67, 197-98
drugs, 122
Dunkirk, New York, 96-97
Durkheim, Emile, 212-13

ecological loops, 190-92
Economic Development Administration, 90
economic development/
structure, 15-18
economic diversity, 192-93,
204
economy. See name of spe-
cific topic or person
education, 129-30, 207,